OPEN DESIGN NOW

WHY DESIGN
CANNOT REMAIN
EXCLUSIVE

AUG 1 4 2012

WITHDRAWN

PROPERTY OF
SENECA COLLEGE
LIBRARIES
@ YORK CAMPUS

ISBN 978-90-6369-259-9
Second printing 2011

Copyright © 2011 BIS Publishers; Creative Commons
Netherlands; Premsela, the Netherlands Institute for
Design and Fashion; Waag Society and the individual
contributors. For image and text credits, see the
respective pages. All texts and images are copyright of
their respective authors.

The editors have made every effort to contact all
copyright holders of the images used in this book. If you
claim copyright of any of the images presented here and
have not been properly identified, please contact the
editors with sufficient proof that you are the copyright
holder. They will be more than happy to make a formal
acknowledgment of your copyright in a future issue.

This work is licensed under the Creative Commons
Attribution-NonCommercial-ShareAlike 3.0 Unported
License, except where stated otherwise.

To view a copy of this licence, visit http://
creativecommons.org/licenses/by-nc-sa/3.0/ or send a
letter to Creative Commons, 171 Second Street, Suite
300, San Francisco, California 94105, USA.

Certain material in this book may be proprietary, and
may for example be or become the subject of industrial
design protection. Inclusion in this book shall not
be construed as implying any license of any sort. No
warranties, express or implied, are made with respect
to any of the specifications, models, instructions or
information contained in this book.

Creative Commons Netherlands Premsela, the Netherlands Institute for Design and Fashion Waag Society

Creative Commons Netherlands aims to advance the use of Creative Commons licences in the Netherlands. Creative Commons Netherlands is a collaboration between Waag Society, Nederland Kennisland and the Institute for Information Law (IViR) at the University of Amsterdam.

Premsela, the Netherlands Institute for Design and Fashion, creates opportunities for the growth of Dutch design from a cultural perspective. Premsela organizes lectures, debates and exhibitions. Its other activities include the publication of Morf, the Netherlands' biggest design magazine, and the international web portal Design.nl.

Waag Society develops creative technology for social innovation. The foundation researches, develops concepts, pilots and prototypes and acts as an intermediate between the arts, science and the media. Waag Society cooperates with cultural, public and private parties.

Bas van Abel is Creative Director at Waag Society. Bas is passionate about developing a wide variety of projects based on open design principles. As co-founder of Waag Society's Fab Lab and the Instructables Restaurant, he is an active member of the international maker and digital fabrication community.

Lucas Evers is Head of the e-Culture Programme at Waag Society. Lucas is involved in projects at the intersection of art, science, design and society, extending the reach of e-Culture to a wider range of technology-informed disciplines.

Roel Klaassen is Programme Manager at Premsela, the Netherlands Institute for Design and Fashion. Roel is a design enthusiast with an academic background in design, psychology and strategic management. At present he's working on the People's Republic of Design programme, a Premsela initiative that aims to stimulate the development of an open design culture.

Peter Troxler is an independent researcher and concept developer with an interest in the overall architecture and design of the social, technological and commercial aspects of enterprises, focusing on companies as permanent organizations and projects as temporary organizations.

ARTICLES

CASES

VISUAL INDEX

ACTIVISM / AESTHETICS:
2D / AESTHETICS: 3D
/ AMATEURISSIMO /
ARCHITECTURE / BLUEPRINTS
/ CO-CREATION / COMMUNITY
/ CREATIVE COMMONS / CROWD
SOURCING / DESIGNERS /
DIY / DOWNLOADABLE DESIGN
/ EVENTS / GRASSROOTS
INVENTION / HACKING /
HACKING DESIGN / HELLO WORLD
/ KNOWLEDGE / MANIFESTOS /
MASS CUSTOMIZATION / OPEN
EVERYTHING / PRINTING /
RECYCLING / REMIX /
REPAIRING / REPRODUCTION /
REVOLUTION / SHARING / SOCIAL
DESIGN / STANDARDS
/ TEMPLATE CULTURE /
TREND: GLOBALIZATION /
TREND: NETWORK SOCIETY /
TREND: SCARCITY OF RESOURCES
/ WYS ≠ WYG

/ BAS VAN ABEL,
LUCAS EVERS,
HENDRIK-JAN GRIEVINK,
AART HELDER

PREFACE

BAS VAN ABEL, LUCAS EVERS & ROEL KLAASSEN

Open design existed before the publication of this book, of course. At the end of the last century, it was defined as design whose makers allowed its free distribution and documentation and permitted modifications and derivations of it. More than a decade later, open design is developing actively and constitutes an influential trend in the world of design.

Bas van Abel, Lucas Evers and Roel Klaassen represent different perspectives on design: respectively emphasizing innovation, sharing and design itself. They agree that open design brings these three qualities together in a natural way. Bas is Creative Director at Waag Society and is passionate about developing a wide variety of projects based on open design principles. Lucas is Head of the e-Culture Programme at Waag Society and is involved in projects at the intersection of art, science, design and society. Roel is Programme Manager at Premsela, the Netherlands Institute for Design and Fashion and is a design enthusiast working on People's Republic of Design, an initiative that aims to stimulate the development of an open design culture.

www.waag.org/persoon/bas
www.waag.org/persoon/lucas
http://nl.linkedin.com/in/roelklaassen

Open design existed before the publication of this book, of course. The term first appeared at the end of the last century with the founding of the non-profit Open Design Foundation, which attempted to describe this new phenomenon.[1] The organization proposed necessary conditions for open design rather than attempting to comprehensively define it: open design was design whose makers allowed its free distribution and documentation and permitted modifications and derivations of it.[2] Around the same time, Reinoud Lamberts launched the Open Design Circuits website[3] at Delft University of Technology for the purpose of developing integrated circuits in the spirit of open source software. The fashion industry was a notable early adopter of open design.[4] More than a decade later, open design is actively developing and has become an influential trend in the world of design. *Open Design Now* looks ahead to the future of design. Using key texts, best practices and a visual index, we sketch a picture of open design based on the knowledge and experience of the present moment. In doing so, we seek to contribute to the development of design practice and at the same time draw attention to the importance of open design among a broad audience of design professionals, students, critics and enthusiasts.

USING KEY TEXTS,
BEST PRACTICES AND
A VISUAL INDEX, WE
SKETCH A PICTURE OF
OPEN DESIGN BASED ON
THE KNOWLEDGE AND
EXPERIENCE OF THE
PRESENT MOMENT.

The three initiators of this book - Creative Commons CREATIVE COMMONS Netherlands; Premsela, the Netherlands Institute for Design and Fashion; and Waag Society - represent three different but complementary perspectives on design. Sharing, design and innovation came together in a natural way in the (Un)limited Design project, which we began together in 2009. The first (Un)limited Design

Contest EVENTS was intended as an open design experiment. Entrants could submit product designs on the condition that they shared their digital blueprints so others could modify and improve their designs or manufacture them using Fab Labs. Creative Commons licences allowed entrants to share their designs without relinquishing copyright. The contest elicited innovative and imaginative designs[5] and led directly to *Open Design Now*.

Open

Digital technology and the internet have irrevocably changed our world. Millions of bloggers are providing serious competition for renowned media and news organizations. The entertainment industry struggles to capitalize on the vast growth of audiovisual consumption. A single individual with internet access can unbalance political relations all over the world. Writers and musicians no longer need printers, publishers, studios or record labels to take a shot at eternal fame. As equipment continues to get cleverer and cheaper, these developments are also affecting physical products and production processes. You can create a 3D design on your computer using free platforms like Thingiverse and make it freely available on a site like the Pirate Bay (or sell it on Etsy) so that it can be manufactured locally all over the world, digitally or otherwise, using a distributed manufacturing service like Shapeways.

Although technological progress is the driving force behind these new forms of design, distribution and production, we must look for and develop more satisfactory forms of intellectual property rights in the near future. The Creative Commons licences were designed to give creative people the freedom to deploy copyright in a flexible manner. They allow a creator to retain all rights while giving permission in advance for his or her work to be shared, distributed and modified – depending on the specific terms stated in the licence. While the licences can no longer be considered innovative, they are being applied in creative new ways. By putting open design on the agenda, Creative Commons Netherlands is expanding the use of open licences into the domain of product design and giving intellectual property back to its creators. After all, before an object is designed and produced, it leads a separate life as an idea, often taking on a range of forms during the process, from a used in production. Open licences can be used to protect every form in between. These licences smooth the way for creativity and innovation, but also remind us of a fundamental issue in design: *that design cannot remain exclusive.*

Digitization BLUEPRINTS has brought unprecedented growth to industries like industrial design, architecture, fashion and media. It has led to technological and professional changes that have also had great social significance. Open design offers unprecedented possibilities for the design of our surroundings, for design as a profession, and for designers – professionals and amateurs alike. The industrial era was mainly about designing products for the masses; in the post-industrial digital era, the masses themselves are seizing the chance to design, manufacture and distribute products.

Design

It is perhaps not surprising that the Netherlands has proven to be a fertile breeding ground for open design. In a culture characterized by a continuous battle to hold the sea at bay, the Netherlands has built up a rich history in adapting and designing the human living environment and can be considered one of the first modern democracies. The relatively open-minded society has allowed experimental design to flourish. This small country has a proportionally high number of designers, most of whom tend not to be highly specialized or tied to an industry. Consequently, they cannot limit themselves to one area and must remain open to other disciplines, inside the field of design and beyond. It is no coincidence that Premsela, the Dutch platform for design, encourages the development of an open design culture. In the 1990s, this mentality led to what became known as conceptual design. Today, a decade later, we can see that an open design philosophy is essential to coping with a changing world. *Open Design Now!*

Now

Where do we go from here? Reading this book could be a good start. It has become an open project; anything else was hardly conceivable. *Open Design Now* is meant as a travel guide to the emerging and expanding world of international open design. Pore over it in your study, take it with you to work and discuss it with your colleagues, and allow it to inspire

you. This book provides an overview of best practices in 'creative innovation', as Waag Society calls it. Or perhaps we should call it 'social and participatory innovation', since the term refers to the continuous search for meaningful applications of technology and design that will benefit the general population.

According to Paul Valéry,[6] creativity springs less from one's own ideas and originality than from a structure that compels new insights. CO-CREATION In his eyes, the true creative never stops searching. Creation itself is the work, the primary goal, an end in itself; in his view, your completed object is no different from anyone else's. The same is essentially true of this book: it is not finished, nor can we claim full credit for its contents.[7]

Textually, *Open Design Now* is structured around feature articles and case studies. Visually, however, it is structured around images that show how open design has changed the way the world looks. Although many of the examples in this book are small in scale, they indicate the promise open design holds for the near future – a future of $50 prosthetic legs, SOCIAL DESIGN DesignSmashes, REMIX FairPhones, Fritzing, Instructables Restaurants, COMMUNITY RepRaps and (Un)limited Design.

13

NOTES

1   Vallance, R, 'Bazaar Design of Nano and Micro Manufacturing
    Equipment', 2000. Available online at http://www.engr.uky.edu/psl/
    omne/download/BazaarDesignOpenMicroAndNanofabrication
    Equipment.PDFaccessed on 17 January 2011.

2   www.opendesign.org/odd.html

3   http://opencollector.org; http://opencollector.org/history/
    OpenDesignCircuits/reinoud_announce.

4   Bollier, D, and Racine, L, 'Ready to Share. Creativity in Fashion
    & Digital Culture'. The Norman Lear Center: Annenberg, 2005.
    Available online at www.learcenter.org/pdf/RTSBollierRacine.PDF,
    accessed 17 January 2011.

5   http://unlimiteddesigncontest.org

6   Valéry, P, 'Cahier', cited in www.8weekly.nl/artikel/1774/paul-val-
    ry-de-macht-van-de-afwezigheid.html.

7   www.opendesignnow.org

INTRODUCTION

MARLEEN STIKKER

The pioneers of our time are not taking the world at face value, as a given from outside; rather, they see the world as something you can pry open, something you can tinker with.

Marleen Stikker developed the 'Digital City' (DDS) in Amsterdam, which was the first European free gateway and virtual community on the internet, a place where many Dutch citizens, organizations, companies and publishers took their first tentative steps on the digital highway. Marleen also founded Waag Society, a media lab developing creative technical applications for societal innovation. Waag Society is also concerned with the social effects of the internet and actively promotes Open Data. For Marleen, "Open design is part of a growing possibilitarian movement. Rooted in information and communication technology, it gives us all the instruments to become the one-man factory, the world player operating from a small back room."

www.waag.org/persoon/marleen

In his novel *The Man Without Qualities*, Austrian author Robert Musil describes two ways of thinking and interacting with the world.

"If you want to pass through open doors you have to respect the fact that they have a fixed frame: this principle is simply a prerequisite of reality. But if there is a sense of reality then there must also be something that you might call a sense of possibility. Someone who possesses this sense of possibility does not say for example: here this or that has happened, or it will happen or it must happen. Rather he invents: here this could or should happen. And if anybody explains to him that it is as it is, then he thinks: well, it probably could be otherwise."[1]

Possibilitarians think in new possibilities, and get all excited when things get messy and life becomes disorderly. In disruption, possibilitarians see new opportunities, even if they do not know where they might lead. They believe, with Denis Gabor, that "the future cannot be predicted, but futures can be invented".[2]

16

Realitarians are operating within a given framework, according to the rules that are given, following to the powers there are. They accept the conditions and the institutions as given, and are fearful of disruption.

Whether a person is a possibilitarian or a realitarian has nothing to do with their creativity. People representing these frames of reference can be found in all professions: entrepreneurs, politicians, artists. In fact, art and design are not avant-garde by definition, and it would be overstating the matter to claim that innovation is an inherent quality in the arts – or science, for that matter.

It would equally be wrong to think that all realitarians are reactionary. There are many different kinds of realitarians. Some play with the given rules, finding better ways to use them, making them more efficient, increasing their moral justice and fairness. Others want to cover all eventualities, seeking to keep everything under control in neatly written scenarios that contain no surprises whatsoever.

When it comes to open design, possibilitarians are enticed and enthused by the new opportunities it could bring, even if they do not know exactly what open design will become, or where it might lead. ACTIVISM Possibilitarians see the disruption that open design brings to the design world, and respond by embracing the potential that is inherent in that disruption.

Possibilitarians engage in open design as a process, trusting their own abilities to guide that process. And as possibilitarians, they pursue strategies to be inclusive, to involve others, to build bridges between opposite positions: North-South, old-young, traditional-experimental. Possibilitarians represent a sharing SHARE culture which is at the core of open design. As such, they trust others to make their own contributions and to build upon what has been shared. Trust, responsibility and reciprocity are important ingredients in an open, sharing culture. These factors have been discussed at length in relation to software development; the debate has been revived in the context of the ongoing informatization of society. As with open data, open design will have to address these questions. And as with open data, open design will have to involve the actual end users, not organizations, panels or marketers. Design will have to identify the fundamental questions, which supersede the design assignments issued by mass-producers or governments. And design will have to develop a strategy of reciprocity, particularly when objects become 'smart' parts of an interconnected web of things, similar to the emergence of the internet.

OPEN DESIGN WILL HAVE TO INVOLVE THE ACTUAL END USERS, NOT ORGANIZATIONS, PANELS OR MARKETERS.

Open design will have to develop its own language for trust. What are its design principles, its ethics, the responsibilities it entails? MANIFESTOS Although a clear answer to these questions is currently lacking, this absence does not prevent possibilitarians from engaging with open design. They know that this trend is not about a dream of the world as a better place, a dream which could too easily be stigmatized as naive and utopian. Possibilitarians also know that only by taking part in the process, by participating and by giving it a direction can those answers be found.

OPEN DESIGN CAN BE VIEWED AS THE LATEST IN A LONG LINE OF SIMILAR DEVELOPMENTS, STARTING WITH THE FIRST PCS – THE ATARIS, AMIGAS, COMMODORES AND SINCLAIRS – THE ARRIVAL OF THE INTERNET, OF MOBILE COMMUNICATION.

Realitarians, in contrast, respond to open design with fear and mistrust. When a fretwork artist recently realized that a laser cutter could achieve within hours what took her four months to cut, she was extremely disappointed and angry with the machine. The positive effect that the machine could have on her work only occurred to her later. This is the Luddite revived, the fear of the machine that might threaten a person's livelihood, that could render irrelevant an individual craftsman's contribution to culture and society.

Realitarians fear that all the energy it costs to create something might be wasted; that the time and effort it took e.g. to write a book would be pointless, that anyone could just go and copy it. Fundamentally, they fear that someone else could commercially utilize something that they have contributed to the public domain. Even Creative Commons CREATIVE COMMONS takes on a threatening aspect in this context, creating a concern that the author will no longer be able to control fair use. Or a designer might argue that open design could result in loads of ugly products,

expressing a concern that if anyone can do it, amateurs AMATEURISSIMO will pollute the beautiful world of design. This is the realitarian speaking.

We've had this discussion in other domains, in other areas: it arose in relation to hacking, and we've experienced it over and over in media and journalism – in the 1960s with the pirate radio stations, in the late 1990s with the advent of blogging. Now it has emerged in the domain of design.

Open design can be viewed as the latest in a long line of similar developments, starting with the first PCs – the Ataris, Amigas, Commodores and Sinclairs – the arrival of the internet, of mobile communication. TREND: NETWORK SOCIETY It is often the same people who are involved in these initiatives again and again. These are the pioneers of our time, people with that hacker-artist-activist attitude. They are not taking the world at face value, a given from outside; rather, they see the world as something you can pry open, something you can tinker with.

So they started to experiment. GRASSROOTS INVENTION The first computers gave them a feeling of autarchy. Suddenly, they were able to use desktop publishing; they produced their own newspapers, they were typesetters, they took responsibility – they got organized and put their opinion out there. This was the first DIY DIY movement that was a parallel campaign. In contrast to the *Parallelaktion* in Musil's novel, it happened beyond the confines of discussion circles: squatting became a parallel movement to the housing market, and they established their own, alternative media infrastructure. In all likelihood, the dynamic of the internet helped it happen. Indeed, in the Netherlands, the first opportunity to experience the internet was created by a possibilitarian movement – De Digitale Stad (the digital city) in Amsterdam. Commercial internet access became available much later.

Open design is rooted in information and communication technology, giving us all the instruments to become the one-man factory, the world player operating from a small back room. Despite this semblance of easy access, many of these resources require the user to be extremely tech-savvy. In addition, purposeful and effective utilization of these

17

resources requires considerable social skills and expertise in social engineering. This combination of technical and social skills is extremely interesting and very rare. Tech-savvy usually carries the connotation of nerdy, socially handicapped and awkward at communication, while the socially adept are generally assumed to lack technical skills.

A similar schism is strikingly evident in education. As a media student, you might finish your degree without ever having made anything yourself, or being responsible for a product. You may have spent your time studying games made by other people, instead of learning to make good games. As a vocational student learning a trade, you might end up sitting at old machines the whole time, never getting to see a 3D printer, or only encountering these relevantly recent developments at the end of your education, or in an external module instead of in the core programme.

In fact, it may be argued that there is a fundamental dichotomy in society, an essential separation between the field of making and the field of science. There is too little science in making, and too little making in science; these two fields are far too disconnected.

Examples of the opposite are emerging, and the connection between modern technology and craft traditions is sometimes aptly named hyper-craft. The implications for education are huge, and hyper-craft broadens the perspectives in education – not only for design, but for all crafts. Hyper-craft as a practice of open design is not primarily concerned with the objects that are being made. Its focus is on the process of making itself and the responsibilities that makers take – for the monsters they may be creating, for the process of creating, and for the ingredients used. PRINTING

Recently, a vocational school in the Dutch province of Brabant took the idea of the Instructables Restaurant and used it as a blueprint for a cross-over programme that combined elements of their hotel and catering education and their design education. Together, they realized an Instructables Restaurant for the CultuurNacht event – students created furniture based on blueprints BLUEPRINTS they had downloaded and cooked meals prepared according to online recipes. The restaurant served 1500 people that night. The

school made a smart addition to the very classical trade of cooking, adding more dimensions, more layers, and creating their first open curriculum.

The agenda of open design – increasing transparency in the production chain, talking about responsibility – is certainly a political agenda. Open design is part of today's possibilitarian movements, such as open data provided by governments seeking greater transparency. The potentially extreme effects of open information initiatives like Wikileaks are becoming apparent in the enormous backlash affecting the people involved. This is a manifestation of the clash between two worlds: the people operating within the bounds of 'reality' fighting back against the challenge to their system.

WHEN ACADEMIC KNOWLEDGE STARTED TO DISAPPEAR BEHIND THE PAYWALLS OF LARGE PUBLISHERS, THE OPEN ACCESS MOVEMENT CREATED NEW WAYS TO MAKE IT ACCESSIBLE AGAIN FOR EVERYBODY.

Open design may appear less extreme: designing is seen as more friendly, more creative, more playful. Much of the unfairness in the field of open design is 'petty injustice'. These incidents include small production runs that are impossible or prohibitively expensive in a mass-production environment – or manufacturers accustomed to mass marketing who decide what will be included in their collection.

These forms of petty injustice are certainly not the only problems in open design, however; there are also profit-driven corporations limiting technical and design solutions, preventing new possibilities from being put to good use. This immediately invokes the global dimension of open design. When international trade agreements become a guise for Western

18

corporations to privatize indigenous knowledge, activists ACTIVISM and librarians deploy open design strategies, documenting and codifying this knowledge and developing protection mechanisms such as the Aboriginal and Torres Strait Islander Library and Archive Protocols in Australia.

When sustainable solutions are locked away in patents, initiatives such as the GreenXchange started by Creative Commons and Nike facilitate easy licensing schemes. When academic knowledge started to disappear behind the paywalls of large publishers, the Open Access movement created new ways to make it accessible again for everybody.

When transnational supply chains blur the provenance of raw materials and the labour conditions of mining, harvesting and manufacturing, fair trade campaigns advocate transparency and propose alternatives, for example the Max Havelaar product range or the Fairphone project.

Disrupting these macro-political movements that privatize the commons or control access to the public domain is the major challenge for open design. An effective response to that challenge starts with understanding and reflecting on what we are doing when we make things.

19

NOTES

1   Musil, R. *The Man without Qualities*. 1933. Trans. S. Wilkins.
     London: Picador, 1997, p. 16.
2   Gabor, D. *Inventing the Future*. London: Secker & Warburg, 1963.
     p. 207.

DIY ADVERTISEMENT

Wiki

live your o

KEA
wn design

ARTICLES

ORCHESTRAL MANOEUVRES IN DESIGN

PAUL ATKINSON

Investigating the roots of open design and identifying its resulting technological, economical and societal changes, Atkinson contemplates the vast consequences this development will have for the design profession and the distribution of design.

Paul Atkinson is an industrial designer, design historian and educator; he lectures and conducts research at Sheffield Hallam University in the UK as a Reader in Design. For Paul, open design is "the internet-enabled collaborative creation of artefacts by a dispersed group of otherwise unrelated individuals. As a purely creative exercise, open design promotes the unprecedented sharing of knowledge between the professional and amateur designer, breaking down unnecessary barriers. When carried out for the common good rather than for capital gain or profit, open design allows the sharing of creative skills between developed and undeveloped nations for humanitarian benefit, countering the ramifications of global product consumerism."

http://shu.academia.edu/paulatkinson

The concepts of open design – the collaborative creation SHARE of artefacts by a dispersed group of otherwise unrelated individuals – and of individualized production – the direct digital manufacture of goods at the point of use – at first sound like something from a utopian science fiction film. And yet, here we are. We can now easily download designs DOWNLOADABLE DESIGN from the internet, alter them at will to suit our own needs and then produce perfect products at the push of a button. Magic.

Back to the Future

In many ways though, there are huge similarities here to much older practices of production and consumption. The emergence of Do It Yourself DIY as a necessity for many is lost in the mists of time, but defined as a leisure pursuit, a pastime, it emerged from a perceived need to 'keep idle hands busy'. In the hours following a long working day, it acted only to bring the Victorian work ethic from the factory into the home. DIY = productive leisure.

In promoting DIY as an amateur pastime, the professional practices of design (which had themselves only appeared a short while earlier) were democratized. The printing of instructional manuals in the form of popular DIY handbooks and magazines enabled anyone having developed the necessary hand skills (which were then passed down from generation to generation) to engage with creative design and production processes and make functional items for themselves.[1] This process of democratization was not all plain sailing – it was one which was strongly rejected by the institutional bodies of various professions, all seeking to protect the livelihoods of their members, and was a source of tension in the relationship between amateur and professional which remains to this day.[2]

At first, technological developments in the design of tools and the development of new materials aided this opening up of professional practice. Some of the key turning points included the emergence of domestic versions of professional power tools, beginning with the electric drill,[3] DIY and the ready availability of new materials such as hardboard, plastic laminates, ready-mixed paints and adhesives. At a time when many products in the home, from furniture to kitchen fittings and from radios to standard lamps, were

produced in relatively small numbers from materials such as wood and metal, these developments effectively de-skilled production processes, meaning that the individual handyman could fairly easily design and build many of the products of everyday life. However, as the professions became more and more specialized and further removed from everyday activities, technology became more complex and esoteric and the mass production of injection-moulded plastic parts became the norm, the design and manufacture of many products moved beyond the capabilities of all but the most dedicated of DIY practitioners, and the creative process moved further away from the hand of the individual. Allied to this, the lack of free time in increasingly busy private lives, and the economies of scale involved in mass production provided further disincentives. Why bother to build a bookcase yourself, when a professionally designed, perfectly well made and highly finished self-assembly version can be bought for less than the cost of the raw materials?

DO IT YOURSELF CAN BE SEEN AS: PRODUCTIVE LEISURE.

This distancing of the professional from the amateur in part contributed to the cult of the connoisseur: the idea of the professional designer as one who knew what was best for everyone, no matter who they were. The grand narrative of modernist design sought singular perfection and brought an elitist view of 'good taste' to the forefront of any design debate. This view held sway and did not even begin to be dismantled until the realization in the 1960s that a single design solution could not possibly fulfil the requirements of such a wide and heterogeneous market, and that the relevance of any particular design was determined by its user, not its creator.[4] Slowly, the opinion of the user grew in importance and more enlightened design practitioners began to promote user-centred design processes, where the observed requirements of the user formed the starting point of creative product development. The logical progression of this view can be seen in the more recent emergence of co-creation design processes, where the user is finally fully involved in the creative process leading to the products they eventually consume. It is a short step from co-creation CO-CREATION or co-design to a position where users take on the responsibility for creative and productive acts in their entirety – a step which technology has now enabled everyone to make. In open design, the cult of the connoisseur has given way to the cult of the amateur:[5] those who know themselves what is best for them.

The processes of technological development that have variously brought amateur and professional closer together or driven them further apart are now acting to potentially remove the barriers between the two completely.[6] The open distribution network of the internet promotes an interactive and iterative process of creative design development amongst a globally dispersed group of potentially anonymous participants: a virtual band of individuals who can coalesce around a particular design problem, and who may or may not include design professionals. COMMUNITY After 'solving' a particular design problem, the band dissolves, only to reform with a different membership around a new problem. Furthermore, the people in this virtual band have at their disposal advanced manufacturing capabilities.

The appearance of Rapid Prototyping HELLO WORLD technologies in the mid-1980s, at first high-level and hugely expensive machines, allowed mass production processes requiring investment in costly tooling to be neatly sidestepped, making it possible to produce one-off products cost-effectively. Low-cost descendants of these – the designs for which are themselves disseminated and downloaded via the internet and made by hand – now enable the desktop manufacture of individualized products in the home. DOWNLOADABLE DESIGN Technology has moved the goalposts from a position of co-creation to one where the user has the capability to completely design and manufacture products by themselves. It is a return, if you will, to a cottage industry model of production and consumption that has not been seen since the earliest days of the Industrial Revolution. What at first glance appears to be a futuristic fantasy is revealed, in fact, to be just the opposite: a recurrence of past ways of doing things.

Orchestral Manoeuvres

We have seen how this situation of open design and production occurred through the technological development of tools and materials, and a change in the standing of the individual's opinion. Both factors increased in importance with the introduction of wide accessibility to the internet and low-cost machines for direct digital manufacture. We can safely assume that open source versions of these machines, such as the 'CupCake' CNC rapid prototyping machine produced by MakerBot Industries[7], the desktop rapid prototyper 'Model 1 Fabber' from Fab@Home[8], or the self-replicating rapid prototyper the 'RepRap'[9], will continue to grow in capability, becoming more and more efficient, more accurate and able to use a wider range of raw materials. Such is the nature of open development.[10]

IN OPEN DESIGN, THE CULT OF THE CONNOISSEUR HAS GIVEN WAY TO THE CULT OF THE AMATEUR – THOSE WHO KNOW THEMSELVES WHAT IS BEST FOR THEM.

It appears, then, that there are two physical aspects to be considered in making such technologies more acceptable to the wider public: the development of more user-friendly interfaces, or more intuitive systems for creating three-dimensional designs in the first place; and the distribution of materials in forms suitable for use in such machines. No doubt web-based supply infrastructures will appear as a matter of course as the demand for materials increases, but many current open design systems still require fairly high-level CAD modelling skills KNOWLEDGE in order to produce designs in a digital form.

Since 2002, I have been leading research projects within the Post Industrial Manufacturing Research Group, initially at the University of Huddersfield and since 2008 at Sheffield Hallam University. This work has explored the development of effective user interfaces to enable the open design of products, with the express intention of increasing amateur involvement in the design process and reducing the distance between amateur and professional. It has pushed such technologies through projects by the industrial designer Lionel T. Dean[11] and by the artist/maker Justin Marshall.[12]

Future Factories

The web portal of FutureFactories allowed observers to watch computer models of organic forms for products such as light fittings, candlesticks and furniture randomly mutating in real time, freeze the design at any point and save the resulting file for later production by rapid prototyping. Marshall's Automake project went a stage further, and gave the user more ability to interact with the design by allowing them to manipulate various computer-generated mesh envelopes within which selected components would randomly be placed by the computer until a finished form appeared, which could then be printed. PRINTING Depending on the mesh chosen and the scale selected, the finished results could range from fruit bowls and vases down to bracelets and rings.

28

The exhibition I curated at the Hub National Centre for Design and Craft in May 2008 EVENTS showed the results of both these projects and allowed visitors to the exhibition to try out the Automake software for themselves. The outputs created were first printed out as colour photographs, becoming part of a growing display wall. A selection of those photographs were printed in 3D AESTHETICS: 3D by the industrial sponsor each week and added to the exhibition. Visitors returned again and again to see the expanding displays, with those whose work was selected and manufactured proudly bringing friends and relatives to see the results of their endeavours. These people said it was the first creative thing they had ever done, and that they could not have achieved it without the Automake system. The system enabled them to engage in a form of design and production that questioned their familiar relationship with the object.

Generative Software

Numerous systems that employ generative software and allow users to manipulate designed forms for pieces of jewellery and then have them produced by lost-wax casting or laser cutting followed soon after. One of the best known is 'Nervous System'.[13] Visitors to their site can either buy ready-made pieces created using their software, or run various simple interactive applets and manipulate screen designs based on organic structures such as amoebas, orchids, lichen and algae to create their own unique pieces, which can then be saved and manufactured by the supplier. AESTHETICS: 3D The result is a growing open design library of unique but closely related forms. The code for the software is also released under a Creative Commons licence to encourage others to produce similar work.

THE GRAPHIC DESIGNER'S ROLE HAS MOVED FROM CREATING FIXED PRODUCTS TO A MORE FLUID DIGITAL PRESENCE, WHERE THEY MAY NOT BE TOTALLY IN CONTROL OF THE CONTENT CONSTANTLY BEING ADDED TO THEIR ORIGINAL CREATION.

These examples underline the value of systems that allow complex three-dimensional forms to be created by users who, for very valid reasons of lack of time and inclination, are unlikely to develop the type of Computer-Aided Design skills and 3D design awareness required on their own. The development of systems to help and support such people in the creation of their own designs should not be seen as a threat to professional designers – who might see their widespread adoption as an affront to their creative expertise and high-level training – but as an opportunity to retain key roles in the design of

BACK TO THE FUTURE: PRODUCTS BECOME PERSONAL AGAIN

CRAFT	MASS PRODUCTION	AUTOMAKE

DESIGNER/   DESIGNER   MAKER/   CONSUMER/
MAKER   CO-DESIGNER   CO-DESIGNER

WORKSHOP   FACTORY   INTERACTIVE
                                     DIGITAL DESIGN   29
                                     PROCESS

VARIABLE   STANDARDIZED   PERSONALIZED
PRODUCTS   PRODUCTS   PRODUCTS

 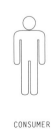   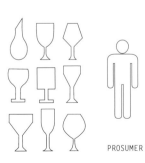

CONSUMER   PASSIVE   PROSUMER
                   CONSUMER

products. It would seem certain that the role of the designer in this situation will change rather than disappear altogether, and that this change in role will bring with it the requirement for a change in the attitude of the designer with respect to their relationship with the finished object, as well as in their relationship to the amateur user. Traditional models of authorship and ownership and the existing legal structures over rights and liabilities do not sit well with open systems of design and production, and trying to maintain them will only lead to heartbreak and disappointment. These lessons have already been learned in the allied creative industries of graphics, film and music production as they have tried to protect their income streams, and need to be heeded here.[14]

Graphic designers have had to learn to cope with the fact that anybody with a computer and the right software has access to the means to create and produce high-quality, finished pieces of graphic design (although the nature of the systems in place often fails to help lay users create anything that would be mistaken for 'professional' work). In many instances, the graphic designer's role has moved from creating fixed, printed products to originating and possibly maintaining a much more fluid digital presence such as websites, where they may not be totally in control of the content constantly being added to their original creation.

The issues that the music industry has had to deal with include not only the enormous and unsettling changes to the processes of how their end products are distributed, but also the opening up of the existing processes of sourcing new, original material. The role of the A+R (Artist and Repertoire) person – acting as a 'professional' arbiter of taste and a filter between the plethora of bands aiming to get recording contracts and those that actually get them – has been replaced by the self-promotion and distribution of music by bands acting as their own producers, which is then filtered first-hand by potential listeners as part of a global online audience. Similarly, film studios have been subjected to huge amounts of 'amateur' AMATEURISSIMO material being made widely available through websites such as YouTube, which is filtered by enormous numbers of viewers rather than by a director.

The analogy alluded to here, between the role of the designer and the role of the film director, music producer, or orchestra conductor for that matter, is a good one. While the director is recognized as the creative force behind the film, it is widely understood that the process of film production is intrinsically a team effort of co-creation CO-CREATION involving a large cast of equally creative individuals. Likewise, an orchestra cannot function well without a conductor, but while the conductor's role is key, the quality of the orchestral music produced relies on the active involvement of all the musicians. Perhaps what we are seeing here is the transition of the designer's role (which in reality has more often than not been one of co-creation in any case, working as they do with teams of engineers, ergonomists, marketing experts and a host of others) to a role more akin to that of a film director or orchestra conductor – with the cast or orchestra in this instance including every end user. The professional designer, I suspect, will become an agent of design, with the audience of end users selecting which designer's system they wish to employ.

THE PROFESSIONAL DESIGNER WILL BECOME AN AGENT OF DESIGN, WITH THE AUDIENCE OF END USERS SELECTING WHICH DESIGNER'S SYSTEM THEY WISH TO EMPLOY.

This anticipated change of role would potentially have a huge impact. The relationship between the designer and the objects they initiate will change, as they might never see or even be aware of the results of their endeavours, changed as they will be by users to suit their own needs. HACKING DESIGN The relationship between the user and the products they own changes too, as they move from being passive consumers of designed products to active originators of their own designs. Indeed, the terms 'amateur' and 'professional' may well disappear as we move into this 'post-professional' era. Design education will also have to change its curriculum, perhaps moving closer to the learning style used in craft training – teaching students to create more meaningful, individual pieces rather than huge numbers of identically mass produced products. Designers will have to learn to develop systems that will be used by others rather than trying to remain the sole author of their own work. And while it might seem daunting for the designer to be further removed from the end product they design, it is in fact a huge opportunity for the designer to become far more closely involved with the process of production than before, with all the associated knowledge and awareness of material quality and behaviour that implies. The challenge will be to create

systems that enable the design integrity of the end result to be retained and perhaps the identity of the original design intention to be perceived, while still allowing a degree of freedom for individual users to adapt designers' work to their own ends.

These orchestral manoeuvres in design will change everything for everybody, but while there may be troubles ahead, it is not all doom and gloom. The innate ability of design to adapt to change will surely be its saviour.

NOTES

1   See Atkinson, P, 'Do It Yourself: Democracy and Design', *Journal of Design History*, 19(1), 2006, p. 1-10.

2   "[P]rofessional attitudes to [amateur design] activities have continued to oscillate between fear and admiration." Beegan, G and Atkinson, P, 'Professionalism, Amateurism and the Boundaries of Design', *Journal of Design History*, 21(4), 2008, p. 312.

3   Wilhelm Emil Fein invented the first electric hand drill in 1895. (www.fein.de/corp/de/en/fein/history.html, accessed 30 September 2010) The device was developed into the 'pistol grip' format common today by Black & Decker in 1916, as they were simultaneously working on producing the Colt pistol. After noticing war-time factory workers were borrowing electric hand drills to do jobs at home, they launched a lightweight domestic version in 1946 (www.blackanddecker100years.com/Innovation/, accessed 30 September 2010).

4   Sir Paul Reilly, Head of the Design Council in the UK, wrote in 1967: "We are shifting perhaps from attachment to permanent, universal values to acceptance that a design may be valid at a given time for a given purpose to a given group of people in a given set of circumstances, but that outside these limits it may not be valid at all." Reilly, P, 'The Challenge of Pop', *Architectural Review*, October 1967, p. 256.

5   'The Cult of the Amateur' is the title of Andrew Keen's polemic 2007 book, which urges caution in allowing the user too much authority in any creative field if the status quo is to be maintained.

6   See Atkinson, P, 'Boundaries? What Boundaries? The Crisis of Design in a Post-Professional Era', *Design Journal*,

Vol. 13, No. 2, 2010, p. 137-155.

7   http://makerbot.com

8   http://fabathome.org

9   http://reprap.org

10 Charles Leadbeater, in his seminal book on open design *We-Think*, gives a variety of examples (including an excellent case study of the Cornish Steam Engine) where collaborative open development has created a much stronger and more successful end product than a protected, closed design. See Leadbeater, C, *We-Think: Mass Innovation, not mass production*, Profile Books, (2nd Ed. 2009), p. 56.

11 http://futurefactories.com

12 www.automake.co.uk

13 http://n-e-r-v-o-u-s.com

14 As Tadeo Toulis wrote: "Failure to appreciate DIY/Hack Culture is to risk having professional design become as irrelevant to the contemporary landscape as record labels and network television are in the age of iTunes and YouTube." Toulis, T, 'Ugly: How unorthodox thinking will save design', *Core 77*, October 2008 (www.core77.com/blog/featured_items/ugly_how_unorthodox_thinking_will_save_design_by_tad_toulis_11563.asp, accessed 30 September 2010).

DVERTISEMENT

FORM

FOLLOW

FORMA

Template CULTURE

REDESIGNING DESIGN

JOS DE MUL

Open design is not a clear and unambiguous development or practice. Jos de Mul names a few of the problems he perceives with open design, without venturing to suggest any indication of how they might be solved. He then goes on to extend his well-documented and widely published 'database' metaphor to design, attempting to define the concept of design as metadesign.

Jos de Mul is a full professor in Philosophical Anthropology and head of the Philosophy of Man and Culture section at Erasmus University Rotterdam, The Netherlands. He is the scientific director of the 'Philosophy of Information and Communication Technology' research institute. His research focuses on the (partly overlapping) domains of philosophical anthropology, philosophy of art and culture, and the philosophy of information and communication technologies. According to Jos, "the open design movement seems to be part of a shift in the world of design from form via content to context, or from syntax via semantics to pragmatics, as my colleague Henk Oosterling expressed it in his Premsela Lecture last year."

www2.eur.nl/fw/hyper/home.html

At the 2010 edition of PICNIC, EVENTS an annual Amsterdam event that aims to bring together the world's top creative and business professionals to develop new partnerships and opportunities, Tom Hulme talked about 'Redesigning Design'[1]: "The design industry is going through fundamental changes. Open design, downloadable design DOWNLOADABLE DESIGN and distributed design democratize the design industry, and imply that anyone can be a designer or a producer." The subtext of this message seems to be that open design[2] is something intrinsically good and should therefore be promoted. Though I generally view open design as a positive development, it is important to stay alert to potential obstacles and pitfalls in order to avoid throwing out the (designed) baby with the proverbial bathwater.

Like other fields influenced by the 'open movement', such as open source software, open science, and open technology, open design is closely connected with the rise of computers and internet. In view of this intrinsic association, the fundamental characteristics of the digital domain are worth examining further. To develop the positive aspects of open design without falling prey to its pitfalls, the designer should not abandon his activities as a designer; rather, the designer should redesign the activities themselves. The designer of the future has to become a database designer, a meta-designer, not designing objects, but shaping a design space in which unskilled users can access user-friendly environments in which they can design their own objects. TEMPLATE CULTURE

Design as Open Design

Openness is a fundamental part of life – and so is closedness. Although organisms have to remain separate from their environment in order to retain their discrete identity, they also need to open themselves up to their environment in order to nourish themselves and to dispose of the by-products of their essential processes. However, whereas the openness of other animals is limited in the sense that they are locked up in their specific environment (their niche or *Umwelt*), human beings are characterized by a much more radical openness. Their world is unlimited in the sense that it is open to an endless supply of new environments and new experiences. This makes human life incredibly varied and rich, compared to

DESIGN AS METADESIGN

In the digital era, we have moved from the computer to the database as material or conceptual metaphor. It functions as a material metaphor when it evokes actions in the material world. Examples of this are databases implemented in industrial robots, enabling mass customization (e.g. 'built-to-order' cars) and bio-technological databases used for genetic engineering. Conversely, it functions as a conceptual metaphor if it expresses a surplus of meaning that adds a semantic layer on top of the material object.

The psychologist Maslow once remarked that if the only tool you have is a hammer, it may be tempting to treat everything as if it were a nail.[10] In a world in which the computer has become the dominant technology – more than 50 billion processors worldwide are doing their job – everything is becoming a material or conceptual database. Databases have become the dominant cultural form of the computer age, as "cinema was the key cultural form of the twentieth century".[11]

They are 'ontological machines' that shape both our world and our worldview. In the age of digital recombination, everything – nature and culture alike – becomes an object for manipulation. The almost unlimited number of combinations that databases offer would seem to prescribe some form of limitation imposed on the possibilities. In the case of open, database-mediated design, this calls for a new role for the designer. The designer should not give up his role as a designer (or restrict himself to his traditional role as designer of material or immaterial objects).

Instead, he should become a metadesigner who designs a multidimensional design space that provides a user-friendly interface, enabling the user to become a co-designer, even when this user has no designer experience or no time to gain such experience through trial and error.

Designing Models

The task of the metadesigner is to create a pathway through design space, to combine the building blocks into a meaningful design. In this respect, the meta-designer resembles the scientist who no longer creates a linear argument, but a model or simulation that enables the user to explore and analyse a specific domain of reality, or a game designer who designs a game space that facilitates meaningful and enjoyable play, if he is successful.

the life of other animals, but at the same time it also imposes a burden on us that animals do not share. Animals are thrown in an environment that is just given to them (which does not exclude, of course, that their environment may sometimes undergo radical changes due to forces beyond their control or understanding), but humans have to design their own world. *Dasein*, or 'being-in-the-world', as Heidegger characterizes the life of human beings, is always design – not only in the sense that they have to shape an already existing world, but in the more radical sense that human beings have to establish their world: they always live in an artificial world. To quote German philosopher Helmuth Plessner, humans are artificial by nature.[3] This is a never-ending process. Over the past few decades, accompanying the development of computers and the internet, we are witnessing the exploration and establishment of a whole new realm of human experience that leaves hardly any aspect of our lives untouched, including the world of design.

Although human beings have, from the very dawn of humanity, been characterized by a fundamental openness, the concept of 'openness' has become especially popular in the last couple of decades. Wikipedia – one of the most successful examples of an open movement project – offers the following definition: "Openness is a very general philosophical position from which some individuals and organizations operate, often highlighted by a decision-making process recognizing communal management by distributed stakeholders (users/ producers/ contributors), rather than a centralized authority (owners, experts, boards of directors, etc.)".[4] In the global information society, openness has become an international buzzword. OPEN EVERYTHING One of the recent developments has been the emergence of open software, from operating systems to a variety of applications. However, the demand for open access not only concerns software, but also extends to all possible cultural content, ranging from music and movies to books. All information (enslaved by copyrights) wants to be free. MANIFESTOS Moreover, open access is not limited to the digital world. An increasing number of scientists are pleading for open science and open technology. They cooperate with the public and demand open access for their publications and databases. The Open Dinosaur project, for example,

37

The Tower of Babel

This implies that the designer's task is to limit the virtually unlimited combinational space in order to create order from disorder. After all, like the infinite hexagonal rooms in the Library of Babel postulated by Jorge Luis Borges[12], most of the (re)combinations of design elements will have little or no value. To some extent, the designer will create these design elements himself, while others will be added by the co-designer. The recombination of the elements will also take the form of an interaction between the possible paths within the design space on the one hand, and the choices of the co-designer on the other. Of course, data mining and profiling algorithms will also play a role by suggesting or autonomously adding design elements (depending on the metadesign). You might ask yourselves

what makes the metadesign presented here essentially different from forms of mass customization that already exist, for example on the Nike website. The answer is that mass customization is part of the project of metadesign, but only part. In the main article I referred to the three dimensions of open design.

In the case of mass customization, as with Nike, the aspect related to openness only exists in the output dimension, and even there the openness is rather limited: a customer can choose from a small range of available colours. It would naturally be impossible to offer a detailed blueprint or road map for exactly what metadesigns will look like; this discussion is merely my reflections on the topic – or perhaps my considerations of a development yet to

come. Creating them will be the task of the meta-designers of the future.

Designability

Some time ago, Kevin Kelly published an article called 'Better Than Free'[13] which advocated a new business model, based on free copies in almost every domain – from music, books and films to your DNA – which should be supplemented by added value. He lists eight 'generative values' that might enhance the value of the free copies, and for which people will be prepared to pay: immediacy, personalization, interpretation, authenticity, accessibility, embodiment, patronage, and findability. I think we should add one more value: designability. It is my belief that this value will encompass all the others, presenting a great challenge for the meta-designer.

which advertises itself on its website as 'crowd-sourcing dinosaur science', involves scientists and the public alike in developing a comprehensive database of dinosaur limb bone measurements, to investigate questions of dinosaur function and evolution.[5] However, in this case, the demand for open access not only targets the results of their research, but also extends their objects. The OpenWetWare organization not only promotes the sharing of information, know-how and wisdom among researchers and groups who are working in biology and biological engineering, it also tries to prevent efforts to patent living matter, such as DNA.

I could list many more examples of the open movement, from open gaming to open love. We seem to be open to everything. In the presence of so many trends towards openness, it does not come as a surprise that we also are witnessing the emergence of an open design movement, albeit slightly later than in many other domains. It seems to be part of a shift in the world of design from form via content to context, or from syntax via semantics to pragmatics.[6] But what does 'open design' actually mean? In his article *The Emergence of Open Design and Open Manufacturing*,[7] Michel Bauwens distinguishes three different dimensions of open design:

Input side
On the input side we have voluntary contributors, who do not have to ask permission to participate, and use open and free raw material that is free of restrictive copyright ACTIVISM so that it can be freely improved and modified. If no open and free raw material is available, as long as the option exists to create new one, then peer production is a possibility.

Process side
On the process side, it is based on design for inclusion, low thresholds for participation, freely available modular tasks rather than functional jobs, and communal validation of the quality and excellence of the alternatives (peer governance).

Output side
On the output side, it creates a commons, using licenses that insure that the resulting value is available to all, again without permission. This common output in turn recreates a new layer of open and free material that can be used for a next iteration.

Making Almost Anything

At the Fab Labs, founded by Neil Gershenfeld at MIT's Center for Bits and Atoms, these three dimensions are merging. Fab Labs give individuals access to tools for digital fabrication; the only provisos are that you must learn to do it yourself, and you must share the lab with other uses and users. Users can use the Fab Lab 'to make almost anything'. This sounds exciting – and indeed, it is. However, there are also some serious problems connected with open design, three of which are associated with the open source movement in general.

> THE DESIGNER OF THE FUTURE HAS TO BECOME A META-DESIGNER, SHAPING ENVIRONMENTS IN WHICH UNSKILLED USERS CAN DESIGN THEIR OWN OBJECTS.

The first problem is particularly linked with open source movements that deal with the production of physical objects. Where any immaterial project is concerned, as long as there is a general infrastructure for cooperation, and there is open and free input that is available or can be created, then knowledge workers can work together on a common project. However, the production of physical goods inevitably involves costs of raising the necessary capital, and the result at least needs to recoup the costs. Indeed. such goods compete with each other by definition; if they are in the possession of one individual, they are more difficult to share, and once used up, they have to be replenished. Thanks to the 3D printer, this problem seems to become less urgent every month. The first consumer 3D printer has been announced for this autumn, produced by Hewlett-Packard. PRINTING Although it will still cost about 5000 euros, it is expected that the price will soon drop below 1000 euros. Nevertheless, the laws of the physical economy will remain a serious constraint, compared to open source activities in the digital domain.

A second problem for the open design movement is that many people are not able or willing to join the open design movement. Human life is an eternal oscillation between openness and closedness, and this holds true for design. Many people do not have the skills, the time or the interest to design their own clothes, furniture, software, pets, or weapons (see below, under the fourth problem).

Third, we should not automatically trust those who think that they are able to design. As long as the individual is happy with the result, this issue does not seem like a big problem. But as soon as the crowd starts sourcing, CROWDSOURCING the varied input might affect the reliability, functionality or the beauty of the design. Unfortunately, crowdsourcing does not always result in wisdom; quite often, all it produces is the folly of the crowds. In *You Are Not a Gadget*,[8] Jaron Lanier argues convincingly that design by committee often does not result in the best product, and that the new collectivist ethos – embodied by everything from Wikipedia to American Idol to Google searches – diminishes the importance and uniqueness of the individual voice, and that the 'hive mind' can easily lead to mob rule, digital Maoism and 'cybernetic totalism'.[9]

Fourth, I want to address an additional problem. We should not forget that the 3D printers and DNA printers PRINTING in the Fab Labs and homes of the future probably will not be used solely to design beautiful vases and flowers; they could also be used to engineer less benign things, such as lethal viruses. This is not a doomsday scenario about a possible distant future. In 2002, molecular biologist Eckhard Wimmer designed a functional polio virus on his computer with the help of biobricks and printed it with the help of a DNA synthesizer; in 2005, researchers at the US Armed Forces Institute of Pathology in Washington reconstructed the Spanish flu, which caused the death of between 50 and 100 million people in the 1920s, roughly 3% of the world's population at that time; to understand the virulent nature of that influenza virus, consider this: if a similar flu pandemic killed off 3% of the world population

today, that would be over 206 million deaths. Although we have to take these problems seriously, they should not lead to the conclusion that we should avoid further development of open design. It should urge us not to ignore or underestimate the potentially dangerous pitfalls of open design, and invent new strategies to face up to them.

NOTES

1 http://.picnicnetwork.org/program/sessions/redesigning-design.html, accessed on 16 January 2011.

2 In this article, for brevity's sake, I use the term 'open design' as a catch-all to cover open source design, downloadable design and distributed design.

3 Plessner, H. 'Die Stufen des Organischen und der Mensch. Einleitung in die Philosophische Anthropologie', in *Gesammelte Schriften*, Vol. IV. Frankfurt: Suhrkamp, 1975 [1928], p. 310.

4 http://en.wikipedia.org/wiki/Openness, accessed on 16 January 2011.

5 http://opendino.wordpress.com

6 Oosterling, H. 'Dasein as Design'. Premsela Lecture 2009, p. 15. Available online at www.premsela.org/sbeos/doc/file.php?nid=1673, accessed 16 January 2011.

7 Available online at www.we-magazine.net/we-volume-02/the-emergence-of-open-design-and-open-manufacturing/, accessed 16 January 2011.

8 Lanier, J. *You Are Not a Gadget*. Knopf, 2010. More information at www.jaronlanier.com/gadgetwebresources.html.

9 Lanier, J. 'One-Half of a Manifesto', on the Edge Foundation's forum. Available online at www.edge.org/3rd_culture/lanier/lanier_p1.html, accessed 16 January 2011.

10 Maslow, A. *The Psychology of Science: A Reconnaissance.* 1966, 2002. Available online at http://books.google.com/books?id=3_40fK8PW6QC, accessed 16 January 2011.

11 Manovich, L. *The Language of New Media*. MIT Press: Boston, 2002, p. 82. Available online at http://books.google.com/books?id=7m1GhPKuN3cC, accessed 17 January 2011.

12 Borges, L. 'The Library of Babel', reprinted in *The Total Library: Non-Fiction 1922-1986*. The Penguin Press, London, 2000, p. 214-216. Translated by Eliot Weinberger.

13 Kelly, K. *Better Than Free*. 2008. Available online at www.kk.org/thetechnium/archives/2008/01/better_than_fre.php, accessed on 16 January 2011.

PEER-TO-PEER ADVERTISEMENT

SHARE
YOUR
GENE
FUTU

P2P.DNA SHARING

THE X/Y FILES

INTO THE OPEN

JOHN THACKARA

John Thackara portrays openness in general as a matter of survival to overcome the legacy of an industrial economy obsessed with control, and open design in particular as a new way to make, use and look after things. He calls upon open designers to take this responsibility seriously.

John Thackara is an author, speaker and events facilitator with a background in philosophy and journalism. He was the first director of the Netherlands Design Institute and programme director in 2007 of Designs of the time (Dott 07), a biennial event in northeast England. John is the initiator of the long-standing pivotal series of events, festivals and projects 'Doors of Perception'. The series connects paradigm-changing designers, technology innovators, and grassroots inventors. For John, "openness is more than a commercial and cultural issue, it's a matter of survival. Open design is one of the preconditions for the continuous, collaborative, social modes of enquiry and action that are needed."

www.thackara.com

In 1909, Peter Kropotkin was asked whether it was possible to learn a trade as difficult as gardening from books. "Yes, it is possible," he replied, "but a necessary condition of success, in work on the land, is communicativeness – continual friendly intercourse with your neighbours."

Although a book can offer good general advice, Kropotkin explained, every acre of land is unique. Each plot is shaped by the soil, its topography and biodiversity, the wind and water systems of the locality, and so on. "Growing in these unique circumstances can only be learned by local residents over many seasons," the aristocratic anarchist concluded. "The knowledge which has developed in a given locality, that is necessary for survival, is the result of collective experience."[1]

The biosphere, our only home, is itself a kind of garden – and we have not looked after it well. On the contrary, we have damaged many of the food and water systems that keep us alive, and wasted vast amounts of non-renewable resources. TREND: SCARCITY OF RESOURCES One of the main reasons we've damaged our own life-support system is that we under-value the kinds of socially created knowledge Kropotkin wrote about. Ongoing attempts to privatize nature, and the over-specialization of knowledge in our universities, continue to render us blind to the consequences of our own actions.

Openness, in short, is more than a commercial and cultural issue. It's a matter of survival. Systemic challenges such as climate change, or resource depletion – these 'problems of moral bankruptcy' – cannot be solved using the same techniques that caused them in the first place. Open research, open governance and open design are preconditions for the continuous, collaborative, social mode of enquiry and action that are needed.

For centuries, the pursuit of knowledge KNOWLEDGE was undertaken in open and collaborative processes. Science, for example, developed as a result of peer review in an open and connected global community. Software, too, has flourished as a result of social creativity in what Yochai Benckler has named 'commons-based peer production'.[2] These approaches stand in stark contrast to the legacy left by the

industrial economy – from cars to power stations – which depends on a command-and-control business model and militant copyright protection. The internet may have made it easier, technically, to share ideas and knowledge – but an immense global army of rights owners and attendant lawyers works tirelessly to protect this closed system of production.

OPENNESS, IN SHORT, IS MORE THAN A COMMERCIAL AND CULTURAL ISSUE. IT'S A MATTER OF SURVIVAL.

The open design experiments you will read about in this book – such as the 60 Fab Labs in operation as we go to press – are nodes within an alternative industrial system that is now emerging. These are the "small, open, local and connected" experiments that environmental designer Ezio Manzini views as defining features of a sustainable economy.[3]

Open design is more than just a new way to create products. As a process, and as a culture, open design also changes relationships among the people who make, use and look after things. Unlike proprietary or branded products, open solutions tend to be easy to maintain and TREND: GLOBALIZATION repair locally. They are the opposite of the short-lived, use-and-discard, two-wash-two-wear model of mainstream consumer products. As you will read in the pages that follow, "nobody with a MakerBot will ever have to buy shower curtain rings again".[4]

Another open source manifesto states, "Don't judge an object for what it is, but imagine what it could become." This clarion call is welcome – but it does not promise an easy ride for open design. Our world is littered with the unintended outcomes of design actions, and open design is unlikely to be an exception. For example, 90% of the resources taken out of the ground today become waste within three months – and it's not axiomatic that open design will improve that situation. RECYCLING On the contrary, it's logically possible that a network of Fab Labs could produce the open source equivalent of a gas-guzzling SUV. The long-term value of open design will depend on the questions it is asked to address.

An important priority for open source design, therefore, is to develop decision-making processes to identify and prioritize those questions. What, in other words, should open designers design? All our design decisions, from here on, need to take into account our natural, industrial and cultural systems – and the interactions between them – as the context for our creative efforts. We need to consider the sustainability of material and energy flows in all the systems and artefacts we design. In reading the articles and case studies that follow in this book, I am confident that these caveats will be embraced by the smart and fascinating pioneers of open design who are doing such fascinating work. Crowds may be wise – but they still need designers.

NOTES

45

1   Kropotkin, P. 'Foreword', in Smith, T, *French Gardening*,
     London: Joseph Fels, 1909, p. vii-viii. Available online at www.
     tumbledownfarm.com/drupal/French_Gardening/Forewords_by_
     Prince_Kropotkin, accessed on 17 January 2011.

2   Benkler, Y, Coase's Penguin, or, Linux and the Nature of the Firm.
     Yale Law Journal, Vol. , Vol. 112, 3, pages 369-446.

3   As discussed in Manzini, E, 'Design research for sustainable
     social innovation'. Available online at www.dis.polimi.it/
     manzini-papers/07.06.03-Design-research-for-sustainable-social-
     innovation.doc, accessed on 17 January 2011.

4   See page 82 of this book.

WHAT'S
OPEN S
OF CU
INNOV

THE GENERATIVE BEDROCK OF OPEN DESIGN

MICHEL AVITAL

A shift in communications infrastructure is an important factor in how open design has taken shape and the possibilities it offers. It is a transition from the 'internet of things' to the things of the internet. Michel Avital analyses the main drivers behind open design, open innovation and open source. He describes the major features of open design and explores the preconditions for open design in relation to four aspects: object, process, practice and infrastructure, with a specific focus on infrastructure.

Michel Avital is an associate professor of Information Management at the Amsterdam Business School, University of Amsterdam, The Netherlands. For Michel, open design "signifies open-access digital blueprints that can be adapted at will to meet situational requirements, and can subsequently be used by consumers to fabricate products on demand by commercial, off-the-shelf production methods. The open design model diminishes the traditional vertical value chain that is formed by designer-manufacturer-distributor-consumer relationships and offers an alternative, open web of direct links between designers and consumers. The resulting short-spanned, transient and non-hierarchical relationships forge dynamic and flexible arrays of design blueprints that are not only user-centred but also user-driven."

http://avital.feb.uva.nl/

'Openness' is a recurring and increasingly frequent theme in recent buzzwords that populate the discourse on the forefront of technology, from *open source* via *open innovation to open design*. A review of related articles in the popular press and trade magazines indicates that the modifier *open* often denotes better, cheaper and faster. Apparently, the qualities inherent in openness or being open have materialized as the underlying enablers that pave the way for creativity, innovation and prosperity. In keeping with the thrust of this volume, this article contextualizes open design, focusing in particular on the characteristics of the infrastructure that are most conducive to its generative capability in relationship to innovation.

The Context of Open Design

Openness pertains to accessibility. Openness is a relative characteristic that refers to the degree to which something is accessible to view, modify and use. The ability to *view* refers to sharing `SHARING` content and the availability of detailed information about the subject matter. The ability to *modify* refers to sharing labour and empowering changes, improvements and extensions of subject matter. The ability to *use* refers to sharing ownership and enabling semi or unrestricted reuse of the subject matter or parts thereof. These are the three fundamental operations that are implied by accessibility. Subsequently, from a systems theory perspective, openness relates to the transparency and permeability of any natural or constructed boundaries. Yet openness is not merely a technical attribute that conveys flow or lack thereof; it is an embedded trait that pervades the structure of a thriving civil society. From a social perspective, openness is a core characteristic of an infrastructure that conveys and reinforces sharing, reciprocity, collaboration, tolerance, equity, justice and freedom. The application of openness, `OPEN EVERYTHING` as implied by various accessibility features, to a growing number of central ubiquitous practices that drive the human enterprise,

JUXTAPOSING ARCHETYPES OF OPEN-X

	OPEN INNOVATION	OPEN SOURCE	OPEN DESIGN
VALUE PROPOSITION AND THRUST	DISTRIBUTED KNOWLEDGE	DISTRIBUTED DEVELOPMENT	DISTRIBUTED MANUFACTURING
CORE OPENNESS FACET	VIEW	MODIFY	USE
PRIME ACTORS	ORGANIZATIONS	DEVELOPER COMMUNITIES	CONSUMERS

has turned into a megatrend that can be labelled the *Rise of Open-X*. Megatrends are widespread trends which have a major impact and are likely to affect all levels – individuals, organizations, markets, countries and civil society – for a long duration. Understanding megatrends TRENDS and their rolling effects can provide valuable information for developing futuristic scenarios and can subsequently help to shape current actions in anticipation of that future. So far, as described below, Open-X has materialized in various configurations that can be classified according to three archetypes: open innovation, open source and open design. The three archetypes are juxtaposed in the table on the previous page as a preliminary overview to point out their different respective value propositions and thrust (as a distributed collective action), core openness orientation, and prime actors involved.

Open Innovation

The value proposition and thrust of *open innovation* is 'distributed knowledge' processes that emphasize the *view-related* capabilities of openness. The prime actors of open innovation are organizations. According to the traditional doctrine, industry leaders self-create the most and the best ideas; innovation should therefore be fostered by internal development teams behind high organizational walls and protected as a trade secret. In contrast, according to open innovation, industry leaders make the best use of internal and external ideas to develop better business models. In other words, superior outcome should be expected with permeable boundaries between a firm and its environment, which allow idea flow, knowledge KNOWLEDGE exchange, and intellectual property trade. Reaching out and tapping into external knowledge resources extends the generative and innovative capabilities of a firm, as demonstrated by industry leaders like Procter & Gamble, Boeing, Philips and many others. The tenets of open innovation have promoted the proliferation of communities of practice and laid the foundations of crowdsourcing. CROWDSOURCING

Open Source

The value proposition and thrust of *open source* is 'distributed development' processes that emphasize the *modification-related* capabilities of openness. The prime actors of open source are developers. The open source concept originated in the software

industry; according to the traditional doctrine, software is developed in commercial software firms by professional personnel, guarded through legal and technical measures, and then licensed for a fee. In contrast, according to the open source business model, software is developed through coordinated peer production by independent volunteers.

THE APPLICATION OF OPENNESS TO A GROWING NUMBER OF PRACTICES THAT DRIVE THE HUMAN ENTERPRISE, HAS TURNED INTO A MEGATREND THAT CAN BE LABELED THE RISE OF OPEN-X.

Subsequently, everyone can freely access the source code, and can modify and redistribute it under the same terms, thus nourishing continuous cycles of improvement, adaptation, and extension in a distributed fashion. Reaching out and tapping into external development resources extends the generative and innovative capabilities of a core project. Inspired by the impact of high-profile projects like Linux and Mozilla Firefox, the tenets of the open source development, licensing and distribution model have promoted the proliferation of open source projects of all sorts – from digital content development (e.g. Wikipedia), via vehicles (e.g. c,mm,n) and beverages (e.g. Free Beer - Vores øl), to 3D printers (e.g. RepRap), just to name a few. OPEN EVERYTHING

Open Design

The value proposition and thrust of *open design* is 'distributed manufacturing' processes that emphasize the *use-related* capabilities of openness. The prime actors of open design are consumers. Although designers undoubtedly play a pivotal role in fostering open design by producing and sharing suitable design blueprints, BLUEPRINTS ultimately the consumers who engage in distributed manufacturing are the core

51

players and *raison d'être* of open design. According to the traditional doctrine, design is mostly a preliminary stage prior to commercial manufacturing and distribution. In contrast, open design is directed toward consumers who engage in fabrication, passing over the conventional manufacturing and distribution channels. Open design implies that the design blueprints are publicly available, sharable, licensed under open-access terms, and distributed digitally in a general design specification file format (e.g. dxf, dwg). Moreover, open design is not black-boxed or exclusive; it implies reconfigurable and extensible design that can be fabricated in distributed and scalable fashions through commercially available, off-the-shelf, multi-purpose means of production.

A structured description of the unique features and boundaries of open design is provided in the table on the next page. The inherent reconfiguration and extension potential of a user-driven open design reinforces the generative and innovative capabilities of consumers. The tenets of open design have inspired the development of public manufacturing facilities networks like Fab Lab, and laid the foundations of open design clearinghouses like Ponoko, Shareable and Instructables. In summary, the distinctions between the three archetypes of Open-X are more a matter of thrust and areas of application. They are not mutually exclusive. All three inherit the core features of openness and naturally overlap to some degree. Open design, for example, is not merely a matter of re-use and distributed manufacturing – it also entails sharing design blueprints and sharing extensions thereof, thus distributing knowledge and development. Building on the working definition of open design and an understanding of its unique features, the remainder of this article will discuss its potential, in particular addressing the infrastructure characteristics that are most conducive to its generative capability in the context of innovation.

Unpacking Open Design

Open design signifies open-access digital blueprints that can be adapted at will to meet situated requirements, and can subsequently be used by consumers to fabricate products on demand by commercial, off-the-shelf production methods. The open design model diminishes the traditional vertical value chain that is formed by designer-manufacturer-distributor-consumer relationships and offers an alternative, open web of direct links between designers and consumers. The resulting short-spanned, transient and non-hierarchical relationships forge dynamic and flexible arrays of blueprints that are not only user-centred but also user-driven.

The discourse on open design encompasses a multitude of considerations: for example, design specification, fabrication, collaborative action, supply and value chain management, business models, legal aspects, technological infrastructure and normative values. The complexity of this ecology can be untangled to some extent by classifying the underlying issues of open design into four interdependent conceptual layers, as follows:

Object layer refers to the *design blueprints* that enable and constrain the specification of the design artefacts. This layer encompasses the design and distribution of open design objects, that is, configurable and extensible blueprints that are available under open access license in online public repositories.

Process layer refers to the *means of production* that enables and constrains the fabrication of the design objects. This layer encompasses open design fabrication, that is, the application and operation of commercial, off-the-shelf machinery like printers, PRINTING laser cutters or CNC machine tools to produce customized products with no custom-built moulds or machines.

Practice layer refers to the *work practices* that enable and constrain the conception of the design processes. This layer encompasses open design culture, that is, the related nomenclature, professional standards, craftsmanship, rules of the trade, code of conduct, rituals and normative values.

Infrastructure layer refers to the underlying *institutional and technical foundations* that enable and constrain the vitality of the design practices. This layer encompasses open design substructure, that is, the related legal system, market structure and technical architecture that govern open design activities and future growth.

LAYERS OF OPEN DESIGN

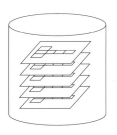

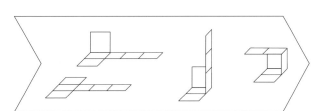

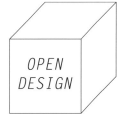

PRACTISE

The work practices that enable and constrain the conception of the design processes. The practice layer encompasses open design culture, that is, the related nomenclature, professional standards, craftsmanship, rules of the trade, code of conduct, rituals and normative values.

OPEN DESIGN

53

OBJECT

Configurable and extensible blueprints that are available under open access license in online public repositories.

PROCESS

The means of production that enables and constrains the fabrication of the design objects.

INFRASTRUCTURE

The institutional and technical foundations that enable and constrain the vitality of the design practices. The related legal system, market structure and technical architecture that govern open design activities and future growth.

The discourse so far is focused on the object and process layers, with some touches upon the practice layer. However, quite surprisingly, despite its fundamental role, the infrastructure layer is virtually ignored.

Designing Generative Infrastructure

The infrastructure that governs open design activities, business models and development is based on the related code of law, market structure and technical architecture, which together enable and constrain most human activity systems in an attempt to balance inherent conflicts and pursue the common good. In a general sense, infrastructures are designed to promote fairness, wealth and operational efficiency. TEMPLATE CULTURE Much has been written about the general nature of infrastructures elsewhere, leaving no need to reiterate it here. Instead, let us elaborate on the generative capability of infrastructure as an additional area of concern that should be considered particularly in the context of developing infrastructure requirements for open design. In view of the generative character of design in general, and open design in particular, developing an appropriate infrastructure should aim to incorporate the structural features that are most conducive to creative processes and products. Building on the concept of *generative design*, I suggest a set of generalizable considerations for designing such infrastructures. More specifically, I propose that the infrastructure of open design should be evocative, engaging, adaptive, and open.

Generative design refers to the design considerations in developing an array of artefacts and interactions that support and enhance *generative capacity* – that is, the considerations in designing systems that are conducive to the ability of a person or group to produce new configurations and possibilities, to reframe the way we see and understand the world, and to challenge the normative status quo.[1] People's generative capacity is a key source of innovation; by definition, generative design aims to encapsulate the design directives that enhance and complement that human capability.

In general, generative capacity refers to having an evocative power or aptitude that can result in producing or creating something, or tapping into a source of innovation. In the context of open design infrastructure, the modifier 'generative' denotes that the noun it modifies is conducive to the production of something innovative or the discovery of new and hitherto unknown design alternatives. In other words, generative design refers here to the design requirements and considerations in developing open design infrastructures – that is, the related code of law, market structure and technical architecture – that augment people's natural ability to innovate. Subsequently, four top-level design directives are suggested for infrastructures, as follows:

Generative infrastructure is evocative
Generative infrastructure inspires people to create something unique. It evokes new thinking and enables them to translate their ideas into a new context. The infrastructure can help to create the environment or conditions that are prone to those insights by generating and juxtaposing diverse frames that are not commonly associated with one another within an underlying context. Systemic features that drive evocative design enable, for example, seeing an object or situation from multiple perspectives, testing it in multiple situations, examining it at multiple degrees of granularity, and exploring multiple overlay configurations.

Generative infrastructure is engaging
Generative infrastructure is enchanting and holds the attention of people by inducing their natural playfulness and 'flow experience'. The infrastructure TEMPLATE CULTURE can help in the creation of engaging environments or platforms that stimulate the users' cognitive spontaneity and playfulness as well as overall positive affect state, thus encouraging further exploration, tinkering and experimentation. Systemic features that drive engaging design enable, for example, fostering positive affect and high spirit that stimulate a state of '*joie de vivre*', activating cognitive spontaneity induced by playfulness, and stirring up curiosity through intriguing challenges.

Generative infrastructure is adaptive
Generative infrastructure is flexible and conducive to effective use by a heterogeneous set of people in their own respective environments and for various tasks within an intended scope. It can be adapted with respect to the type of users or groups that it

54

THE DISTINCT FEATURES OF OPEN DESIGN

	OPEN DESIGN IS...	OPEN DESIGN IS NOT...
ACCESS	AVAILABLE, SHARABLE, LICENSED UNDER OPEN-ACCESS TERMS	CONCEALED, PROTECTED, LICENSED FOR A FEE
BLUEPRINTS	SPECIFIED BY COMMON DIGITAL NOTATION LANGUAGE	SPECIFIED BY PROPRIETARY NOTATION LANGUAGE
DERIVATIVES	RECONFIGURABLE AND EXTENSIBLE	BLACK-BOXED AND FIXED
EXCLUSIVITY	REPRODUCIBLE	LIMITED TO A FINITE SERIES OR ONE-OFF
MEANS OF PRODUCTION	FABRICATED BY COMMERCIAL, OFF-THE-SHELF, MULTI-PURPOSE MACHINES	FABRICATED BY ARTISAN HANDWORK, CUSTOM-BUILT MACHINES OR MOULDS
MANUFACTURING PROCESS	SUBJECT TO DISTRIBUTED AND SCALABLE PRODUCTION	SUBJECT TO CENTRALLY CONTROLLED AND PRESET BATCH PRODUCTION
POTENTIAL	GENERATIVE	CLOSED-ENDED

55

serves in diverse problem spaces. It is also simple to understand and easy for anyone to master. The infrastructure can help in the creation of adaptive systems or platforms that are flexible yet powerful enough to enable the generation of a continuous stream of new ideas and configurations. Systemic features that drive adaptive design enable, for example, user-induced tailoring and customization to meet situated needs, self-production of complementary extensions and features that meet new or initially unforeseen needs, automatic system-induced adaptation, and overall scalable functionality with no regard to size-related attributes.

Generative infrastructure is open
Generative infrastructure accentuates permeable boundaries and transparency that promote co-production, cross-fertilization and exchange of any kind. The infrastructure ARCHITECTURE can help in the creation of open systems or platforms that provide connectivity, enable transparency, allow information sharing, and encourage dialogue with no regard to institutionally or culturally imposed boundaries. Systemic features that drive open design enable, for example, free and unrestricted access to information, communication among all stakeholders, and the easy integration of third-party extensions by independent boundary-spanners. In summary, from the generative requirement perspective, infrastructures of open design should be evocative, engaging, adaptive and open. However, while the last two directives are clearly implied in the discourse of open design, the first two have not yet been addressed. Subsequently, the inclusion of evocative and engaging features in the infrastructure of open design, let alone in the discourse concerning its requirements, is strongly recommended. Although this conclusion might not be obvious for legislators, policymakers, managers, and engineers, it should be quite intuitive for designers. The expected proliferation of open design has far-reaching implications that are likely to extend well beyond design practices as such and have significant socio-economic effects on a global scale.

Another Brave New World
Open design presents entrepreneurs and agile companies with a grand opportunity to expand existing markets, to develop new ones, and to capture large shares from current market leaders. Mobilizing open design to generate organizational value and to boost its market position requires radical strategic and operational changes. However, the tight coupling between design and production, which has so far been instrumental in fostering economies of scope and competitive advantages for the current industry leaders, is now likely to hinder their agile capability and their ability to take advantage of the new vistas that are beginning to be afforded by open design.

PEOPLE'S GENERATIVE CAPACITY IS A KEY SOURCE OF INNOVATION; BY DEFINITION, GENERATIVE DESIGN AIMS TO ENCAPSULATE THE DESIGN DIRECTIVES THAT ENHANCE AND COMPLEMENT THAT HUMAN CAPABILITY.

The adoption of open design practices by established industry leaders, let alone run-of-the-mill manufacturers, where the dominant culture and mode of product design has been shaped and reshaped over long periods, is likely to pose multiple challenges to these organizations at all levels, from the boardroom to the production floor. Subsequently, the resistance to change in these organizations is expected to reinforce the current tight coupling between product design and industrial manufacturing. Just as Amazon could conquer the market share of established retailers that were unable to adapt quickly enough to the new marketplace of e-commerce, emerging market players based on open design business models are likely to cannibalize the turf of established manufacturers that are entrenched in the old model of industrial production.

56

From Push to Pull

Open design paves the way to the next iteration in the massive shift from push to pull business models. In general, push business models are based on top-down value chains where a line of a few mass-produced products is distributed broadly through value-driven downstream marketing techniques. In contrast, pull business models are based on bottom-up value chains where a line of customer-configured products are distributed individually through features-driven upstream marketing techniques. Whereas push models are based on economies of scale and emphasize cost efficiency, pull models are based on flexible manufacturing and emphasize mass ustomization. In previous centuries, most artefacts – from shoes to carriages – were custom-designed and built on demand by a craftsperson.

Building on push business models, the industrial revolution almost wiped out cottage manufacturing and shifted its lion's share to production lines and mass-scale manufacturing in factories that offer economies of scope and scale. Consequently, the resulting abundant supply of affordable products was instrumental to massive market expansion, higher living standards, and growing wealth across the board. This prosperity has come at the expense of product variety and personalization, as most notoriously conveyed by Ford's remark "any color as long as it's black". `MASS CUSTOMIZATION`

OPEN DESIGN INFUSES 'DO IT YOURSELF' WITH A WHOLE NEW MEANING THAT GOES FAR BEYOND COST SAVINGS OR THE JOY OF CRAFTING.

The advent of the internet has bestowed a new communication infrastructure that made it possible not only to exceed the economic accomplishments of industrialization, but also to offer an unprecedented variety of products and personalization thereof.

The latter has been accomplished through pull business models and upstream marketing that take advantage of automated fulfilment and logistics centres supported by fast, wideband, many-to-many communication networks. The extent of product variety and personalization has been attained and fortified in three main phases enabled by the accessibility (i.e. ability to view, modify and change) afforded by the internet. In the first phase, *retailers* have introduced consumers to the ability to view up-to-date, rich and targeted information about off-the-shelf products, thus enabling them to make informed decisions. Then, in the second phase, *manufacturers* have introduced consumers to the ability to *modify* base products and specify a customized configuration thereof, thus enabling them to fine-tune a product according to their preferences. Finally, in the still-nascent third phase, *designers* have introduced to consumers the ability to *use* blueprints for self-managed fabrication, thus enabling them to gain full control over the features of the resulted product as well as its production process. In summary, as in a stage model, every phase builds upon the previous one to bring the consumers closer to the designers and to provide them with more control over what they get, how it is produced, and how it is delivered.

The Road Ahead

Open design is still nascent, yet it provides a springboard for radical changes in the way we acquire almost anything that is currently mass-produced. Open design presents a new way of design that complements new methods of fabrication, commonly branded as 3D printers `PRINTING` of all sorts. Open design infuses 'Do It Yourself' with a whole new meaning that goes far beyond cost savings or the joy of crafting. It allows consumers to be in charge and offers them an opportunity for full customization of an artefact, including a choice of features, materials and delivery options. It allows for continuous innovation and localization, which in turn has major implications for consumers in shoestring economies as well as in developed countries. It also provides a fertile ground for the development of new forms of organization, new business models, new supply chain structures, new varieties of products and services, and the like, as demonstrated in the many cases in this volume. Nonetheless, traditional design and mass manufacturing practices have been extremely valuable since the Industrial Revolution REVOLUTION and are unlikely to disappear in the future. Although the threat to the dominant technologies and practices may seem implausible, open design presents a clear alternative that may grow strong once it reaches a critical mass in the right socio-economic conditions. Open design is not a threat to designers' livelihood. Quite the contrary; it opens new vistas and new opportunities and is likely to generate increased consumer appreciation of the role of designers. Moreover, it is likely to bring designers closer to the intended and unintended applications of their designs. Grand opportunities also imply undeveloped land. There is much development to do in all four layers of open design – the object, process, practice and infrastructure layers. To a large extent, the discourse mirrors the field; the most immediate attention is required in shaping practices and laying the foundations of the support infrastructures.

Conclusion

It has been suggested that open design stands for accessible design in the form of blueprints that are publicly open to view, modify and use under open-access terms. Moreover, open design often implies that the design blueprints are available via open-access digital repositories, that they can be adapted at will to meet situational requirements, and that they can be used by consumers to fabricate products on demand by commercial, off-the-shelf means of production. DOWNLOADABLE DESIGN Open design is generative. It is conducive to continuous re-design, adaption, refinement and extension. Open design is a potent elixir that mitigates stagnation and awakens generative action.

58

NOTES

1   See Avital, M. and Te'eni, D. 'From Generative Fit to Generative Capacity: Exploring an Emerging Dimension of Information Systems Design and Task Performance', *Information Systems Journal*, 19(4), 2009, p. 345-367.

COMMUNITY ADVERTISEMENT

IDEA
INGS
BODY

DBC Design By Community

AUTHORS AND OWNERS

ANDREW KATZ

Andrew Katz traces the origins of the problems of copyright legislation and practice when confronted with the natural, human, social mode of creative endeavour. Building on developments in open source software, he outlines how designers could benefit from a similar model and reveals the differences between the digital and the analogue realm.

Andrew Katz is a former software engineer and partner at Moorcrofts LLP in Marlow, Bucks, UK, specializing in advising clients on intellectual property and other aspects of open source software. For Andrew, "a design is an open design if it bears four freedoms. One: The freedom to use the design, including making items based on it, for any purpose. Two: The freedom to study how the design works, and change it to make it do what you wish. Three: The freedom to redistribute copies of the design so you can help your neighbour. Four: The freedom to distribute copies of your modified versions of the design to others so the whole community can benefit from your changes. Access to the design documents is a precondition for these freedoms."

www.moorcrofts.com

We are reaching the end of a great historical experiment. Printing (starting with Gutenberg-style presses `PRINTING` and leading to huge industrial Heidelberg printing machines), radio broadcasting, 78s, vinyl, CDs, cinema, television: all these discoveries formed the technological backdrop for this experiment. All are (or were) media based on the principle of one-to-many distribution. To understand how this experiment was initiated, and how it is reaching its end, we need to understand a little of the nature of the businesses involved in these activities, and how the law enabled them to attain, and retain, that nature. `WYS ≠ WYG`

AS THE PUBLIC GREW ACCUSTOMED TO THE IDEA OF PASSIVE CONSUMPTION, CREATIVITY BECAME INCREASINGLY MARGINALIZED.

64

The one-to-many broadcast distribution model distorted our perception of creativity. A key characteristic of one-to-many distribution is the role of the gatekeeper: the corporation which decides what we, the public, get to read, watch or listen to. The roles of creator and consumer are starkly defined and contrasted. As the public grew accustomed to the idea of passive consumption, creativity became increasingly marginalized, at least in those areas covered by copyright. `ACTIVISM` Creativity was perceived as capable of flourishing only through the patronage of the movie studios, the record companies or the TV stations.

The industrial technology behind printing, broadcasting and vinyl duplication is expensive. Copyright law grants a monopoly which enables the distributors of media to invest in the capital infrastructure required for their packaging and distribution. These are the businesses which grew fat on the monopolies so granted, and they succeeded in convincing the public that it was the corporations' role to provide, and the public's role to pay and consume.

The original social approach to creativity did not become extinct as the dominant producer/consumer mode became established, even for media (like music, for example) where it applied. Andrew Douglas's film *Searching for the Wrong-Eyed Jesus* shows that a visitor to the late 20th century Appalachians of the American South may well be asked: "What instrument do you play?" If the visitor answers: "I don't play any", the questioner will go on to say: "Ok, so you must sing."

Steven Johnson in *Where Good Ideas Come From* makes the convincing case, based on a mass of evidence, that the social mode is more effective at maximizing creativity than relying on lone inventors and creators sitting in their garrets and sheds. Lone creators make good central figures in a compelling narrative – one reason why this meme is so popular. However, examining the truth behind the narrative often reveals that any creative work has much broader parentage than the story suggests. James Boyle in *The Public Domain* reveals the story behind the Ray Charles song *I Got a Woman*, tracing it backwards to Gospel roots, and forwards to the YouTube mashup George Bush *Doesn't Care About Black People*, which sprang to prominence in the aftermath of Hurricane Katrina. To be sure, companies sometimes tried to foster a social model *within* the organization, but as Johnson points out, the benefits of social creation increase very dramatically with the size of the pool of participants, due to network effects. Until company silos are able to combine, the beneficial effects are relatively small.

Technology is Expensive

The internet has proved hugely disruptive. `TREND: NETWORK SOCIETY` The sharing and social nature of Web 2.0 has enabled the rediscovery of the natural, human, social mode of creative endeavour. The social side of the internet is dominated by individuals acting in their private capacity, outside the scope of businesses. Companies were initially wary of losing control over the activities of their staff, and regarded internet social activities as time-wasting at best. In the worst-case scenario, businesses saw online social networking as a potential channel for employees to leak the company's valuable intellectual property, and were therefore often slow to see the benefits of social interaction in terms of benefits to their creativity. As they have seen the benefits accrue to their competitors, however, companies are starting to embrace a more open mode of business.

A return to the social mode is not without its setbacks. The internet radically lowered the barrier to entry for collaborative participation, and consequently increased the number of potential contacts that an entrant can make. SHARING This immensely powerful engine of creativity comes with a brake that inhibits its full capacity: the effect of unfit-for-purpose copyright laws.

The copyright laws of the broadcast era do more to assist the incumbent gatekeepers (the film companies, music companies and so on) than to promote the social mode of CO-CREATION collaboration. A side effect of the digital world is that almost every form of digital interaction involves copying of some sort. Whereas copyright law had nothing to say about sharing a book with a friend by lending it to her, in the digital realm, lending her a digital copy of Nineteen Eighty-Four to read on her e-book reader or computer involves a form of copying which may potentially violate copyright law.

The broadcast-model gatekeepers have used this unintended side effect of copyright law to their advantage, taking action against private individuals who had no intention of monetary gain, including mash-up artists, REMIX home video enthusiasts and slash fiction authors. Incumbent rights holders, fearful of losing their profitable monopoly-based businesses, have sought to extend their rights ever further by lobbying governments (frequently successfully) to legislate for new and increased intellectual property rights, extending such rights far beyond their original purpose and intention. To put the issue in context, it is necessary to ask a fundamental question: what is copyright for?

Thomas Jefferson was one of the most lucid writers on the topic. He understood well the unique nature of knowledge:

> "If nature has made any one thing less susceptible than all others of exclusive property, it is the action of the thinking power called an idea, which an individual may exclusively possess as long as he keeps it to himself; but the moment it is divulged, it forces itself into the possession of every one, and the receiver cannot dispossess himself of it. Its peculiar character, too, is that no one possesses the less, because every other possesses the whole of it. He who receives an idea from me, receives instruction himself without lessening mine; as he who lights his taper at mine, receives light without darkening me. That ideas should freely spread from one to another over the globe, for the moral and mutual instruction of man, and improvement of his condition, seems to have been peculiarly and benevolently designed by nature, when she made them, like fire, expansible over all space, without lessening their density in any point, and like the air in which we breathe, move, and have our physical being, incapable of confinement or exclusive appropriation. Inventions then cannot, in nature, be a subject of property."[1]

A Monopoly is a Bad Thing

Jefferson did admit that creative people should be given a limited right of exclusive control over their creations. A monopoly is inherently a bad thing, a fact that was recognized in the late 18th century, as it is today. Nonetheless, a monopoly of control in the form of copyright or a patent was the most convenient way of enabling the creators to be remunerated for their work. And once the monopoly expired, the idea would be freely available to all and would become part of the common heritage of mankind, to be used without restriction by anyone. The necessary (but limited) monopoly includes 'copyright'. The principle that the restrictions should be the minimum possible to achieve that aim should be copyright's golden rule. That golden rule has been repeatedly ignored. The scope of protection has increased steadily over the last three hundred years, to the extent that the protection granted in Europe to the author of a novel, for example, lasts for seventy years after his or her death. Materials that are not restricted by intellectual property are considered to be 'in the public domain'. Commentators have become increasingly strident in arguing that the public domain is a public good; it is likely that Jefferson would have agreed. In the same way that common land is an area where anyone can allow their animals to graze, the public domain has been described as a commons of knowledge, where potentially anyone can graze on the intellectual creations of others. The public domain has one crucial difference from a commons in the tangible world: a meadow open to all can easily be over-grazed and ruined, so that it becomes of use to no one (sometimes referred to as the 'tragedy of the commons'). It is impossible to exhaust the commons of knowledge and ideas.

The Tragedy of the Commons

The modern 'tragedy of the commons' is that, just as the internet makes it easier to pass ideas and knowledge KNOWLEDGE from one person to another (for "the moral and mutual instruction of man, and improvement of his condition"), it seems that legislation and the more extreme activities of the rights holders are making it more difficult for those ideas and knowledge to enter the commons in the first place. This is because the duration of intellectual property is constantly being extended (will the early Mickey Mouse films ever enter the public domain?), and so is its scope, as evidenced by the patenting of genes or plants. Increasingly, people are becoming aware of the value of the commons and are seeking to protect it. At the same time, we are gradually realizing that the monopoly granted by intellectual property laws is a blunt instrument, and that people are prepared to create for reasons other than the expectation of payment for the use of their creation. Copyright law does not always have to work against the commons. Free and open source software has been an undeniable success. Gartner confidently states that all businesses today use at least some free software in their systems; the Linux Foundation is predicting that free software will underpin a $50 billion economy in 2011. Following from these and other successes, the applicability of the open source model has been considered in other contexts.

The Creative Commons Licenses

One of the most prominent open source models has been the Creative Commons CREATIVE COMMONS movement. Founded in 2001, Creative Commons has written a suite of licences which were inspired by the GNU/GPL, but which are intended for use in relation to a broad range of media, including music, literature, images

GNU/GPL AND BSD LICENSES

In the late 1980s, computer programmer Richard Stallman realized that copyright law could be turned inside out to create a commons of computer software. The method he proposed was simple, but brilliant.

Software is protected by copyright. The software business model used in the 1980s involved granting customers permission (the licence) to use a specific piece of software. This licence was conditional on the customer not only paying the software publisher fee, but also adhering to a number of other restrictions (such as only using the software on one computer). Why not, Stallman reasoned, make it a condition of the licence that if you took his software and passed it on (which he was happy for people to do), then they had to pass it on, together with any changes they made, under the same licence? He called this sort of software 'free software': once a piece of software has been released under this sort of licence, it can be passed on freely to other people, with only one restriction: that if they pass it on, in turn, they must also ensure that it is passed it on in a way that guarantees and honours that freedom for other people.

In time, he reasoned, more and more software would be released under this licence, and a commons of freely available software would flourish. The most widely used version of the licence is the GNU General Public License version 2, known as the GPL. In the 19 years since it was issued, it has become the most commonly used software licence. The GPL is the licence at the core of Linux, the computer operating system which powers Google, Amazon and Facebook, and which enabled Red Hat to forecast revenue in excess of $1Bn in financial year 2010-11.

The software commons envisioned by Stallman not only exists; by any measure, it has been an overwhelming success. Its success can be measured in countless ways: the number of participants creating software for that GPL commons, the number of open source software programs in use, or the environments in which such software can be found. More than 90 of the 100 most powerful computers in the world run on GPL software, not to mention mobile phones and in-car entertainment systems; open source software is at the core of the business offerings of such large companies as IBM and Red Hat.

The Commons Analogy

The success of free software cannot be solely attributed to the GPL. The GPL extracts a price for using the commons. To risk taking the analogy too far, a landowner who has property adjoining the GPL commons and who wants to use it also has to add his own land to the commons. (Remember, this is the magical land of ideas which cannot be ruined by over-grazing.) This will have the effect of increasing the size of the commons as more and more adjoining landowners want to make use of the commons and donate their own land in the process. However, many of them may not want to join this scheme, either because they do not want to add their own land to the

and movies. The licences are drafted to be simple to understand and are modular, in that the rights owner can choose from a selection of options. The *attribution* option requires that anyone making use of the work makes fair attribution to the author; the *share alike* option is akin to the GPL, in that if a licensee takes the work and redistributes it (whether amended or not), then the redistribution needs to be on the same form of licence; the *no derivatives* option means that work may be passed on freely, but not modified, and the *non-commercial* option means that the work can only be used and distributed in a non-commercial context. There are now millions of different works available under a Creative Commons licence: Flickr is just one content hosting site which has enabled Creative Commons licensing as a search option. There are, at the time of writing, nearly 200,000,000 Creative Commons-licensed images available for use on Flickr alone.

Similar sites provide music and literary works under a Creative Commons licence. Creative Commons provide a legal infrastructure for designers and other creatives operating within the digital domain to adopt this model. They also offer an effective choice as to whether an appropriate model is GPL-style share-alike, or BSD style. Where designers' DESIGNERS work moves into the physical world, matters become much less straightforward. The movement of hardware design into the commons has been difficult. The fundamental issues can be summarized as follows:

→ In the digital world, the creator has the choice of whether a GPL or BSD model is appropriate. This choice does not translate well to the analogue world.

→ Digital works are relatively easy to create and test. on low-cost equipment. Analogue works are more

commons, or because they have already pledged their land to another commons.

Is it possible to generate a commons of ideas without forcing participants to pay the price of entry; without requiring that they add their own adjoining land to the commons? Is the compulsion of the GPL necessary, or is the social and community dynamic powerful enough to allow a similar commons of ideas to spring up on its own?

The software industry has given us several outstanding examples of this. Apache, the most popular web server software in the world, used by many of the world's busiest web sites, is issued under a licence which does not ask users to pay the GPL price. Anyone can take the Apache code, and modify it and combine it with their other software, and release it without having to release any sources to anyone else. In contrast to the GPL, there is no compulsion to add your software to the Apache commons if you build on Apache software and distribute your developments, but

many people choose to contribute in return even without this compulsion. FreeBSD, to take another example, is an operating system bearing some similarity to GNU/Linux which is licensed under a very liberal licence allowing its use, amendment and distribution without contributing back; nonetheless, many people choose to do so.

Free Riders

A parallel development to the GPL was the BSD licence, first used for the Berkeley Software Distribution (BSD). As opposed to the GPL, the BSD licence only requires the acknowledgement of the original authors, and poses no restrictions on how the source code may be used. As a result, BSD-licensed code can be used in proprietary software that only acknowledges the authors.

The GPL tackles an issue called the free rider problem. Because BSD does not compel people to contribute back to the commons, those who take advantage without contributing back are called free riders. The question is whether free riders really are a

problem (as the GPL band would maintain), or whether they are (as the BSD band would maintain) at worst a cost-free irritant, and at best, a cadre of people who will eventually see the light and start to contribute, once they recognize the benefits. Supporters of both the GPL and BSD models of licensing have similar aims. In both cases, they seek to support a software commons which will enable the social mode of creativity to flourish.

While the BSD model could subsist in the absence of copyright, GPL relies (perhaps ironically) on copyright law to enforce its compulsion to share. It still remains an open question as to whether the better model is to use licensing to compel people to participate in the software commons, thus reducing the free rider problem (as with GPL), or whether voluntary engagement will result in a more active community (as with Apache). Designers working outside the digital domain will rarely have the chance to choose a GPL-style option.

difficult to create, test and copy, which creates barrier-to-entry problems.

→ Digital goods are easy to transport; analogue goods are not. This creates a barrier to the communication necessary to get the maximum benefit out of network effects.

The barrier to entry for any participant in a digital project is remarkably low. A low-cost computer and basic internet access are all that is required to have a system capable of running the (free) GNU/Linux operating system, accessing (free) project hosting sites like sourceforge.com or koders.com. A vast range of tools required to develop software (such as GCC – the GNU Compiler Collection) are also available as free software. Copying purely digital works is trivially easy. Physical (or 'analogue') objects are a different matter. Hardware development is likely to require more intensive investment in equipment (including premises in which the hardware can be placed), not just for development, but for testing. Electronic digital hardware is probably closest to software in terms of low barrier to entry: for example, the open-source Arduino microcontroller project enables an experimenter to get started with as little as $30 for a basic USB controller board (or less, if the experimenter is prepared to build the board). Arduino's schematics, board layouts and prototyping software are all open source. BLUEPRINTS However, Arduino-like projects represent the lowest barrier to entry in the hardware world.

Complications of Analogue

An Arduino-style project is essentially a hybrid of the analogue and the digital domains. Prototyping software makes it possible to develop Arduino-based hardware in the digital domain, where it retains all the characteristics of the digital world: ease of copying, the ability to upload prototypes to fellow contributors for commentary, assistance and the chance to show off.

RIGHTS AND LICENSING SCHEMES

68

The re-use of designs is governed mainly by copyright, design rights and patents. Traditional open licensing schemes have been based on copyright, as this is the main intellectual property right which impinges on software, the most fertile ground for openness.

Software licensing schemes include the GPL (which enforces copyleft) and BSD (which doesn't). Software licences rarely work properly when applied to other works. For literary, graphic and musical works, the Creative Commons suite is more effective. They allow both copyleft (*share alike*) and non-copyleft options. They may work well when applied to underlying design documents, which are covered by copyright, and control the distribution of those documents, as well as the creation of physical objects from them, but (depending on the jurisdiction) their protection is unlikely to extend to copying the physical object itself. Some efforts have been made to create licences that cover hardware; the TAPR Open Hardware Licence is one example. However, these efforts have frequently been criticized for their lack of effectiveness.

www.opensource.org/licenses/index.html

CREATIVE COMMONS AND DESIGN RIGHTS

Creative Commons licensing is fundamentally based on copyright, and there is little clarity or consensus on how such licenses would operate in relation to design rights across the myriad different jurisdictions and types of rights.

Those designers operating purely in the realm of copyright will find that there is already an existing structure of support in terms of Creative Commons licences and associated communities. Where other forms of intellectual property impinge, matters are far more murky. The Creative Commons licences are arguably drafted to be sufficiently broad as to cover unregistered design in certain circumstances. However, since they were not drafted with design rights in mind, it cannot be assumed that the copying of a three-dimensional object will automatically fall within the scope of such a license.

www.creativecommons.org

These are characteristics which enable network effects, and which make the open source model very powerful. It is only when the project is implemented as a physical circuit board that these characteristics are lost.

The analogue world is not always so simple. One of the most ambitious open source projects is the 40 Fires/Riversimple hydrogen car project, which has developed a small urban car (the Hyrban) powered by hydrogen, using a fuel cell/electric drivetrain. Elements of the design (such as power control software or the dashboard user interface) can be developed largely in the digital domain, but the development of motors, brakes, the body shell and so on are strictly analogue only. `WYS ≠ WYG` Not only do these analogue elements present a large barrier to entry for interested tinkerers, but they also tend to restrict their ability to participate in the development community: a necessity if network effects are to work. It is, clearly, difficult to upload a car to a development site and say "can you tell me why the windscreen leaks?"

COPYRIGHT PROTECTS THE EXPRESSION OF AN IDEA. RETAINING THE SAME IDEA, BUT RECASTING THE EXPRESSION OF IT IN A DIFFERENT FORM, DOES NOT INFRINGE ON THE COPYRIGHT.

Another significant issue is the lack of access to design software at a low cost. Software developers have access to high-quality tools like development environments and tools available for free under free software licences. There is no similar suite of CAD software, and proprietary CAD software is notoriously expensive. The barrier to entry is raised once again.

Many of these issues are surmountable, given time. Ever-improving simulation software means that more and more testing and prototyping can be undertaken in the digital domain. The introduction of 3D printers `PRINTING` like the RepRap means that it is becoming increasingly affordable and feasible to print physical objects, such as gears, from a variety of plastics. The lack of suitable CAD software is being addressed by a number of projects.

For designers, progress in open source tools, increased connectivity and so on makes the establishment of open source communities ever more feasible. The legal issues, however, are less straightforward.

So far, we have concentrated on copyright issues. In some ways, other forms of intellectual property pose greater challenges. Copyright protects the expression of an idea. Retaining the same idea, but recasting the expression of it in a different form, does not infringe on the copyright. The story of two people from warring tribes meeting, falling in love, and dying in tragic circumstances can be told in a myriad of different ways, each with their own independent copyright, none of which infringes on anyone else's copyright. This has two practical consequences. The first is that if a creator creates something which he or she has not copied from something else, then the creator will not be in breach of copyright, even if their creation turns out to be very similar, or even identical, to someone else's. The second is that if a component of something is found to be infringing on a copyright, it is possible to salvage the project by recasting the same idea in a different expression. `REMIX`

Design Rights

Copyright also has the advantage of being (reasonably well) harmonized worldwide, and has also proved amenable to hacking (e.g. by Richard Stallman) `HACKING` so that it can be used to guarantee openness in the code it covers. However, other forms of intellectual property protection are more problematic for designers.

This issue is linked to the distinction between the analogue and digital domains. Designs almost invariably start with some sort of drawing or description, which is protected by copyright as a literary or artistic work. Often, this material will be digital in nature. At this point, it is similar to software. Licensing options include the suite of Creative Commons licences. Once an item is created in the physical world, a different set of legal considerations applies.

69

STRUCTURE OF INTELLECTUAL PROPERTY

The rule of thumb for intellectual property is that all works are considered to
be in the public domain, with intellectual property protection as the exception.
However, this exception is highly diversified. Copyright protects the creative,
original expression of an idea, whereas patents protect the idea itself and its
technical specifications. Design rights cover aspects such as shape, texture,
colour, materials, contours and ornamentation. Other forms of protection
include trademarks, database rights and performers' rights.

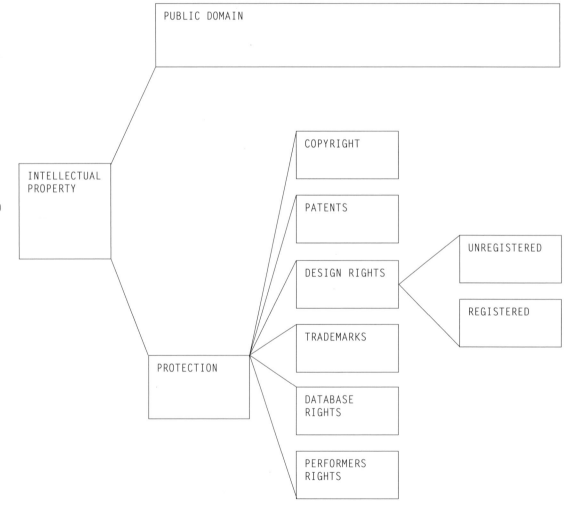

70

The most obvious is design right. Unfortunately, design right is complex and uncoordinated. There are many different types of design rights, and they differ from country to country. In the UK, for example, there are four separate design right regimes operating simultaneously. Depending on the right in question, they cover aspects such as shape, texture, colour, materials used, contours and ornamentation. Registered designs are in many ways similar to patents; in fact, they are sometimes called petty patents or design patents. Infringement can be unintentional, and independent creation is irrelevant. Unregistered designs are more in the nature of copyrights, and are vulnerable to infringement only where copying has taken place. The very fact that registration of design rights is required in itself provides a barrier to entry for collaborative projects, whereas copyright arises automatically and without the necessity of registration. On a collaborative project, who will pay for the preparation of a design registration, and who will make the application and maintain it?

Patents

Patents provide a particular problem for both programmers and designers, as they can impinge on both the digital realm and the analogue realm. Patents are a protection on the idea itself. Regardless of how that idea is expressed, its expression would represent patent infringement. Independent invention does not excuse patent infringement. The only way to be sure that an invention does not infringe a patent is to do an exhaustive check in patent offices worldwide. Such checks are very rarely carried out, since the expense is enormous and creates a vast barrier to entry for small businesses. US law in particular applies a positive disincentive to search: if a search is undertaken, then the searcher can be deemed to have knowingly infringed a patent – even if their reasonable determination was that the patent was not infringed – and will be liable to triple damages as a consequence. Pressure groups are lobbying worldwide for a reform of the patent system and process, but at present it is clear that the system benefits incumbent large companies with an existing patent portfolio.

The upshot of the intellectual property issues is that the BSD model is the only viable option in the hardware, analogue world. In contrast, those operating wholly in the digital domain (which includes programmers,

but which can also extend to digital creatives such as filmmakers, novelists or graphic designers) have the ability to choose whether they prefer the GPL model to the BSD model, for a number of reasons. In brief, the two main reasons are as follows:

Copyright, being largely universal, automatic, unregistered and long-lasting, is better suited to the development of a copyleft model than other forms of intellectual property. The difference in cost between copying and reverse engineering WYS ≠ WYG (which is vast in digital world, but much smaller in the analogue world), makes the copyleft a less compelling problem. A more detailed discussion of these reasons is needed to clarify why they are pertinent.

THE SYSTEM BENEFITS INCUMBENT LARGE COMPANIES WITH AN EXISTING PATENT PORTFOLIO.

If a GPL model were applied to hardware designs, in order to be effective, it would need to impinge on the ideas underlying the design (patents), or on the visual characteristics of the design (design rights). A GPL-style model based on patents would likely fail because of the cost, complexity, and time involved in applying for the patents – not to mention the necessity of keeping the invention secret prior to its publication, since part of the application process squares badly with the open source ethos. If the model were based on design rights, it would fail in relation to registered design rights, for the same reasons as for patents. If it were based on unregistered design rights, it would be unlikely to work because the scope and length of protection would be too short, and because the rights are insufficiently universal (although there is some scope for a limited GPL-style model in relation to unregistered design rights). Even if a GPL model were feasible in the world of hardware, there is an economic reason why it would be unlikely to work. The reasoning is as follows: the digital world makes things extremely easy to copy. Imagine a programmer wants to create some software based on a program with similar functionality to a word processor released under the GPL. The options are either to take the original GPL program, modify it, and release the result under the GPL; or to take the GPL program, reverse-engineer it, and rewrite a whole new program from scratch, which would be unencumbered by copyright restrictions. There is a vast difference in the amount of work involved in the two scenarios, and any programmer is likely to consider very seriously adopting the easier, cheaper and quicker option (modifying the original), where the 'cost' is licensing under the GPL. However, to offer a different example, even if there were a functioning mechanism for applying share-alike to a mechanical assembly, an engineer wishing to reproduce the mechanical assembly would, in effect, have to reverse-engineer it in order to set up the equipment needed to reproduce it. Copying a digital artefact is as simple as typing:

```
cp old.one new.one
```

Copying an analogue artefact is vastly more difficult. REPRODUCTION Consequently, there is little difference between slavish copying, which would invoke GPL-like restrictions, and reverse-engineering and re-manufacturing, which would not. In this case, it is much more likely that the 'cost' of GPL-like compliance would be greater than the benefits of having a GPL-free object. In conclusion, even if GPL-style licences were effective in the physical world, economics would tend to disfavour their use.

It can therefore be stated that designers operating in the analogue realm are likely to be restricted to an openness model more akin to BSD than to GPL. Their challenges are to make this model work, and to discourage free riders with a combination of moral pressure and a demonstration that playing by the community norms will be beneficial both to them, and to the community as a whole.

Benefiting from Connected Creativity

Designers and creators are increasingly able to benefit from the promise of the connected, social mode of creativity. The way was paved by free software pioneers, who skilfully hacked HACKING the copyright system to generate a commons which has not only generated a huge global business, but also provided the software which runs devices from mobile phones through to the

most powerful supercomputers. It provides the software which gives the developing world access to education, medical information and micro-finance loans and enables them to participate in the knowledge economy on similar terms to the developed nations.

DESIGNERS AND CREATORS ARE INCREASINGLY ABLE TO BENEFIT FROM THE PROMISE OF THE CONNECTED, SOCIAL MODE OF CREATIVITY.

The challenge for designers and creators in other fields is to adapt the model of software development to their own field of work, and to counter the extensive efforts of incumbent beneficiaries of the broadcast era to use ever more draconian legislation to prop up the outmoded business models. Ultimately, the social mode will win: it takes one of humanity's defining characteristics, the fact that we are highly social and community-oriented, and uses it as the foundation of the entire structure. One-to-many works against this fundamental trait, but Nature will ultimately triumph.

NOTES

1   Jefferson, T. Letter to Isaac McPherson, 13 August 1813. *The Writings of Thomas Jefferson*. Edited by Andrew A. Lipscomb and Albert Ellery Bergh. Washington: Thomas Jefferson Memorial Association, 1905. Vol. 13, p. 333-334. Available at http://press-pubs.uchicago.edu/founders/documents/a1_8_8s12.html, accessed 11 January 2011.

GENERATIVE ADVERTISEMENT

Volumizr

IDEAS
BECOME
OBJECTS

MADE IN MY BACKYARD

BRE PETTIS

Envisioning the potential of open source tools to facilitate making, Bre Pettis retraces the thorny and convoluted path from wanting to produce self-replicating robots, through a series of prototypes, to being at the core of a little universe of 2,500 MakerBots. He reports just a few examples of what makers and artists have made with the MakerBot and wonders what the future might hold.

Bre Pettis makes things that make things. Passionate about invention, innovation, and all things DIY, Pettis builds infrastructure for creativity. He is one of the founders of Makerbot, a company that produces robots that make things. He is also one of the founders of NYCResistor, a hacker collective in Brooklyn, and he co-founded the digital design sharing site Thingiverse.com. Besides being a TV host and video podcast producer, he has created new media for Etsy.com, hosted Make Magazine's podcast Weekend Projects, and has been a schoolteacher, artist, and puppeteer. Bre says: "When I design something, I share it so that others can modify it, hack it, and use it however they like. That's open design."

www.brepettis.com

2007: Pizza around the Clock

In 2007, I was actively recruiting hardware hackers in New York City to be part of NYCResistor, a hackerspace where we could make anything together. I met Zach at an NYCResistor microcontroller study group. After hearing about self-replicating robots, I spent the autumn in a corner of a film studio, where some friends of his were letting him work on RepRap robots `REPRODUCTION` when films weren't being made. We spent a lot of time working on the McWire RepStrap, a 3D printer `PRINTING` made out of plumbing pipes. We would meet up, solder some new boards that he had designed from tutorials on the internet, swear at broken traces, and in general just have fun. One of the things to come out of this time was a commitment to LEDs. I remember him turning to me and remarking that he had not put LEDs on a PCB. At that point, we made a solemn vow that no electronics board would ever make it through the design process again without blinking LEDs.

We did not have a working machine yet, but for months on end, we seemed just hours away from getting it to work. We were close enough that I ordered my own plumbing pipes and bent aluminium to take to Vienna, Austria, where I had an artist-in-residence spot with Monochrom, an artist collective in the Museum Quarter. I enlisted the help of the local hackerspace; the entire crew there, including Marius and Philipp Tiefenbacher, and Red, helped out for a week straight. Back in those days, we had to make our own wiring harnesses for everything, and it took forever. The code wasn't working yet, but it was constantly very close to working. We ate pizza round the clock.

2008: Printing Vodka Shot Glasses

This first Austrian experiment was beautiful. `HELLO WORLD` It worked for about a minute before the first-generation electronics burned traces and let the magic smoke out. The extruder was made from a mix of ballpoint-pen hardware and angled aluminium that was ground down with a Dremel, a handheld rotary grinder. We pulled stepper motors from old disk drives and scanners found in the depths of the Metalab archive. We had planned to print out shot glasses at Roboexotica, the cocktail robotics festival `EVENTS` in Vienna that happens every winter, but our machine failed completely; we couldn't even print out swizzle sticks. Even more shame was heaped on our failure

when we were awarded the 'lime' award, which is reserved for non-functioning robots. I left the machine in Vienna with Marius and Philipp. By the next year's Roboexotica festival, they had fixed it up and got it working. Through a combination of brute force and alchemical magic, they spent the cocktail festival of 2008 printing out shot glasses that they promptly filled for visitors with a horrid Scandinavian concoction of vodka and Fisherman's Friend throat lozenges. Robots and alcohol are a fantastic combination.

FINALLY, THE ORDINARY PERSON IS IN THE UNIQUE POSITION OF BEING ABLE TO MAKE ALMOST ANYTHING WITH OFF-THE-SHELF MODULES, PARTS, COMMUNITY AND SHARED CODE.

Back in the States, after I had left the McWire machine in Vienna, NYCResistor had found a location and the hardware hacking club was in full swing. Starting with nine people, we created a wonderful clubhouse for hardware hackers. The NYCResistor motto is 'Learn, Share, and Make Things'. Early on, we chose to collectively share our tools, and we pooled our money to buy a $20,000 laser cutter. The team at NYCResistor is a special group of people who are not afraid to push technology forward and with a tendency towards the absurd; almost anything is possible. Electronics have gotten to the place where creating the electronics of your dreams has become a real possibility. Microcontrollers like the Arduino are accessible. Blogs like *Make Magazine* and *Hackaday*, as well as countless personal blogs, are fantastic resources for tinkerers. Finally, the ordinary person is in the unique position of being able to make almost anything with off-the-shelf modules, parts, community and shared code.

On a Saturday in August 2008, Zach and I started Thingiverse to give people a place to share digital designs for things. We had been telling people that downloading designs would be possible someday. Since nobody had created a library of digital designs that allowed people to share their work under open licences, we created it ourselves. Thingiverse is now a thriving community where sharing runs rampant and creativity is found in abundance.

Later that year, Zach got a Darwin up and running, but that design had so many flaws that getting it to work was a challenge. It extruded plastic for a few minutes before this model joined the ranks of machines that release the magic smoke. It was very disappointing. He had spent years trying to get a machine working, and then it worked for only a few minutes before failing completely. We had developed a taste for 3D printing by working on the RepRap project, and we wanted more. That early McWire machine and the RepRap Darwin REPRODUCTION showed us that creating an inexpensive 3D printer was possible. We promptly quit our jobs.

That winter, in December of 2008, Zach and I were at the 25th Chaos Communication Congress. EVENTS Zach gave a talk about RepRap and I spoke about living a prototyping lifestyle. We got home and somehow came to the conclusion that we should start a company to make 3D printers that could be made with the tools we had at hand (the laser cutter) and as many off-the-shelf parts as possible. In January of 2009, we formed MakerBot Industries. Adam Mayer, another friend from NYCResistor, got involved; since he had spent 10 years working on firmware and software for embedded devices, he was immediately charged with making the software functional and friendly.

2009: MakerBot Industries

When we started MakerBot, we set different priorities than RepRap had done. Rather than focusing on self-replication, we wanted to make our first MakerBot the cheapest 3D printer kit that anyone could put together and have it actually work. Those first few months of MakerBot were intense. While prototyping during the first two months, we rarely left NYCResistor. We went through two whole cases of Top Ramen instant noodles and drank countless bottles of Club Mate, a carbonated and caffeinated soft drink from Germany. Powered by caffeine and carbohydrates, we used the tools we had at hand, a laser cutter, and off-the-shelf parts to create the MakerBot Cupcake CNC kit. We went to our friends for funding: Jacob Lodwick, who started Connected Ventures, and Adrian Bowyer, who initiated the RepRap project. They invested some money in us so we could start ordering the electronics, parts, motors and other things we needed to get the first kits together.

We worked hard on those first prototypes. After two months of work, we got the first machine to work at 8:15 on the 13th of March, 2009. As soon as it worked, we threw it in a Pelican case and took off to SXSW, the big music, film and interactive festival in Austin, Texas, where we shared it with the world for the first time. I set up shop in bars and printed endless amounts of shot glasses and twelve-sided dice. The machine printed flawlessly for the entire week. We had been able to pull together 20 kits; we expected to sell 10 of them that first month and have 10 in stock to sell the next month. When all 20 sold out in two weeks, we started staying up late running the laser cutter making the parts.

WE MAKE 3D PRINTERS TO OFFER AN ALTERNATIVE TO CONSUMERISM.

The buyers of those machines were brave. The electronics came unassembled and required SMD soldering, not a trivial task even for seasoned tinkerers with Heathkit assembly experience. Still, they were putting them together and they worked! The MakerBot Google group buzzed with chatter, shared pro tips and stories. Thingiverse, which up until then had been mostly a repository for DXF files for laser cutting, started seeing more and more 3D-printed designs.

Our mission at MakerBot is to democratize manufacturing. We make 3D printers to offer an alternative to consumerism. A year and a half after we began, there are now 2500 folks with MakerBots, and those people are living in a future where they can 3D print the tangible products of their imagination. They get to make a choice between buying something

MAKERBOT TRAVEL SCHEDULE

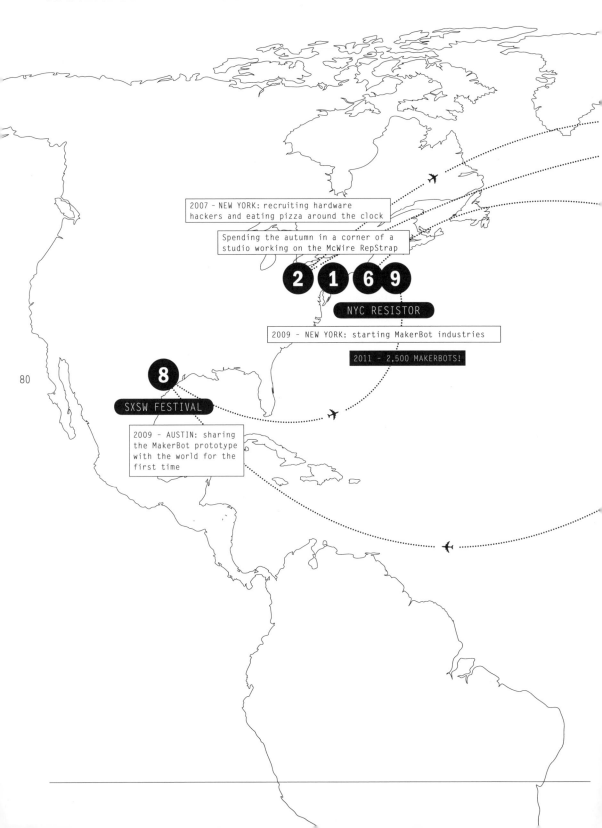

2007 – NEW YORK: recruiting hardware
hackers and eating pizza around the clock

Spending the autumn in a corner of a
studio working on the McWire RepStrap

2 1 6 9

NYC RESISTOR

2009 – NEW YORK: starting MakerBot industries

2011 – 2,500 MAKERBOTS!

8

SXSW FESTIVAL

2009 – AUSTIN: sharing
the MakerBot prototype
with the world for the
first time

80

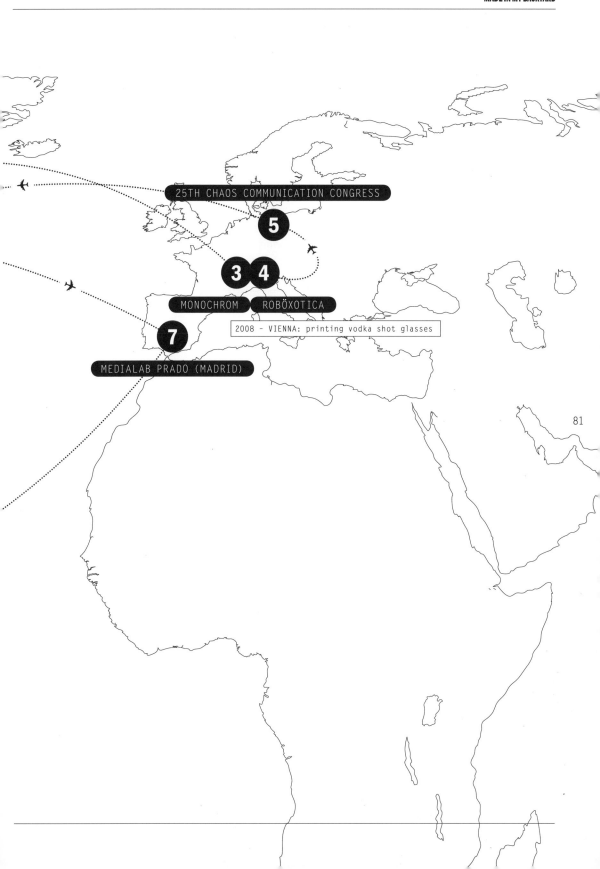

25TH CHAOS COMMUNICATION CONGRESS

5

3 **4**

MONOCHROM   ROBÖXOTICA

2008 - VIENNA: printing vodka shot glasses

7

MEDIALAB PRADO (MADRID)

81

and 3D printing it. DOWNLOADABLE DESIGN Kids that grow up in a household or classroom with a MakerBot have the option to 3D print the things they want as an alternative to shopping. If a MakerBot Operator needs a doorknob, they can check Thingiverse to see if someone else has made it. (There are 22 things tagged 'knob' on Thingiverse.[1]) If you don't like the knobs made available by the community of digital designers, you can download the designs and modify them if they are shared under an open licence, or you can design your own. This idea of sharing and being able to customize and modify other people's designs is a powerful force in the universe. It goes beyond doorknobs to all sorts of practical and beautiful objects.

Designing things for 3D printers is still at an early stage. The programs have traditionally been set up as CAD programs, with a learning curve similar to Photoshop. Only recently have we seen programs like openSCAD that are designed for programmers who are interested in programming dynamic and parametric objects. Software engineers are now able to transform code AESTHETICS: 3D into real physical objects.

82

MakerBot operators report that fixing things around the house is a point of pride for them. Thingiverse user Schmarty created his own shower curtain rings when his local store was out of stock. He shared the design on Thingiverse, and now nobody with a MakerBot REPRODUCTION will ever have to buy shower curtain rings again. On the thing page for the curtain rod rings, Schmarty says:

> "It's a story that can happen to anyone. You move to a new town and leave your shower curtain behind. 'No problem,' you think, 'I'll just pick up a new liner at the pharmacy down the street.' So, you trek to the local pharmacy and find the shower curtain liner you were looking for, only to discover that they are out of shower curtain rings, hooks, anything made for holding up a shower curtain! Facing down defeat and the very real possibility that you will have to take a dirty, inefficient bath, you come to a stunning realization: You're a MakerBot owner. You live for these moments."

Schmarty made his curtain rings in openSCAD and shared the source files, so you can download them and make curtain rings to your own specifications. One Thingiverse site user has already uploaded a design for a derivative variation with spikes.[2]

When we made the MakerBot, we were limited by the size of our laser cutter. AESTHETICS: 2D That meant that the first model, the MakerBot Cupcake CNC, can only make things that are 100x100x120 mm. That size is big enough to make things that are slightly larger than a coffee mug. Architects in particular complained about this, until Thingiverse user Skimbal created an amazing modular cathedral.[3] There are 10 different cathedral pieces that can be modularly connected to make your own customizable and expandable cathedral! This print pushes the limit of what a MakerBot can do. One of the limitations is in regard to overhangs. A MakerBot can do overhangs of around 45 degrees. It will still print things with overhangs, but they'll turn out 'fluffy' and require cleanup and trimming after printing. AESTHETICS: 3D

The MakerBot is open source. You can download the schematic and board files, the DXF laser-cutter files, and the software, firmware and parts lists. This allows MakerBot users to truly own their MakerBot inside and out. Charles Pax was one of the first to take advantage of this. He wanted to put the electronics on the inside of his MakerBot, so he modified the DXF laser-cutter files to accommodate an alternative power supply and gave his MakerBot a clean form factor. Unsatisfied with having to reset the machine after each print, he developed the MakerBot Automated Build Platform. Charles now works in the R&D department at MakerBot Industries, pushing the technology of personal fabrication forward.

Because it's an open platform, you can swap out the tool heads easily. Besides the MakerBot plastruder, which extrudes plastic to create a programmed 3D shape, we've launched the MakerBot Unicorn Pen Plotter, which artists can use as a drawing tool. We also created the MakerBot Frostruder so that anyone can use their MakerBot to decorate cupcakes or print with anything that you can fit inside a syringe. This opens up a whole new range of possibilities for artists, chefs and DIY bio-experimenters. MakerBot operators have also used the stepper motors to create beautiful music. Bubblyfish, an 8-bit artist, has composed music for the MakerBot; many others have converted midi files to play their favourite music on the MakerBot.

MakerBot Operators are a great community for each other. When Cathal Garvey (creator of the DremelFuge[4]) had a mouse problem, he wanted to catch the mouse without killing it, so he put a bounty out for a better mousetrap. He said that he would pay $25 to anyone who could make a MakerBottable mouse trap that actually caught his mouse. The day after he made the call for a MakerBot operators to design a better mousetrap, eight new designs for a mousetrap showed up on Thingiverse!

2010: Thing-O-Matic

Throughout 2009 and 2010, we have constantly updated both the software and the hardware of the MakerBot Cupcake CNC. Now, in autumn 2010, we've launched our second machine, called the Thing-O-Matic, which incorporates all the updates. This new machine has a new way of moving the print bed, which moves down along the Z axis as an object grows in height during printing. All the tolerances are tighter, and we have increased the build area to allow users to make bigger things.

AT MAKERBOT INDUSTRIES, WE ARE EXCITED ABOUT THE FUTURE. THIS NEW INDUSTRIAL REVOLUTION IS STILL IN ITS EARLY DAYS.

At MakerBot Industries, we are excited about the future. This new industrial revolution REVOLUTION is still in its early days. Ordinary people are taking up the tools of manufacturing, fabrication and production. I love to check Thingiverse.com to see what new possibilities have emerged during the night. There are so many opportunities for anyone who has the passion and interest to explore the frontier of personal manufacturing. With the tools at hand and the community of sharing that has developed around the MakerBot, the future is bright. Exciting innovations and amazing things are emerging.

2011: 2,500 MakerBots

When we first started MakerBot, we would wonder, "What will people do with it?" We knew that anything could happen; sure enough, we've shared the excitement as people shared their work. Now, with 2,500 MakerBots in the wild and more shipping every day, I am curious what the community will do together. What kinds of problems can 2,500 MakerBots solve? What kind of projects can we, as a worldwide community of sharing, SHARING do together?

NOTES

1   www.thingiverse.com/tag:knob/
2   www.thingiverse.com/thing:3465
3   www.thingiverse.com/thing:2030
4   www.thingiverse.com/thing:1483

COMMONS-BASED PEER PRODUCTION

THE USER-GENERATED CONTENT OF THE 21ST CENTURY

ﷺ Swarmz. The content providers.

LIBRARIES OF THE PEER PRODUCTION ERA

PETER TROXLER

Mapping the landscape of commons-based peer production, Peter Troxler analyses the arena of open source hardware and looks into various initiatives being spawned by fabrication labs, trying to identify their business potential and asking how these initiatives contribute to giving people more control over their productivity in self-directed, community-oriented ways.

Peter Troxler is an independent researcher and developer with a history as a project manager, theatre director, community steward and industrial engineer. For Peter, "open design is a practice that borrows its operating principles from open source software and applies them in the domain of design. It conveys knowledge about its products transparently, communicating its nature within the products themselves.

As a peer-oriented form of production, it makes production tools, methods and experience accessible to everybody as a common infrastructure; it gives people options for controlling their productivity. It is continually evolving, appearing and reappearing in various shapes, sometimes producing contradictory manifestations."

www.petertroxler.org

In today's society, individuals often collaborate in producing cultural content, knowledge, and other information, as well as physical goods. In some cases, these individuals share the results and products, the means, methods and experience gained from this collaboration as a resource for further development; CO-CREATION this phenomenon is referred to as commons-based peer production.

Commons-based peer production is most widely practiced in the area of software development: open source software. The most prominent examples of open source software are the Linux operating system and the Apache web server. Open source is not the exclusive domain of software, however; it has spread into other domains, from culture and education to knowledge discovery KNOWLEDGE and sharing. Examples include the many people who use Creative Commons licences, CREATIVE COMMONS the Blender movies, VEB Film Leipzig, the countless initiatives in open education, the SETI@home project, Wikipedia, Open Street Map, or Slashdot. Commons-based peer production is generally attributed to digital revolutions: the widespread availability of new, digital information technologies.[1]

While its origins can indeed be traced back to digital development, commons-based peer production goes beyond the purely digital domain. A number of open source hardware projects currently aim to produce tangible goods through a peer-production approach, not to mention 'fabbing' initiatives (abbreviated from fabrication) that seek to make it possible for anyone to manufacture their own goods.

Perhaps these initiatives are emerging because many "physical activities are becoming so data-centric that the physical aspects are simply executional steps at the end of a chain of digital manipulation", as Shirky suggests.[2] Then again, perhaps the commons-based peer production model "provides opportunities for virtuous behavior" and so "is more conducive to virtuous individuals".[3]

Yochai Benkler argues that "in the networked information economy – an economy of information, knowledge, and culture that flow through society over a ubiquitous, decentralized network – productivity and growth can be sustained in a pattern that differs fundamentally from the industrial information economy of the twentieth century in two crucial characteristics. First, non-market production (...) can play a much more important role than it could in the physical economy. Second, radically decentralized production and distribution, whether market-based or not, can similarly play a much more important role".[4] TREND: NETWORK SOCIETY

The business, or rather, the benefits of commons-based peer-production are not uniquely monetary.[5] The rewards include indirect mechanisms, such as the positive effects of learning *on future earnings* or enhanced reputation, which in turn can lead to future (paid) contracts for consultancy, customization, maintenance or other services. The business also includes what economists call hedonic rewards: not consumption, but the act of creation gives pleasure to the prosumers. Peer recognition is another physiological reward, involving ego gratification. This part of the business is an exchange of production for consumption that does not rely on monetary means.

Open Source Hardware

Since 2006, Philip Torrone and Limor 'Ladyada' Fried have been curating Make Magazine's *definitive guide to open source hardware projects* MANIFESTOS that started out as a holiday season spending guide to 'gifts that give back'.[6] Under the heading *Million Dollar Baby* – probably alluding to the underdog nature of open source hardware – they presented fifteen examples of companies at O'Reilly's Foo Camp East in May 2010:

Adafruit Industries, makers of educational electronic kits; *Arduino*, the open source computing platform; *Beagle Board*, a manufacturer of open development boards for computers; *Bug Labs*, known for their modular Lego-type computer hardware; *Chumby*, standalone Internet content viewers; *Dangerous Prototypes*, Dutch hackers turned entrepreneurs who sell an open source reverse engineering tool; *DIY Drones*, for open source unmanned aerial vehicles (autopilot drones); *Evil Mad Scientist Labs* and their fun educational projects; *Liquidware*, who make Arduino accessories; Makerbot Industries, the company behind *MakerBot 3D printers* and the sharing platform Thingiverse.com; *Maker Shed*, the shop behind *Make* Magazine and Maker Fair; *Parallax*, education in microcontroller programming and interfacing; *Seed Studios*, for Chinese Arduino derivatives; *Solarbotics*, for solar kits, robot kits and BEAM robotics; *Spark Fun Electronics*, for education and prototyping electronics products.

All these companies are selling open source hardware and creating some kind of community around them. Together, they generate a turnover of about US$ 50m, or so Torrone and Limor estimate. They reckon that there are currently about 200 open source hardware projects of a similar kind. The open source hardware community will reach a turnover of US$ 1b by 2015, according to the forecasts made by Torrone and Limor. Some of these communities have seen exponential growth recently, such as the RepRap community.[7]

Kerstin Balka, Christina Raasch and Cornelius Herstatt went to great lengths to collect examples of open source hardware projects through Open-Innovation-Projects.org. In 2009, their database consisted of 106 entries, 76 of which were truly open development of physical products, or open design. Open design as defined on that site is characterized by revealing information on a new design free of charge, with the intention of collaborative development of a single design or a limited number of related designs for market exploitation. Among others, their database includes community projects such as Openmoko, Fab@home, OpenEEG, One Laptop Per Child, SOCIAL DESIGN Mikrokopter, or RepRap.

IT IS NAÏVE TO BELIEVE THAT OPEN SOURCE SOFTWARE PRACTICES COULD BE COPIED TO AND APPLIED IN THE OPEN DESIGN REALM WITHOUT ANY ALTERATION, IGNORING THE CONSTRAINTS AND OPPORTUNITIES OF MATERIALITY.

Balka, Raasch and Herstatt used this database of open design projects for statistical studies to identify similarities and differences in open source software projects.[8] They found that, "in open design communities, tangible objects can be developed in very similar fashion to software; one could even say that people treat a design as source code to a physical object and change the object via changing the source".[9] However, they also find that "open parts strategies in open design are crafted at the component level, rather than the level of the entire design"[10] and that "the degree of openness differs significantly between software and hardware components, in the sense that software is more transparent, accessible, and replicable than hardware".[11] WYS ≠ WYG Indeed, despite the many academic discussions that support such a view, it is naïve to believe that open source software practices could be copied to and applied in the open design realm without any alteration, ignoring the constraints and opportunities that the materiality of design entails.

Fabbing

Besides these single-aim or single-product projects, there are other initiatives promoting commons-based peer production primarily by sharing designs and encouraging people to 'make things'. Some are about making things for the fun of it; GRASSROOTS INVENTION the Maker Faire in the USA, *Make Magazine* and *Craft Magazine* are all good examples. Some initiatives are about easy sharing, distribution and promotion, such as Ponoko, Shapeways and Thingiverse. Others involve more serious or more ambitious social experiments, such as the Open Source Ecology with their experimental facility, Factor E Farm.[12]

And there are initiatives of commons-based peer production that could be summarized under the heading of 'shared machine shops'.[13] These initiatives are typically centred around workshops equipped with hand tools and relatively inexpensive fabrication machines (e.g. laser cutters, routers, 3D mills). Users produce two-dimensional and three-dimensional objects that once could have only been made using equipment costing hundreds of thousands of euros. They use digital drawings and open source software to control the machines, and they build electronic circuits and gadgets.

89

100k-Garages is "a community of workshops with digital fabrication tools for precisely cutting, machining, drilling, or sculpting the parts for your project or product, in all kinds of materials, in a shop or garage near you".[14] Most of these workshops are located in the USA and Canada (about 180), with five shops in Europe and two in Australia. 100k-Garages are essentially establishing a network of distributed manufacturing shops that produce their users' designs for a fee. They are providing a professional manufacturing service, rather than offering shop access for makers to make their own things themselves. Through quality of workmanship and standardization of equipment – the network is sponsored by ShopBot Industries, a maker of CNC routers – they are establishing a platform which guarantees the making end of it and frees users to focus on design. Ponoko, one of the preferred sharing platforms, enables further exchange.

TechShop is a group of workshops that are equipped with typical machine shop tools (welding stations, laser cutters, milling machines) and corresponding design software. TechShops are mainly based on the 'gym model': a monthly subscription buys users access to tools, machines, design software, and other professional equipment. Courses on how to use the tools are offered, too, for a fee. Located in Menlo Park, San Francisco and San Jose, CA, Raleigh, NC, Portland, OR, and Detroit, MI, they cater to a US-based clientele.[15] Chris Anderson describes them as an "incubator for the atom age";[16] according to his account, the facilities are mainly used by entrepreneurs who come to a TechShop for prototyping and small batch production. The online member project gallery, however, shows such diverse projects as a 3D scan of an alligator skeleton, custom-made sports equipment, movie props, a laser-cut gauge for bamboo needles, a laser-etched laptop and an infrared heater for an arthritic dog.

Hackerspaces are another venue where peer production takes place, self-defined "as community-operated physical places, where people can meet and work on their projects".[17] Emerging from the counterculture movement,[18] they are "place[s] where people can learn about technology and science outside the confines of work or school".[19] Equipment and funding are collective endeavours.

A hackerspace might use a combination of membership contributions, course fees, donations and subsidies to sustain itself. Activities in hackerspaces evolve around computers and technology, and digital or electronic art. Hackerspaces are founded as local initiatives following a common pattern. The Hackerspaces ecosystem comprises several hundred member locations world-wide, of which roughly half are either dormant or under construction.[20] Becoming a hackerspace is essentially a matter of self-declaration – an entry on the hackerspaces.org wiki is sufficient – which lowers the barrier to entry enormously, at least for advanced computer users. However, this low barrier to entry is probably also the reason for the relatively large number of 'registered' but dormant hackerspaces. Collaboration `CO-CREATION` between Hackerspaces has recently begun in the form of 'hackathons'; these marathon sessions currently do not seem to extend beyond displaying the activities happening at the spaces taking part.[21]

THE OPEN SOURCE LABEL CONFERS A CERTAIN COOLNESS IN SOME CIRCLES OF A GADGET-CRAZY WORLD.

Fab Lab, short for fabrication laboratory, is another global initiative with a growing number of locations around the world. Fab Labs have a more conceptual foundation, as they emerged from an MIT course entitled 'How To Make (almost) Anything'.[22] While there is no formal procedure on how to become a Fab Lab, the process is monitored by MIT, and MIT maintains a list of all Fab Labs worldwide. At the moment of writing, the Fab Lab community `COMMUNITY` comprises about sixty labs, with another fifty to open in the not-too-distant future. There are a few collaborative projects within the community, and a number of initiatives to exchange designs and experience between the labs. Similar to the hackathons, but occurring more regularly and systematically, all the labs around the world can get in contact with each other through a common video conferencing system hosted at the MIT which is used for ad-hoc meetings, scheduled conferences and the delivery of the Fab Academy training programme. Academic publications note a number of examples of Fab Lab projects. Mikhak and colleagues report on projects in India, at Vigyan Ashram Fab Lab just outside the village of Pabal in Maharashtra, and at the Costa Rica Institute of Technology in San Jose, Costa Rica. The projects in India are about developing controller boards to facilitate more accurate timing of the diesel engines they use to generate electrical power, and developing devices to monitor milk quality not at the collection centres and the processing plants, but at the producer level. The Costa Rican projects revolve around wireless diagnostic modules for agricultural, educational and medical applications, for example monitoring a certain skin condition in a rural village.[23] SOCIAL DESIGN

In *FAB: The Coming Revolution on Your Desktop*, Neil Gershenfeld lists examples of what students at MIT made in his course on 'How to Make (almost) Anything'. The list includes a bag that collects and replays screams, a computer interface for parrots that can be controlled by a bird using its beak, a personalized bike frame, a cow-powered generator, an alarm clock that needs to be wrestled with to turn it off, and a defensive dress that protects its wearer's personal space.[24]

Arne Gjengedal reports on the early projects at the Norwegian MIT Fab Lab at Solvik farm in Lyngen. His list includes the 'electronic shepard' (sic) project that used telecom equipment RECYCLING to track sheep in the mountains, the 'helmet wiper' for clearing the face shield in the rain, the 'wideband antenna' for the industrial, scientific and medical (ISM) radio band, the 'Internet 0' project for a low-bandwidth internet protocol, the 'perfect antenna', and the 'local position system' for positioning of robots in the lab.[25]

Diane Pfeiffer describes her own experiments and projects in the context of distributed digital design. Her experiments were *Lasercut News*, *Digital Color Studies & Pixelated Images*, *Lasercut Screen*, and *Lasercut Bracelets* (which she sold at a local shop); the projects she worked on were *Distorted Chair* and *Asperatus Tile*.[26]

The Business Promise

All those initiatives represent various aspects of a commons-based peer production ecosystem (non-market or radically decentralized production) or are at least contributing to the emergence of such an ecosystem.

Torrone and Fried have shown how a regular and sizeable market has grown around open source hardware. Those open source hardware businesses clearly operate under market conditions and their production is not radically decentralized. Indeed, Torrone and Fried's agenda might even be said to 'prove' that open source hardware results in marketable products. Evidently, the open source label confers a certain coolness in some circles of a gadget-crazy world. OPEN EVERYTHING

Yet many of these open source hardware components – Arduino and MakerBot being the most prominent examples – are providing open source ingredients to a peer production ecosystem at a price that outweighs the pain of sourcing all the parts, having to deal with manual assembly, or facing issues of incompatibility. As components, they can become building blocks of higher-order machines. In that sense, they function as a platform for open source development. As far as the components themselves are concerned, they are open source in the sense that their internal structure and functioning are made transparent and potentially modifiable. BLUEPRINTS

As flat-packed, self-assembly, open source machines, they are the choice of many peer-producers and form an important basis for highly decentralized – and highly customized – production. It becomes possible to own machines at the price of building them rather than the price of buying them pre-assembled. DOWNLOADABLE DESIGN And their open source nature makes it easier to adapt them to specific requirements or even repurpose them in novel ways.

Rather than commoditizing ingredients, 100k-Garages commoditize one part of the making process: the cutting. If there is a dense enough network of such facilities in any particular region, this makes a certain practical sense in terms of efficiency and safety, given the somewhat demanding fabrication process of a ShopBot CNC router as compared to a laser cutter.

'LIBRARIES' OF THE PEER PRODUCTION ERA

The fabbing universe could be described on two dimensions, characterizing initiatives as more reproductive or more generative in their nature, and as more infrastructure-oriented or more-project oriented in their approach.

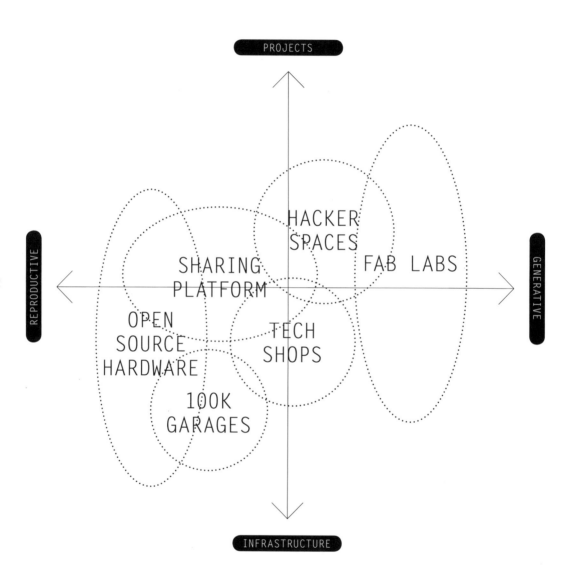

However, it establishes a division of labour, and it deprives user-clients from accessing potential learning experiences and therefore potentially contributing to a more general commons. The result is that the ShopBot remains a commons apart, and somewhat closed at that.

TechShops, Hackerspaces and Fab Labs are all providing facilities and knowledge as part or rather as a basis of a commons. The environment in which TechShops operate is strictly commercial. Peer production might happen by accident, but there seem to be no incentives to support it. As an 'incubator for the atomic age', they remain safely in the market arena, yet they are effectively creating opportunities for decentralized prototyping and production.

In contrast, Hackerspaces live up to their name, definition and history by building on non-market, sometimes even anti-market MANIFESTOS commons-based principles. Their core focus is doing personal and collective projects. And Hackerspaces are far from exclusive; they frequently include casual users who might spend a lot of time in hackerspaces. Nick Farr even speculates that those casual users are "perhaps making more significant contributions than regular members, but decline to officially join for many different reasons."[27]

The Fab Labs' commitment to a commons is clear from how they are structured. Fab Labs subscribe to a charter which, among other things, stipulates open access, establishes peer learning as a core feature and requires that "designs and processes developed in fab labs must remain available for individual use". In the same clause, however, the charter also allows for intellectual property to be protected "however you choose". Underlining this point, it explicitly continues that "commercial activities can be incubated in fab labs", while cautioning against potential conflict with open access, and encouraging business activity to grow beyond the lab and to give back to the inventors, labs, and networks that contributed to their success.[28] Fab Labs incorporate an interesting mix of characteristics that might seem contradictory at first, but might well be considered the best practical approximation of Benkler's networked information economy. TREND: NETWORK SOCIETY

Books, Libraries, and the Choices of Self-Directed Productivity

Open source hardware – as components or production equipment – not only embodies the technical knowledge of products and production the way that traditional components and machines once did. In sharp contrast to the opaque and impenetrable black boxes of advanced 20th-century engineering, WYS ≠ WYG they give users access to that knowledge as a result of their open source design. Akin to books, which seem meaningless to people who cannot read, but open their content to those who have achieved literacy, open source hardware reveals its technicalities to those who grasp that language.

If open source hardware can be compared to the 'books' of commons-based peer production, then TechShops, Hackerspaces and Fab Labs are its libraries. Traditional libraries act as common points of access to knowledge coded in books, and in fact offer locations where knowledge can be produced. Similarly, copy shops allow anybody to produce their own range of print products, from cards to books, T-shirts and mugs. Cyber-cafés also provide access to knowledge, as locations where everybody can link into a common information and communication infrastructure. Those new labs are the places that provide general access to the tools, methods and experience of peer production. Indeed, the National Fab Lab Bill presented to the US Congress in 2010 EVENT argues along these lines, aiming "to foster a new generation with scientific and engineering skills and to provide a workforce capable of producing world class individualized and traditional manufactured goods".[29]

The business proposals of open source hardware and the various fabbing initiatives are not equally straightforward in every case. As discussed, commons-based peer production has found ways to generate monetary returns by selling open source products, charging memberships fees in open source communities, or providing paid education and manufacturing services. To some extent, the strong appeal of commons-based peer production can probably be attributed in part to its hedonic rewards: the pleasure of being creative, the pride of recognition by peers, the feeling of achievement and status. However, there are no clear examples of indirect mechanisms deriving tangible benefits

93

from these hedonic rewards, such as makers getting corporate development assignments or contracts as product managers thanks to their reputation in open hardware design. If such examples exist, they are not being discussed openly. And commons-based peer production has yet to realize its potential as a platform for many more developers and producers to generate a substantial income under market or non-market conditions.

As Yochai Benkler notes, it is "important to see that these efforts mark the emergence of a new mode of production, one that was mostly unavailable to people in either the physical economy (...) or in the industrial information economy."[30] The initiatives of commons-based peer production give more people more control over their productivity in self-directed and community-oriented ways. The variety of the initiatives give people a range of fundamentally different options to choose from, and indeed requires them to make those choices instead of accepting a mode of consumption that has been predetermined by a lobby of the current "winners in the economic system of the previous century."[31]

94

Even if the emergence of open source hardware and fabbing initiatives only dates back a few decades, commons-based peer production is still in its early days. Nobody knows yet whether the one and only correct, long-lasting and sustainable approach to this new mode of production has been found yet – or even if such a uniform approach will ever emerge. REVOLUTION It seems much more likely that the current trend will develop into a plethora of different models that embrace various aspects of commons-based peer production, with users switching between different models as appropriate. It will be interesting to see whether and how traditional businesses will be able to adapt to a new reality of real prosumer choice.

NOTES

1 See e.g. Benkler, Y. *The Wealth of Networks. How Social Production Transforms Markets and Freedom*. New Haven and London, Yale University Press, 2006.

2 Shirky, C. 'Re: [decentralization] Generalizing Peer Production into the Physical World'. Forum post, 5 Nov 2007 at http://finance. groups.yahoo.com/group/decentralization/message/6967, accessed on 30 August 2010.

3 Benkler, Y and Nissenbaum, H. 'Commons-based Peer Production and Virtue'. *The Journal of Political Philosophy*, Vol. 14, No. 4, 2006, p. 394.

4 Benkler, Y. 'Freedom in the Commons: Towards a Political Economy of Information', *Duke Law Journal*, Vol. 52, 2003, p. 1246f.

5 See also Benkler, Y. 'Coase's Penguin, or, Linux and The Nature of the Firm', *The Yale Law Journal*, Vol. 112, 2002.

6 Available online at http://blog.makezine.com/archive/2006/11/ the_open_source_gift_guid.html

7 Jones, R, Bowyer, A & De Bruijn, E. 'The Law and the Prophets/ Profits'. Presentation given at FAB6: The Sixth International Fab Lab Forum and Symposium on Digital Fabrication, Amsterdam, 15-20 August 2010. Available at http://cba.mit.edu/events/10.08.FAB6/ RepRap.ppt, accessed 30 August 2010.

8 Balka, K, Raasch, C, Herstatt, C. 'Open Source beyond software: An empirical investigation of the open design phenomenon'. Paper presented at the R&D Management Conference 2009, Feldafing near Munich, Germany, 14-16 October 2009. See also: Balka, K, Raasch, C, Herstatt, C. 'Open Source Innovation: A study of openness and community expectations'. Paper presented at the DIME Conference, Milan, Italy, 14-16 April 2010.

9 2009 study, p. 22.

10 2010 study, p. 11.

11 Idem.

12 Dolittle, J. 'OSE Proposal – Towards a World-Class Open Source Research and Development Facility'. Available online at http:// openfarmtech.org/OSE_Proposal_2008.pdf, accessed 6 June 2010.

13 Hess, K. *Community Technology*. New York: Harper & Rowe, 1979.

14 100kGarages. Available online at www.100kgarages.com, accessed 30 August 2010.

15 TechShop is the SF Bay Area's only open-access public workshop. Available online at http://techshop.ws/, accessed 30 August 2010.

16 Anderson, C. 'In the Next Industrial Revolution, Atoms Are the New Bits', Wired, Feb. 2010. Available online at www.wired.com/ magazine/2010/01/ff_newrevolution/all/1, accessed 4 June 2010.

17 HackerspaceWiki. Available online at http://hackerspaces.org/ wiki/, accessed 30 August 2010.

18 Grenzfurthner, J, and Schneider, F. 'Hacking the Spaces' on monochrom.at, 2009. Available online at www.monochrom.at/ hacking-the-spaces/, accessed 30 August 2010.

19 Farr, N, 'Respect the past, examine the present, build the
    future', 25 August 2009. Available online at http://blog.
    hackerspaces.org/2009/08/25/respect-the-past-examine-the-
    present-build-the-future/, accessed 30 August 2010.

20 List of Hackerspaces. Available online at http://hackerspaces.org/
    wiki/List_of_Hacker_Spaces, accessed 30 August 2010.

21 Synchronous Hackathon. Available online at http://hackerspaces.
    org/wiki/Synchronous_Hackathon, accessed 30 August 2010.

22 Gershenfeld, N, FAB: *The Coming Revolution on Your Desktop. From
    Personal Computers to Personal Fabrication*, Cambridge: Basic
    Books, 2005, p. 4.

23 Mikhak, B, Lyon, C, Gorton, T, Gershenfeld, N, McEnnis, C, Taylor,
    J, 'Fab Lab: An Alternative Model of ICT for Development'. Paper
    presented at the Development by Design Conference, Bangalore,
    India, 2002. Bangalore: ThinkCycle. Available online at: http://
    gig.media.mit.edu/GIGCD/latest/docs/fablab-dyd02.pdf, accessed
    11 July 2010.

24 Gershenfeld, op.cit.

25 Gjengedal, A, 'Industrial clusters and establishment of MIT
    Fab Lab at Furuflaten, Norway'. Paper presented at the 9th
    International Conference on Engineering Education, 2006.
    Available online at: www.ineer.org/Events/ICEE2006/papers/3600.pdf,
    accessed 3 March 2010.

26 Pfeiffer, D, *Digital Tools, Distributed Making & Design*. Thesis
    submitted to the faculty of the Virginia Polytechnic Institute
    and State University in partial fulfilment of the requirements for
    the Master of Science in Architecture. Blacksburg, VA: Virginia
    Polytechnic Institute and State University, 2006.

27 Farr, N, 'The Rights and Obligations of Hackerspace Members',
    19 August 2009. Available online at http://blog.hackerspaces.
    org/2009/08/19/rights-and-obligations-of-hackerspace-members/,
    accessed 31 August 2010.

28 Fab Charter, 2007. Available online at http://fab.cba.mit.edu/
    about/charter/, accessed 11 January 2011.

29 H.R. 6003: To provide for the establishment of the National Fab
    Lab Network (…). Available online at www.govtrack.us/congress/
    billtext.xpd?bill=h111-6003, accessed 13 Oct 2010.

30 Benkler, Y, 'Freedom in the Commons: Towards a Political Economy
    of Information', *Duke Law Journal*, Vol. 52, 2003, p. 1261.

31 Idem, p. 1276.

PREMIUM ADVERTISEMENT

With My OpenCard, I never have to worry about intellectual property rights anymore.

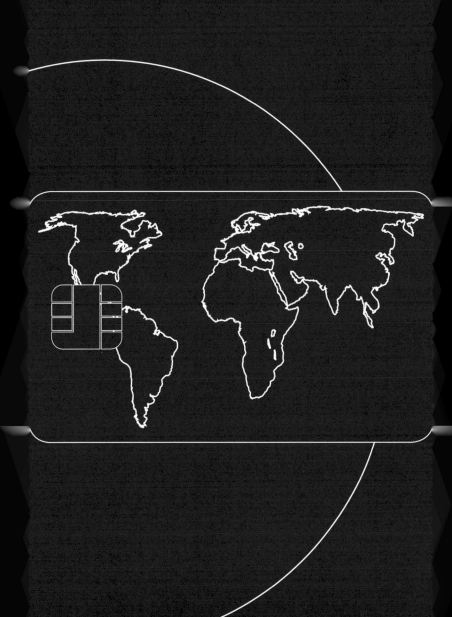

THE OPENCARD. PREMIUM SHARING.

NO MORE BESTSELLERS

JOOST SMIERS

The present copyright system is beneficial for a few best-selling artists while providing no benefits at all for most creative professionals. Joost Smiers explores ways to improve the market, including the financial situation of most artists and designers, and to keep the sources of knowledge and creativity in common hands instead of privatizing them.

Joost Smiers is a Professor Emeritus in Political Science of the Arts at Utrecht School of the Arts, The Netherlands, and has been a visiting professor at the Department of World Arts and Cultures, UCLA, Los Angeles. He has written, lectured and researched extensively on decision-making in cultural matters worldwide, on new visions of creative and intellectual property, copyright and the public domain, on freedom of expression versus responsibility, and on cultural identities. For Joost Smiers, "the appropriate term is not open design, but the open designer. The open designer does not spend any time suing other designers. Originality? Any image has been inspired by many other images."

http://en.wikipedia.org/wiki/Joost_Smiers

It was in 1993 that I started to realize that intellectual property rights – such as copyrights and patents – are steadily privatizing most of the public knowledge and creativity that our communities have developed and cultivated over centuries. Around the same time, I heard that farmers in India were staging massive protests. They faced the threat that seeds they had used for years to plant their crops would be slightly modified (or 'improved') by multinational agricultural companies like Monsanto, and that this tiny change would make those companies the owners of this 'new' knowledge. KNOWLEDGE What those farmers and their grandparents, and generations before them, had developed in their communities over the course of centuries could, with a single stroke of the pen, become the sole and exclusive property of a major corporation. These are the selfsame corporations, most of which are based in Western countries, that dominate agricultural markets all over the world.

IS THIS WHAT IP RIGHTS ARE REALLY DOING? PRIVATIZING KNOWLEDGE AND CREATIVITY ON A MASSIVE SCALE?

I was suddenly overwhelmed by a sense of cynicism. Is this what intellectual property rights are really doing? Privatizing knowledge and creativity on a massive and unprecedented scale? What could possibly justify such a bold move? It was a small step for me to extrapolate these principles from the seeds of Indian farmers to copyrights on works of art and design, which is another form of privatization. Certainly, it could be argued that every new contributor – every person who modifies or adapts seeds, words, music, design, or chemical processes – adds something to what has been developed by his predecessors. But is this a valid reason to hand over absolute ownership to the latest producer, keeping in mind that we will need this knowledge and creativity for further developments? Privatization in this context means that the product can no longer be used for common purposes, unless the 'owner' of this knowledge and creativity grants permission – and

we pay the price that 'owner' sets for it. Never before in recorded history, in any culture, has intellectual misappropriation taken place on such a grand scale as what we have seen in the Western world over the past century, expanding exponentially since the 1990s.

It soon became clear to me — long before Napster and the increasing popularity of open source software — that we have to seriously question whether or not we really need to have intellectual property rights. My main concern, in the context of copyright for artists, entertainers and designers, was that they should have the chance to make a living. There can be no doubt that the present copyright system is extremely beneficial for a few best-selling artists, and fails almost entirely to benefit the majority of creative professionals. How can the market be improved to include a better financial situation for most of the artists and designers? Moreover, can we achieve that goal by keeping the sources of our knowledge and creativity in common hands instead of privatizing them?

During the 1990s, more people started to feel uneasy with our current copyright system, partly due to the opportunities offered by digitization. Concepts like free culture, open source and Creative Commons became fashionable. ACTIVISM However, these concepts and the practices associated with them are less than helpful when it comes to creating a fairer market for creative professionals. With such a strong emphasis on 'free' access and sharing, how can this be the right answer for artists and designers seeking to earn a living from their work? In addition, these developments do nothing to reform current structures and power relations, in which a few huge enterprises dominate cultural markets. Aside from issues of democratic process, such companies artificially exclude from public view all artists who are not big stars, essentially pushing them out of the limelight. To assure a reasonable income for many artists and to stop the privatization of our common knowledge and creativity, a more fundamental answer must be found for the challenges we face.

What if We Would Abandon Copyright?

Suppose we were to leave copyright law behind us. Would it then be possible to structure a market in such a way that protection by copyright law would become unnecessary? The first question that springs to mind is what we would want to achieve in that cultural market. The answers follow from imbalances in the current structure.

→ Many more artists should be able to earn a reasonable income from their work.

→ The resources of production, distribution and promotion should have numerous owners, and access should be given more liberally.

→ An extensive database of knowledge and artistic creativity should exist in the public domain, freely available to all.

→ Audiences should not be overwhelmed by PR efforts aimed at marketing a small number of top stars. Instead, people should be freely exposed to a wide variety of cultural expressions, from which they can make their own choices.

How might all this be achieved? My starting point, which may come as a surprise, is the cultural entrepreneur. This individual could be the artist or designer himself, or someone who represents him or her, or a producer, publisher or commissioning client. The major characteristic of an entrepreneur is that he or she takes a risk in a chosen field, which in itself presents its own specific opportunities and threats. In this case, our field could be defined as 'cultural activity', a sweeping title which could also refer to the entertainment industry or to various forms of content production. The field in which the cultural entrepreneur operates bears some similarities to any other business; the cultural entrepreneur should think and act pro-actively. This individual should, in other words, be capable of staying one step ahead of the competition, try to stay on top of potential threats and opportunities, and be acutely aware of what is happening, both in his or her immediate surroundings and in the wider world.

However, a factor seldom mentioned in the context of entrepreneurship is the conditions that facilitate or obstruct risk-taking behaviour. How could such a market be constructed? How should the balance of power be organized, and what kind of regulations should set the limits and offer opportunities for the scope of entrepreneurship?

The Two Controlling Markets

The present cultural markets exhibit two forms of negative dominance. The first is copyright law. Copyright in its current form gives the owner control over the use of a work, with all the consequences that this entails. As an investment protection, it works well for best-sellers, pop stars and cinematic blockbusters, but at the same disrupts the diversity in cultural markets in ways that are harmful for cultural democracy. The second form of market control, monopolization, is often inadvertently overlooked in debates on this topic. Simply put, a limited number of conglomerates worldwide have a strong grip on the production, distribution, promotion and creation of films, music, books, design, visual arts, shows and musicals, as well as the conditions for how these creative expressions are received. Their influence also extends – even more than expected – into the digital domain.

These two forms of market domination go hand in hand. The exciting challenge is to find out whether eliminating both forms of market domination would create a more normal level playing field – whether it would be possible to achieve an environment in which no single party is able to control or influence the market or the market behaviour of others to any substantial degree. In this context, I feel that it is crucial for many cultural entrepreneurs – creative professionals, their representatives, agents, producers, publishers and so on – to actually be able to fully take part in the market.

What is currently keeping them from this level of participation? There is no single answer to that question. Yes, there are thousands and thousands of artists and designers producing work and therefore theoretically taking part in the market. However, they are often pushed out of public view by the omnipresence of the major cultural conglomerates. They do not have a fair chance to trade. Under these circumstances, it is made extremely difficult, to say the least, to bear the risk inherent in entrepreneurship.

In essence, access to the cultural market – and therefore to audiences, clients and the opportunity to earn money – is severely limited for the vast majority of cultural entrepreneurs, but wide open for a few cultural giants, which continue to grow through mergers.

The Power of the Giants

These huge enterprises also hold the copyright to a vast number of the products that they market. As copyright holders, they have an even greater stranglehold on the market, as they are the only ones that can determine whether, how and where a vast quantity of work is used. They decide which cultural products are available in the market; they dictate which kinds of content are considered acceptable and appealing, and can determine the atmosphere in which they are enjoyed, consumed or used. Their works may not be changed or undermined, either, and alternative narratives would be banned.

The majority of cultural entrepreneurs have minimal access. Many, even the mid-level ones, enter a market – if they succeed – where a few giants determine the atmosphere and appeal of what they themselves have on offer, often having to compete against big stars and 'famous' designers. DESIGNERS In this doubly dicey position, where a few major players not only dominate the market but also determine the atmosphere of the cultural playing field, it is not entirely impossible to succeed, but it is very difficult for many smaller and mid-level entrepreneurs to achieve any kind of profitable position in which they can survive.

A Proposal for a New Market

To achieve a level playing field in this cultural market, I see no other alternative than to undertake two simultaneous courses of action: first scrap copyright, and then make sure that no market domination of any kind exists with regard to production, distribution and marketing. So how does this work?

Abolishing copyright means it is no longer attractive for entrepreneurs to invest lavishly in blockbuster films, best-selling books or rising pop stars. After all, there is no longer any protection making those works exclusive. If this system were to be implemented, anyone could, in principle, change or exploit the works the next day. So why make such exorbitant

investments any longer? Naturally, it is not forbidden. Anyone who wants to can go ahead, but the investment protection that copyright offered – that privileged exclusivity – is no longer available.

THERE SHOULD BE MANY DIFFERENT PLAYERS IN ALL MARKETS, AND SOCIETY SHOULD BE RESPONSIBLE FOR IMPOSING THE CONDITIONS.

Does that mean, for example, that there will be no more epic films made? Who knows? Perhaps in an animated form. Is that a loss? Maybe, maybe not. It would not be the first time in history that a genre had disappeared due to changing production circumstances. Historically, as genres have vanished, others have appeared to replace them and become incredibly popular. It is not unthinkable that people will get used to the change very quickly. Moreover, there is no reason to offer investment protection to large-scale productions supported by excessive marketing that, in fact, pushes true cultural diversity to the outermost fringes of the market.

The second course of action I propose is to normalize market conditions. This may be even more drastic than abolishing copyright, a proposition which has become increasingly feasible over the past few years. As stated previously, no one party should control prices, quality, range, employment conditions, market access for other parties, or anything else, in any market. Similarly, no one party should be able to act with impunity, without regard for any other social considerations. In other words, there should be many different players in all markets, and society should be responsible for imposing the conditions under which they operate.

What applies to the economy in general surely applies even more to our human communication through artistic media. What we see, hear and read contributes extensively to the forming of our identities, in the plural. It cannot be stressed enough that there should therefore be many, many enterprises in the cultural field; instead of being pushed away from public attention by excessively strong forces, they should be able to offer their cultural wares from totally different perspective. I view that point as non-negotiable.

The Consequences

If such a dramatic restructuring took place, what would the result look like? There would no longer be any conglomerates dominating the production, distribution, promotion and creation of creative work or dictating the conditions for how artistic works were received. The scale of such enterprises would be reduced considerably, ranging somewhere between medium-sized and small. How could this landslide of change be brought about? Most countries have regulatory tools at their disposal in the form of competition or anti-trust laws, which are intended to level the playing field in every market – including the cultural market.

What should be happening is a fundamental investigation of anything that hints at an excessively dominant position in cultural markets, including design. That investigation should, perhaps, be one of the primary aspects of cultural policy. Imagine that large combinations of capital, assets, market positions, and production and distribution facilities were to be divided into many smaller pieces. After all, this is what we have been discussing for the cultural and media sectors in our societies. It may come as a surprise that this is even more necessary in the highly networked digital world, where it tends to be 'winner-take-all'.

Suppose that the cultural market could be normalized, that a level playing field could be attained. Can the objectives I formulated earlier be achieved there? I think so. There are no longer any obstacles to many cultural entrepreneurs taking the plunge and accepting the risks. Enterprise always entails risk; it goes with the territory. There have always been some artists and entrepreneurs who have dared to brave those risks. In this new market, many of these cultural entrepreneurs can take risks with more confidence. Irrepressibly, those entrepreneurs will evolve in every corner of the cultural universe, serving audiences with a varied range of artistic creations and performances. What used to be niche markets can begin drawing larger audiences than had ever been deemed possible.

If the cultural conglomerates' overkill marketing is no longer being dumped onto the populace en masse, then current and potential audiences are more than likely to develop interests in a wider variety of trends. Why not? Man is essentially a curious creature and has individual preferences on how he would like to be entertained or accompanied, as evidenced by the varied expressions of culture that people seek out as comfort in moments of grief. If those preferences are no longer being drowned out by a dominant few, then more room is created for far more individual choice.

Despite that individuality, man is also something of a pack animal. TREND: GLOBALIZATION People will therefore in all probability cluster more around one particular artist than around others. That artist then becomes a 'well-seller'. In our imagined scenario, the artist can never take that supreme step up to become a best-seller, since the market conditions that made that possible are simply no longer there. A normalized market for the public domain of artistic creativity and knowledge has turned out to be extraordinarily beneficial in our example. After all, artistic material and knowledge can no longer be privatized, and therefore remain the property of us all. There is not a single company left that can monopolize production, processing and distribution, either.

Now it gets interesting: how well does this thought experiment translate into practice? Could a real, functioning market conceivably be created under the conditions that I have formulated, in which devious thieves will be unable to seize their opportunity before taking to their heels? In other words, can numerous artists, their representatives, intermediaries, commissioning parties or producers earn a good living in that market? Are the risks of enterprise acceptable? Do they also have reason to believe that their work will be treated with the appropriate respect?

Let's start with the question as to whether it is likely that creative work will be used by others without payment. Is there any reason to assume that another cultural entrepreneur will pop up and exploit it immediately after release? In principle,

103

that would indeed be possible without copyright law. Nevertheless, there are several reasons why this is unlikely. First of all, there is the 'prime mover' effect. The original publisher or producer is the first in the market, which gives him an advantage. Naturally, with digitization, that prime mover effect can diminish to a few minutes, but that's not an insurmountable problem in itself. Most artistic work is not famous enough for free-riders to fall on it like hawks. Moreover, an increasingly important factor is that artists and related entrepreneurs add a specific value to their work that no one else can imitate. Building up a reputation may not be half the work, but it is a significant factor. Remember, we are assuming that there are no longer any dominant parties in the market. There are no longer any big companies to think they could easily 'steal' a recently published and well-received work because, for example, they control the distribution and promotion channels. In this scenario, they simply no longer exist.

AS A NORMAL MARKET EMERGES, MANY ARTISTS AND DESIGNERS WILL BE EARNING BETTER THAN EVER BEFORE.

In the absence of copyright, there can now be no question of theft; still, free-rider behaviour is an undesirable occurrence. In fact, there are twenty, thirty, forty, or innumerable other companies that could come up with the same idea. With this reality in mind, it becomes less likely, even very unlikely, that another company will put the money and effort into remarketing a work that has already been released. Should one be concerned that someone other than the initiator and risk bearer merrily walks off with a work that belongs to the public domain? It won't come to that. Investments go hopelessly up in smoke when numerous parties are willing to take a free-rider gamble. In that case, the first creator almost certainly remains the only one to continue exploiting the work; no one benefits from trying to take it over.
Let me remind you that the two courses of action I proposed earlier have to be taken simultaneously.

Abolishing copyright should not be an isolated action. It has to be accompanied by the application of competition or anti-trust law and market regulation in favour of diversity of cultural ownership and content. Only then there will be a market structure that discourages free-rider behaviour.

It can happen that a specific work does really well. In that case, another entrepreneur could include it in his repertoire, make 'legal' copies, or promote it in his own circles. Is that a problem? Not really, since he or she will not be the only one able to do so. Moreover, if the first entrepreneur has gauged the market accurately and remains alert, then he will have a good head start on all others. The first entrepreneur can also offer the work in a less expensive version, for example, which doesn't encourage competition. Nevertheless, successful works will certainly be exploited by others. That does not pose a serious problem, as the work has obviously already generated a lot of money for the author and the first producer or publisher. A legal copy or new presentation then only serves to enhance the author's fame, which he or she can capitalize on `CREATIVE COMMONS` in many different ways.

The Power to the Masses
I already mentioned briefly above that, if the market is structured as I propose, the phenomenon of best-sellers will be a thing of the past. That would be culturally beneficial, as real room is created in the artists tastes of people world-wide, encouraging a far greater diversity in forms of artistic expression. The economic consequence is that a tremendous amount of cultural entrepreneurs, including designers, can operate profitably in the market without being pushed out of the limelight by the big stars. At the same time, it has been established that some artists and designers often succeed in attracting more publicity than others. This will not make them best-sellers, as there are no longer any mechanisms for boosting them to worldwide fame. They become well-sellers. Besides being a nice position to be in as an artist, it would also be economically beneficial for the artists and for their producers, publishers and other intermediaries.

Another appealing effect is that the income gap between artists would take on more normal proportions. Before, the difference between rising stars and the rank and file was astronomical. In my scenario, the well-sellers may earn more than many other artists, but the differences are more socially acceptable. At the same time, another change is taking place, which is perhaps even more drastic. As a normal market emerges, many artists, designers and related intermediaries will be earning better than ever before. In the past, these people generally had a hard life, hovering around break-even point and often ending up in the red. Now, a substantially greater number will sell quite a bit better. This will allow them to scramble up above break-even point. They might not become well-sellers, but they don't have to.

In the scenario we have explored here, a significant improvement has already been achieved, because their activities have become profitable. That is a giant step forward for the income of the artist and, at the same time, an enormous improvement for the risk-bearing entrepreneur (who may also be the artist or designer). The business is no longer in a permanent state of insecurity, barely making ends meet. Moreover, as the investment becomes more profitable, it becomes possible to build up capital to finance for further activities. It also becomes easier to take a risk on artists who deserve a chance – who should be published, who should have the opportunity to perform and so forth – but have not yet had the chance.

One surprising aspect of the economic and financial crisis that swept the world in 2008 is that, for the first time in decades, the idea of markets being organized in such a way that the structure does not solely serve the interests of shareholders and investors has entered the debate. A high price has been paid for the idea that they knew what they were doing and would automatically work to serve the common good. The neo-liberal notion that markets regulate themselves should be abandoned; it simply isn't true. Every market, anywhere in the world, is organized in one way or another that serves certain interests more than others. Once this realization dawns, it will be a weight off our shoulders. We can then start constructively considering how we can organize markets – including cultural markets – to enable them to serve a broader spectrum of interests. There are exciting times ahead, not without their potential pitfalls, but with ample opportunity for these ideas to take hold and flourish.

105

COLLABORATIVE ADVERTISEMENT

HOW OPEN ARE YOU?

Open AED. The Collaborative Lifesaving Device.

THE BEGINNING OF A BEGINNING OF THE BEGINNING OF A TREND

PETER TROXLER

This portrait of open designer Ronen Kadushin reveals his vision of 'opening' industrial design and putting the designer firmly back in the centre of the design process. It tells of successful examples of Ronen's design practice – the Hack Chair, the Italic Shelf – showing how Ronen works as a designer and revealing how he envisages earning a living from Open Design.

Ronen Kadushin is an Open Designer and design teacher, based in Berlin, Germany. He designs furniture, lighting and accessories. According to Ronen, "Open Design aims to transform industrial design to become relevant in a globally networked information society. For him, Open Design is based on two preconditions: An Open Design is CAD information published online under a Creative Commons license to be downloaded, produced, copied and modified. An Open Design is produced directly from file by CNC machines and without special tooling. These preconditions infer that all technically conforming Open Designs and their derivatives are continuously available for production, in any number, with no tooling investment, anywhere and by anyone."

www.ronen-kadushin.com

"I'm smelling the beginning of a beginning of a beginning of a trend," Ronen said to me when I visited him at his Berlin Mitte flat in September 2009. He moved to the city "with his wife and dog to work on Open Design", to explore how today's products could regain their contemporary relevance in relation to "the grand vision of human society", as expressed in the internet. "You don't get to have many adventures as a professional designer", DESIGNERS he said in his lecture at Premsela's Unlimited Design Forum, 11 May 2010. "I'd say this is a good adventure. A revolution REVOLUTION in product development, production and distribution is imminent due to the disruptive nature of the internet and the easy access to CNC machines. Open Design is a proposal to make it happen. Its aim is to shift industrial design, making it relevant again in a globally networked information society." TRENDS

developed his view of "Open Design" (the capitals are his) quite a bit, from the early 2009 *Introduction to Open Design*[2] to the *Open Design Manifesto*[3] of September 2010. MANIFESTOS

Ronen's interest in open design stems from his Master's thesis, which he completed at Middlesex University in 2004. Before that, Ronen had studied industrial design at the Bezalel Academy of Art and Design in Jerusalem and graduated *cum laude* with a Bachelor of Design in 1991. He went on to work in furniture design in Tel Aviv at Studio Shaham and for Znobar, and in London at Ron Arad's One-Off studio. In 2005, he moved to Berlin to found his open design venture and to become a lecturer at the Universität der Künste (UdK). In 2010, he taught open design at Burg Giebichenstein University of Art and Design, Halle, as a visiting professor.

MY AIM IS TO MAKE INDUSTRIAL DESIGN RELEVANT AGAIN IN A GLOBALLY NETWORKED INFORMATION SOCIETY.

110

I first heard about Ronen Kadushin at an event showcasing projects using CC licences,[1] which was held in a former military barracks in Zurich in January 2009. It was not until August 2009 that I first met Ronen in person; we were launching the first (Un)limited Design Contest in Vierhouten, the Netherlands, at Hacking at Random, the 2009 international technology & security conference. EVENTS This big family get-together of European hackers was attended by over 2000 people. The contest was intended to promote open design; as its number-one proponent, Ronen seemed just the right person to kick it off. Unknowingly, we were inviting Ronen into a community he had only recently discovered for himself; his memories of the event still bear the glow of his first explorations in open design.

Ronen gave a fascinating talk on Open Design on that occasion; it was only his first stop on a series of subsequent talks that took him to Vienna, Tallinn and London. In the time that I have known him, Ronen has

I LOOKED AT OTHER DESIGN FIELDS, SUCH AS GRAPHIC DESIGN AND GAME DESIGN, AND THEY WERE HAVING A FIELD DAY ON THE INTERNET! CREATIVITY WAS BOOMING. BUT INDUSTRIAL DESIGN WASN'T EVEN A BLIP ON THE RADAR.

Ronen has been preoccupied with bringing the ideas of open source software to the world of industrial design: sharing the source code for designs over the internet, allowing anybody to download, copy and modify it and to use it to produce their own products. "I looked at other design fields, such as graphic design and game design, and they were having a field day on the internet! Creativity was booming. But industrial design wasn't even a blip on the radar." Sharing CAD files on the internet under a permissive license is the first condition of Open Design. The second condition is that Open Design products must be able to be produced on CNC machines, directly from the CAD file, without requiring specialist tooling such as moulds or matrices.

WE'RE TALKING ABOUT A NEW MOVEMENT IN ITS INFANCY HERE: PEOPLE ARE TAKING THEIR FIRST STEPS WITH THE TECHNOLOGY, PRODUCING THE STUFF THEY JUST NEED.

Designs that adhere to these two conditions – and the associated derivative designs that evolve from them – are continuously available for production, in any number, with no tooling investment, anywhere and by anyone. For Ronen, this is no longer just an aspiration. "We're talking about a new movement in its infancy here. People are taking their first steps with the technology, producing the stuff they just need." Yet these early adopters are more into making things for the sake of making, regardless of what they create, whether it's some mechanical toy or a decoration for their laptop.

Perhaps just for the sake of validating the Open Design movement, Ronen designed a chair: the Hack Chair.
"If you're in a design movement, in a style, or if you're an individual designer, you would probably want to do a chair that would embody the basic attitudes and points of view or technologies. The chair is a central object in our culture and a central object in design. So the Hack Chair is my first Open Design chair. DESIGNERS I wanted it to be an object or a chair that makes you say, 'I've never seen anything like this before.' At the same time, the Hack Chair is very sculptural, very dangerous, but also very funny; it's pure expression. I had no buyer for it. I was not working for some producer who told me how to design it so it could be sold. I suppose it won't be a bestseller, but that's not the point. I did it because it helps me make a

statement about being an independent designer. It says loud and clear that I'm able to design something like this, and share it, and make it open; if you want to make the chair more cushy and comfortable, it's an open design. Go ahead, make it comfortable, add your nice round radiuses. I see the Hack Chair as very concise: my story, in a very basic product. Hack."
HACKING DESIGN

Of course Ronen's Hack Chair employs certain procedures that are considered 'clever' in design, such as producing a three-dimensional object out of a single, two-dimensional sheet of metal. Ronen has been doing this for years, and has even given the technique a name: 'thinology'. He wanted to invest this chair with a sense of his own aesthetic preferences:
"I was designing the chair so everything would look wrong and be as unconventional as possible; an un-chair, a chair that has a look that makes you stop and consider your own self, reassess your relation to an object that is not the expected. You may not enjoy its beauty, but you'll enjoy the conflict between its appearance and your experience of sitting and of chairs in general. I could have designed it to be straight and rounded and nice, but I chose not to.

"The chair has conflict in it. There is some anger in it, there is some humour in it; there are many things in it that I want my viewer to experience. I don't want them to just go out and buy it in the first place. It will be available to purchase shortly, but it is also open. There is an important connection between it being open and the way it looks. This is my choice; you have other choices, and you can have different points of view. If you're a designer, or if you want to be a designer, or if you think you are a designer, you could make your own version. You are actually welcome to make your version.

"It looks edgy and sharp, but it's quite sittable. It's not the first chair to have a user-object conflict, but it's the first one I've made."

Ronen just sent me some photos from his Hack Chair exhibition, Recent Uploads, at Berlin's Appel Design gallery. He extended the Hack Chair and produced several permutations. The exhibition was truly process-oriented. The walls were decorated with the

111

remains of the 2D cut-outs. `AESTHETICS: 2D` Throughout the evening, Ronen would take new sheets of metal and fold them, within a matter of a minute, into yet another *Hack Chair* derivative, a clear nod to the active process of creation rather than the finished product. People could sit in the chairs and interact with them; there were also miniature versions that the audience could buy and fold themselves. It was an intriguing concept – and indeed, the exhibition chairs were all sold out.

When sharing his own designs, Ronen offers friendly production instructions:
"In order to produce this object, you need to be somewhat proficient with handling DXF files, have knowledge of laser-cut part `AESTHETICS: 2D` production, have two good hands and a creative personality that thrives on experimentation. If you have all these, there's a good chance you are an industrial designer or design student; if not, welcome aboard.

I AM SAYING: PLEASE COPY. BUT IF YOU WANT TO MAKE A BUSINESS OUT OF IT, THEN CALL ME AND WE'LL DISCUSS ROYALTIES. IT IS MY INTELLECTUAL PROPERTY, AFTER ALL; THAT'S THE BOTTOM LINE.

"Please note that you can use this design as many times you like, change it, send it to others, and express through it any personal point of view and creativity, as long as you follow the Creative Commons licence."

The Creative Commons license that he applies allows anybody to reproduce and modify his designs. There are only two limitations: these modifications and derivatives must be shared under the same license, and the licence prohibits commercial uses.

"I am saying: please copy. But if you want to make a business out of it, then please call me and we'll discuss royalties. It is my intellectual property, after all; that's the bottom line. If you want to use it, I would love you to use it; we can talk about it. But if you're making money out of it, then I would like a share `SHARING` of it also. That's the principle behind my design.

"Open Design is not an intellectual property trap. It is not something I do to get money out of suing companies. I consider my audience to be designers and makers and anyone who is interested in creating. The intellectual property rights, the Creative Commons license I publish it under, these are just a legal framework that supports my work, but they are not at the centre. The centre is creativity through designing objects."

Ronen is well aware that his ability to prosecute somebody is fairly limited, particularly if a big manufacturer copied his designs illegally, without his consent.
"Copyright protection gives you the big guns, but can you afford the ammunition? You can register your intellectual property, but you don't usually have the money to defend it. This is life; the big fish eat the little fish."

"Suppose you have a good bicycle. You like it and you want to keep it, so you buy a really nice lock for it. If a thief truly wants your bicycle, no matter how good your lock is, he will find a way to steal your bicycle. Intellectual property protection is exactly the same. I'm not saying that I'm leaving my bicycles completely unlocked; they have a lock. But the lock says, 'hey, why don't you take a ride and give it back when you're finished.' So you can take it out for a test drive, but if you want to keep it, I'm asking you to buy it from me, and I am willing to sell it to you. If you want to produce it, I will let you do it. There are many other options available too. People should just be honest about it."

And many people are honest. While Ronen gets many emails asking if he's really serious about sharing his designs, he does not get to see most of the private copies or modifications. An exception was São Paulo-based designer Oswaldo Mellone, who produced a Hanukkah design based on Ronen's *Candle Holder*[1] and sold it at a gallery; proceeds went to a local educational project.

SUPPOSE YOU HAVE A GOOD BICYCLE. YOU LIKE IT AND YOU WANT TO KEEP IT, SO YOU BUY A REALLY NICE LOCK FOR IT. IF A THIEF TRULY WANTS YOUR BICYCLE, NO MATTER HOW GOOD YOUR LOCK IS, HE WILL FIND A WAY TO STEAL YOUR BICYCLE. INTELLECTUAL PROPERTY PROTECTION IS EXACTLY THE SAME.

Ronen is not out to squeeze every eurocent he could possibly get from every user of his designs; he does not even see recovering production expenses as a truly commercial enterprise.

"My answer to this is always, you're welcome to sell them to cover your expenses; it would be my pleasure to have you make some money out of it."

He occasionally makes some money himself, too. In September 2009, his original prototype of the *Italic Shelf* was included in the Phillips de Pury & Co. auction 'Now: Art of the 21st Century'. The estimate was around four to five thousand pounds; the shelf sold for six and a half thousand pounds, plus the 25% commission for the auction house, bringing the final sales price to GBP 8,125.

"The interesting thing about selling in an auction is that buyers usually research the background of what they might be going to buy, because each piece has a name, a designer's name, a history, and so on. They probably knew beforehand that the shelf was

Open Design and that anybody else could copy it and build it, so there is an interesting conflict between the rarity of an object and the fact that anybody can copy it. Even so, they got the prototype. There is no real difference between the prototype and a copy. So putting yourself in that situation is an interesting concept. I wanted to do it that way, displaying things in a gallery. It takes Open Design and the concomitant legal copying of an object and brings about a confrontation with the collector's situation, collecting rare things or limited editions. The limited edition is exactly the same as any other copy to be produced anywhere by anybody, legally. This is an interesting intellectual puzzle."

The only thing that differentiates the original from any other original copies is a little brass plaque on the edge of the shelf, incised with the words 'RONEN KADUSHIN 2008/ITALIC SHELF PROTOTYPE', naming the Open Designer as the author.

In the meantime, Ronen is garnering increasing attention with his Open Design products. His *Square Dance* coffee table already made it into Wired in 2009. *The iPhone Killer* which he launched in a style worthy of Steve Jobs, presenting it at Premsela's Unlimited Design Forum in 2010, landed him a prominent spot on some of the most widely read web publications: *Wired, BoingBoing, The Huffington Post*. Ronen knows how the Net ticks; with no real marketing budget to speak of, his self-created media ripples are not to be underestimated. And he is certainly enjoying his '15 megabytes of fame' on the internet.

Yet Ronen's real Open Design business is clearly geared towards the producers of lighting and furniture accessories. It's a business-to-business thing. If we're talking about royalties and serious marketing, and production and branding, and so on, this is what I'm looking at.

THERE'S NO REAL DIFFERENCE BETWEEN THE PROTOTYPE AND A COPY.

113

"If an accessory producer or lighting manufacturer would want to include it in their collection, then we would have to sit down and work out the details: not just royalties, but the whole concept. There is no big company today – no big producer, no mid-sized producer, not even a small producer – that is doing something that is in any way connected to Open Design. There is mass customization, MASS CUSTOMIZATION yes, but not Open Design as such. I would like to convince the producer that it could be to his advantage to try it out, and it would not cost him more to try it out. Actually, it could be a marketing pitch for the company to position itself as the first business to embrace Open Design. This claim would be very likely to benefit the company that does it."

The real benefit for a producer that adopted the principles of Open Design would of course be that a second and third Open Design product would not incur any extra costs for tooling. They would only have to care about marketing, packaging, production. However, the companies Ronen has spoken to so far have not considered this concept to be relevant. "They are investing in tooling to make a specific product. If a company produces something made of plastic, or that involves tooling by definition, Open Design becomes irrelevant. Making it open would also not make it relevant for any other user to make modifications. They don't have the equipment, they don't have the know-how, KNOWLEDGE they don't have the money; it's too complicated."

> I'M NOT PLEADING, "OH PLEASE, PLEASE, DO MY DESIGN FOR A 3% ROYALTY", WITH THE MANUFACTURER EQUIVOCATING, "NO, WELL, MAYBE LATER", AND THEN CHANGING IT AND SO ON.

Ronen still believes that c ommercial adoption of open design could be possible. Yet he's not a fundamentalist about his own ideas; he is not pushing open design to companies. Rather, he is introducing it gradually, helping companies develop a basic understanding that they have 'this type of designer' in their network of contexts, a designer who sees things a little differently. This approach seems to be paying off; Ronen secured a rather large project about two years ago. "The company approached me because they liked the Open Design concept, and they liked the product that resulted from this concept. I was never put at a disadvantage, I was never mistreated; quite the opposite."

So one day, Ronen dreams, another producer might approach him, asking him to become their chief designer. "What I would like to see is not about getting money from other people. I just want to be ... let's call it an 'art director' on this kind of projects. I want to be in a position where I can influence how people understand what quality is, how to make the connection between the producer, Open Design and consumers, to search for the next stage, things like that. That would put me in a very comfortable position; I would enjoy that. But it will take time. I'm waiting patiently, no hurry. I'm doing other things at the moment. But my plan is to introduce this concept to companies."

Ronen's Hack Chair has all the characteristics of an open design product. It is native to the internet, and was clearly designed to use the internet as a marketing and distribution channel.
Ronen believes that "if you do something this way, it will be watched, viewed, produced, copied, talked about, blogged about in more places than if it was a closed design, if it was a normal design".

"So, in this situation, the designer is at the centre of an enterprise. If I meet a manufacturer, we're talking eye-to-eye. I'm not pleading, 'oh please, please, do my design for a 3% royalty', with the manufacturer equivocating, 'no, well, maybe later', and then changing it and so on. It's really about having control of your creative output.

"At a fairly low cost, a designer can select suitable producers and sell products at a price he or she thinks it appropriate. It is a flexible venture that adapts easily to the customers' needs and locations, and it is scalable in terms of quantities. The presence of the designs on the web gives a large number of designers, producers and entrepreneurs access to creative content to experiment with. It can be considered as a business opportunity, on a 'try before you buy' basis. It also creates space for new business practices that are unknown in 'normal' circumstances", Ronen writes in his 2009 Open Design primer.[4]

AT A FAIRLY LOW COST, A DESIGNER CAN SELECT SUITABLE PRODUCERS AND SELL PRODUCTS AT A PRICE HE OR SHE THINKS IT APPROPRIATE.

Ronen talks about his experiences with design schools and how they see open design. "Students are kind of suspicious, but once I tell them how I make money out of it, why people don't copy from me, they get it; they understand that I'm on to something here. And the design professors complain that it's not working for them anymore; they say that design is not what it used to be. So maybe we are discovering a new opportunity, a new approach here."

This new approach as proposed in Ronen Kadushin's concept of Open Design has another interesting aspect as well. "You're designing for a consumer, but you're also designing for a user. Somebody has to use it as a design, to change the design. And this distinction causes a lot of confusion in students. They don't know how to handle it until they are pretty far into the projects."

However, once they finally understand the concept, some students produce very interesting transformations. In a course on open design at the Institute of Advanced Architecture in Barcelona, students converted the *Square Dance* table into what they imagined could become a shelter for use in South America. For another design, they took the idea behind the construction of the *Italic Shelf* to

build a church hall. Ronen is fascinated by what these students are doing: "They are turning Open Design into architecture."

In the future, maybe ten years from now, Ronen imagines a couple walking down the street, peeking into the shop windows of designer outlets and saying to each other, "God, I simply can't stand this Open Design junk anymore, it's everywhere. Can't they come up with something else?" So there still will be designers, their products will still be sold in design shops, and there will still be couples going shopping to furnish their new home.

But maybe the situation will have changed fundamentally. Maybe the producer will have disappeared altogether, or perhaps just have taken on a completely different role. Ronen is searching how to make his vision of Open Design a reality: "I have to find a way to ensure that my creativity will not stop at the producer's front door. I will be independent in pursuing that goal."

NOTES

1   http://creativecommons.org/licenses/by-nc-sa/3.0/

2   Kadushin, R. *Open Design. Exploring creativity in IT context.* An Industrial Design education program by Ronen Kadushin, 2009. Available at http://www.ronen-kadushin.com/uploads/2382/Open%20 Design%20edu3.pdf, accessed 11 January 2011.

3   Kadushin, R. *Open Design Manifesto.* Presented at Mestakes and Manifestos (M&M!), curated by Daniel Charny, Anti Design Festival, London, 18-21 September 2010. Available at http://ronen-kadushin.com/uploads/2440/Open%20Design%20Manifesto-Ronen%20 Kadushin%20.pdf, accessed 11 January 2011.

4   Kadushin, 2009, op.cit.

PRODUCTS BECOME INFORMATION BECOMES PRODUCTS.

Vectorizr ⊕

JORIS LAARMAN'S EXPERIMENTS WITH OPEN SOURCE DESIGN

GABRIELLE KENNEDY

The mediocracy of the middle classes dominates the current mass production design. In a world less controlled by branding and regulations, a new breed of designers can contribute to an altered, more honest economy.
An interview with Dutch designer Joris Laarman, contemplating his relationship to modernism and the modernist roots of open source design and digital fabrication.

Joris Laarman started Joris Laarman Lab in 2004 in partnership with filmmaker Anita Star. Joris Laarman Lab is an experimental playground set up to shape the future. It tinkers with craftsmen, scientists, engineers and many other young, motivated people.
It wants to give meaning to technological progress and show the beauty of how things could work, using a hands-on approach imbued with a sense of poetry.

Joris describes open design as "a complex theme that has not yet revealed all its twists and turns. Essentially, open design offers a new economic model for design that distributes power among creative professionals and local manufacturers, rather than concentrating it in centralized industrial brands."

www.jorislaarman.com

There's always something special about the top crop of Dutch design graduates, but every once in a while one comes along that makes everyone sit up and take notice. In 2003, that was Joris Laarman. His *Reinventing Functionality* project at the Design Academy of Eindhoven fused function with ornament and was snatched up by Museum Boijmans Van Beuningen in Rotterdam.

DESIGN MUST ACCEPT SOME OF THE RESPONSIBILITY FOR CREATING MANY OF THE WORLD'S CURRENT PROBLEMS.

Since then, he has earned a reputation for himself as a designer with visionary ideas and a concern for societal issues. His first project out of school, the *Bone Furniture* range, was exhibited in the Friedman Benda gallery in New York, a limited edition series made from marble, porcelain and resin. While he calls it an "annoying coincidence" that much of his work has spawned major contemporary trends, it also testifies to its relevance to the issues that matter.

Furniture That Can Be Grown

Both those early projects clearly expressed Laarman's highly specific views on modernism. The *Bone* range DESIGNERS resulted from a cooperative partnership with car manufacturer Opel, using software to design a series of artworks based on the organic way that bones form. Car parts are designed with the help of topology optimization software to increase strength and maximize the efficient use of materials. Furniture, as it turns out, can also be 'grown' by adding and removing material to maximize its strength and functionality.

Laarman's stance is that functionality and extravagance are not mutually exclusive. Where modernism went wrong, and how its core advantages need to be readdressed, are what drive his research. What he is looking for are design solutions that possess a revolutionary quality. Much of his current

research repudiates how things are currently done and patiently pursues a better way not just to manufacture, but also to distribute design.

Seen in this light, design must accept some of the responsibility for creating many of the world's current problems. More importantly, it can play a key role in fixing them. In 2009, Laarman opened his Amsterdam studio to the public for the first time. His purpose was to share his thinking and his process. He wanted to reveal how design experimentation and research can create answers, not just pretty objects.

"In galleries and in Milan, people only ever see perfect pieces," he says. "In this exhibition, I wanted people to see the research part of design, what is behind all the pretty shapes, and how they could eventually be of use in the world. I wanted people to understand what the future of design could look like using technological progress."

Laarman hit a wall when he was researching open source design and digital fabrication. He realized that design had taken a wrong turn somewhere along the way and was now failing society. "I am not necessarily against how design is now," he says, "but I do think the internet can provide a more honest way to design, make, distribute and sell things." Not modernism, then; what's needed is a new -*ism*. It takes some audacity for such a young designer to criticize the industry. Laarman has gone beyond theoretical criticism, underlining his opinion with some tangible ideas that he wants to try out – hopefully with the support of his contemporaries.

I DO THINK THE INTERNET CAN PROVIDE A MORE HONEST WAY TO DESIGN, MAKE, DISTRIBUTE AND SELL THINGS.

"I started to think of my work and of design in general as a sort of laboratory," Laarman says. He explains it as a place where solutions might be found to the predicament created by over-production in the post-industrial age. "I'm not condemning the whole design industry," he says, "or even questioning it. There is a lot of very good industrial production, and that will never go away, but I think it will soon be joined by another revolution made possible by the internet." REVOLUTION

Despite its failures and the role it played in creating over-production, Laarman's research kept bringing him back to modernism – not as an aesthetic per se, but as a philosophy. In 2010 Laarman was selected by Ingeborg de Roode, curator of industrial design at the Stedelijk Museum in Amsterdam, to participate in the Modernism Today series. "I guess she sees me as a sort of contemporary version of Rietveld," DESIGNERS says Laarman. "That is an interesting comparison, and I see some connection." 100 years ago, Gerrit Rietveld experimented with technology and materials; Laarman does the same today. His aesthetic is not in the tradition of De Stijl, but his values most certainly are.

The Modernist Roots (of Open Design)

In line with those values, it made good sense to fuse Rietveld's world of ideas and experiments with open source design and digital fabrication; both could be argued to have modernist roots. Open source has been revolutionizing the cultural content universes of music and software for almost a decade, so why shouldn't it also be able to change the way design is both made and distributed?

"I think true modernists wanted open source design one hundred years ago," says Laarman, "but back then it wasn't possible. Rietveld published manuals about how to make his chairs, but nobody could really use that information, because there were no networks of skilled artisans. His designs look simple, but are difficult to construct. These days, we can distribute knowledge in a way that can potentially bring craftspeople back to the centre stage of design – not in an idealistic, naïvely romantic way, but in an economically sound way. All we need are the networks, and cheaper and more accessible digital manufacturing technology." One of modernism's core flaws was the huge amount of power that ended up in the hands of a few big factories and design firms. The movement was supposed to be about the democratization of design – that was their big idea – but somewhere along the line it became nothing more than an aesthetic. Of course there are some obvious differences between modernism and open source design. Modernism produced an international and generic style. Industrialization led to mass production, which meant production had to be centralized and its products transported across the globe from countries with the lowest wages at great environmental and economic expense. Information and knowledge were kept closed and protected by copyrights; even if they had been accessible, it would have been impossible for an individual to use the design data without access to exorbitantly expensive production tools. The quality of design produced was and continues to be guaranteed by the producer; in turn, the producer and the retailer divide the majority of sales revenues.

I THINK TRUE MODERNISTS WANTED OPEN SOURCE DESIGN ONE HUNDRED YEARS AGO.

Open source design, on the other hand, has the capacity to conserve culture and decoration as well as traditional skills by utilizing new technology. Digital production makes mass customization possible. Open source makes information and knowledge public; in addition, it has low entry costs, quality control takes place in the form of peer review by the public, and revenues are divided between craft and creativity. Also, because the products of open source design can be produced locally, transportation costs are drastically reduced.

What open source design does is redistribute knowledge KNOWLEDGE and the means of production. It has the potential to change everything that we know about design, from manufacturing to education. Open source design is anti-elitist insofar as it can create fairer and more honest prices. It is democratic and helps to create self-determination in an individual's

121

COMPOSITION OF SALES PRICE

Under the current system, a designer takes his or her
design to a manufacturer, who makes it and then takes it to
a shop that sells it. If he is lucky, the designer gets 3%
ex factory. The brand adds 300% and the shop doubles that
again.

RETAIL

BRAND

FACTORY

DESIGNER

122

immediate environment. Ultimately, it takes power away from the huge multinationals and from production hubs like China and India and hands it back to craftspeople – those individuals rendered irrelevant by industrialization. In short, open source design could feasibly become this century's new -ism.

ULTIMATELY, IT TAKES POWER AWAY FROM THE MULTINATIONALS AND PRODUCTION HUBS LIKE CHINA AND HANDS IT BACK TO CRAFTSPEOPLE – THOSE INDIVIDUALS RENDERED IRRELEVANT BY INDUSTRIALIZATION.

"This does not mean that anyone can make good design or that more rubbish can be produced," Laarman says. "Just because everyone has a digital camera doesn't mean that everyone is a photographer. I am not in favour of amateurism, but the way I envision the system working, the good will eventually be filtered from the bad." AMATEURISSIMO

Less Production Is Needed, Not More.
Statistics show that up until the Industrial Revolution, a similar amount of products were being produced every year. With industrialization came increased wealth and prosperity, which lead to massive increases in production. The result was more waste, more environmental damage TREND: SCARCITY OF RESOURCES and a surge in unemployed artisans. The average Western person today has access to more things than Queen Victoria owned during her reign. "The tragedy is that the vast majority of what is being today made lacks creativity and quality and isn't really needed," Laarman says. "The over-production of mediocrity for the middle classes has created a difficult economic situation, and there is nothing that can be done about it within the current system."

If digital design went local, imagine what this would mean for small producers. "Right now, most people are just talking about digital fabrication," says Laarman, "but it is happening, and I think can eventually take over. I am not going to say it will change the world, but it will change the way things are made. 3D printing is still very limited, AESTHETICS: 3D especially in terms of materials, but as digital manufacturing technology evolves, anything is possible."

One possible scenario would be for local communities to invest in technology. "There are already all kinds of initiatives popping up that give individuals the opportunity to start their own small production facilities," Laarman says. "We are looking into setting up a sort of professional Fab Lab, for instance, where any design based on a digital blueprint could be mass-customized and made."

It could work. The RepRap machine, for example, is an open-branded DIY 3D printing machine. HELLO WORLD The RepRap is a machine that you can make yourself (and that can reproduce itself!) REPRODUCTION that can in turn make other gadgets. "Right now, this sort of thing is the domain of geeks for geeks, but once it becomes more professional, it will be ready for more general usage," Laarman says.

123

THE AVERAGE WESTERN PERSON TODAY HAS ACCESS TO MORE THINGS THAN QUEEN VICTORIA OWNED DURING HER REIGN.

Open source design and local digital fabrication could also revolutionize education, which has mostly become outdated and irrelevant. "We could tie the platform into trade schools," Laarman says. "Education has fallen behind and kids are not being taught what is needed. Digital manufacturing should be taught in schools, especially at the vocational school level."

These developments are slow, however, because open source design remains the great unknown, with many unanswered quandaries. The new, innovative nature of the ideas works both for and against them; instead of inspiring images of a world less controlled by branding and regulations, open source design ends up sounding chaotic, with too much choice and an over-abundance of experimentation and waste. Issues of copyright and profit-sharing scare off many, leaving a lot of the earliest experimental platforms looking unprofessional and insecure. MANIFESTOS

But the problem for most of the current websites selling open source design is they lack professional participation. What's needed is more of the best and most visionary design minds debating and devising ways to make it all work. "What is happening so far isn't really making a difference, but it does show that there is huge potential," Laarman says.

Creative Commons CREATIVE COMMONS has made some interesting inroads. It is a new type of copyright that protects a designer (or anyone else) so that they can make licensing agreements with suitable producers or limit use of their ideas to personal use only. "It works in an idealistic sense if everybody plays nice," says Laarman. It is still limited, though, and resembles a small-scale iTunes dominated by amateur musicians playing a limited number of instruments. What is needed next is a professional digital platform, or a network where people can meet, access and share information about how and where to have design digitally manufactured.

124

DIGITAL MANUFACTURING SHOULD BE TAUGHT IN SCHOOLS, ESPECIALLY AT THE VOCATIONAL SCHOOL LEVEL.

Make-Me.com

One exciting project already under way, albeit in its nascent stages, is Make-Me.com, a cooperative venture involving Laarman, the Waag Society, Droog Design and some early internet pioneers. For designers, it means uploading their design for general distribution. For consumers, it means being able to access and customize design. For local producers, it means using licensing agreements to make the things that people want. "It reduces our carbon footprints and allows for more customization," says Laarman.

THAT IS WHAT WE DO. WE TAKE SOMETHING FROM THE PAST AND SHAPE IT INTO SOMETHING NEW.

Make-Me.com plans to operate like an app store. You go there to get what you want. Some of it is free and some of it is paid for; some are designed by amateurs and some by professionals. "The amateurs and the professionals have to compete against one another," Laarman says. "You find the chair you want online via us and you go to the local Fab Lab to have it produced on the spot. The platform is linking consumers to craftspeople and digital fabrication tools."

Make-Me.com as an open source platform is not limited to design. "It is for journalists, architects, businesspeople, scientists – even a place you could go to for a new haircut," says Laarman. Big pharmaceutical companies, for example, don't want to invest in research on diseases that only affect small numbers of people, because there is no money to be made. An open source platform could open up possibilities for DIY bio-labs where scientists and doctors could access research and make their own medicines. "Anyone can use Make-Me.com to distribute information in a new way."

Designers, however, fear what all this means for them in terms of copyright. They think production companies protect their intellectual property, the quality of their designs, and guarantee them an income. What that fails to recognize is that copyright is a complicated question. Who really owns an original idea? Is anything truly and completely original? Every creative person pilfers and borrows ideas from everywhere; referencing what came before is a natural part of the creative process. "That is what we do," says Laarman. "We take something from the past and shape it into something new." REMIX Via Creative Commons licensing, it might become possible to profit from someone stealing your idea.

What limits the scope of open source at this point goes beyond legal concerns. For it to work, a whole new economic model would need to be devised and accepted. Under the current system, a designer takes his or her design to a manufacturer, who makes it and then takes it to a shop that sells it. "If he is lucky, the designer gets 3% ex factory," Laarman says. "The brand adds 300% and the shop doubles that again. It's ridiculous how little of the cut a designer gets. If we used digital tools and changed the way stores work, the ratio would be able to favour creativity and the craftsman."

However, test-driving a new model will require a platform like Make-Me.com. It has to be large scale, and it will need to attract big-name designers and brands so that people can see it working. It's a tough chicken-and-egg situation: unless designers feel that their financial income and copyright dues are guaranteed, they are not going to take the risk – and without enough designers taking the risk, it will be virtually impossible to erect the solid infrastructure to ensure smooth, safe and legal operations. It will take a coordinated leap of faith from educational facilities, designers and craftspeople for anything like this to work.

None of these obstacles are insurmountable. What Laarman wants is to be a part of the experiment and to be a contributing member of that generation who will be defining the parameters and creating the way forward. It is that vision which distinguishes him from a lot of his contemporaries – he has the commitment and the patience. He knows that this is something big and wants to do whatever it takes to make it work. "Right now, I am making very expensive, limited-edition designs," he says. "That is a good way to fund the experiments and start a business, but eventually what I'd like to be able to do is provide open source versions of my work for everyone. That is my goal."

He knows he doesn't have all the answers, but Laarman is working through all these problems one by one. "I don't want to say that this idea could take over the entire production world," he says, "but it can certainly help craftspeople to make things that are not standardized or mass produced. If a world-wide network of craftspeople grows, then this could potentially really change things."

Closed Societies Fail

Whichever way you look at this, design cannot continue as is. Design reveals a lot about society, and closed societies fail; like organisms that shut themselves off from their environment, a society that shuns reality will eventually die. Likewise, closed design is outdated. Open source, whether it can be what designers want or even understand at this point, is one way for design to play a real role in building a new, more honest economy. A world with less mass production, less waste, less transportation and less standardized design STANDARDS can only be interpreted as a win-win situation for all concerned.

Another decade of discussion is needed before open source design will ever be able to make a tangible difference. Interestingly, the same arguments being used against the phenomenon now are the very same arguments that were once used against the introduction of democracy. The ruling elite will always feel threatened by the idea of giving power to the people.

125

WHAT I'D LIKE TO BE ABLE TO DO IS PROVIDE OPEN SOURCE VERSIONS OF MY WORK FOR EVERYONE.

VERSION-MANAGED ADVERTISEMENT

UPGRADE TO NEARLY PERFECT.

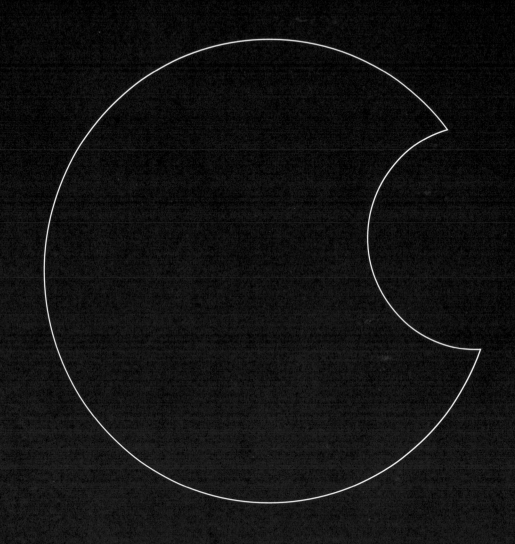

Different Thinking.

DO IT WITH DROOG

ROEL KLAASSEN & PETER TROXLER

Renny Ramakers talks about Droog's latest project Downloadable Design, about making money, designing for the masses, the development of the design profession, and Droog Design's recent experiments and research in sustainability, local production, co-creation, upcycling and collective revitalization of the suburbs.

Renny Ramakers is the director of Droog Design in Amsterdam, The Netherlands. She is trained as an art historian; after her studies she decided to specialize in design and to make history herself by creating projects which stretch the borders of design thinking and create interaction with the public. Renny curates design exhibitions, is a judging panellist on various design boards and gives lectures and leads workshops worldwide. For Renny, "open design means that you're open towards the user, that you open yourself to the user. Not by conducting market research and so on, but by being open to people, by giving people something to do, by interacting, by not planning everything right down to the last detail."

www.droog.com/renny-ramakers

Roel Klaassen: Looking at recent and future developments in design in the Netherlands, Droog has played an important part, perhaps even a key role. One of your latest projects is about design that can be downloaded. Are you giving your designs to users so they can modify them?

Renny Ramakers: We started the *Downloadable Design* DOWNLOADABLE DESIGN project together with Waag Society because we saw that designers these days make products that could be downloaded very easily, but aren't available for download. Take Jurgen Bey's design for our store in New York, for example. Even though it's based completely on laser cutting, it is constructed from so many parts and its assembly involves so much manual labour that it is not possible at this stage to offer it as a downloadable design.

We've seen the idea of flat-pack products that you assemble yourself, and are seeing the growth of the 3D printer, PRINTING which can now be used to create physical objects from various designs. These concepts looked interesting, so we thought: let's see if we can build a platform for these kinds of designs. Together with early internet pioneer Michiel Frackers and designer Joris Laarman, we are now working on the realization of this platform, which will be released as Make-Me.com.

We set up the project with the aim of achieving a number of goals. First, we wanted to eliminate some of the many steps between design and production, so the products become cheaper, similar in a sense to what IKEA has done. Compressing the process is an important reason. We know from our experience with producing designs that it may take up to two years before a finished product reaches the shops. Two years is a tremendously long time, so it's interesting to explore whether designers would be able to design products without this second part of the process. It could be a very interesting development. Second, if you produce locally, you cut down on the need for transport. Reducing transport adds an ecological benefit. Third, local production on demand means that you don't need to have your products in stock. This constitutes an economic advantage. From the consumer's perspective, providing everybody access to design products also has value. Design is everywhere: even the most inane magazines feature design. However, a high level of design isn't available

to most end users; our products are just too expensive for the people who read those magazines. As a result, people end up going to stores like IKEA. We think that *Downloadable Design* will make it possible for us to bring our products within reach for people who would not otherwise be able to afford them. All these end users would have to do is assemble the product themselves.

> TAKE JURGEN BEY'S DESIGN FOR OUR STORE. EVEN THOUGH IT'S BASED ON LASER CUTTING, IT IS CONSTRUCTED FROM SO MANY PARTS AND ITS ASSEMBLY INVOLVES SO MUCH MANUAL LABOUR THAT IT IS NOT POSSIBLE AT THIS STAGE TO OFFER IT AS A DOWNLOADABLE DESIGN.

This leads me to another aspect: do it yourself, or DIY. DIY There are countless DIY shows on TV; DIY is everywhere. So we thought: what if we not only made design products cheaper, but also introduced more variety. How many times have you found almost the perfect table, but it's only 80 cm wide and you need a table that's 90 cm or 120 cm wide to fit in your living room? In so many cases, your house is too small or too big for the standard sizes. What if you could adapt all these measurements to suit your space? That would be hugely practical, much more functional. Or you could choose your own colour, to make it your own thing. Downloadable design is also a form of co-creation. CO-CREATION

Challenging the creativity of designers is yet another reason, and a very important one. Designers have to adapt their design process to the platform. They have to figure out which parameters of the product can vary, while still earning a profit. What we did here was not just to ask the designers to design a product and have the consumer choose a colour or a pattern; that's already been done. We asked them to be creative and think of completely different ways for consumers to interact with the design. We also challenged designers to consider how they would make money on their design. We asked them to be creative in what they would offer for free and what they could be offering for an added fee. What if there could be layers in a design? For example, a product could be more expensive if it bears the designer's signature. The business model requires creativity, too, and it is the most challenging part. As I said, we were inspired by laser cutting and digital technology, but our focus is not limited to digital technology; we also want to revitalize craftsmanship.

We plan to set up a whole network of small studios for highly skilled crafts; as I've discovered, it is not easy for small-scale workshops to survive. This network of craftspeople is as important to us as the 3D printers and laser cutters. The emphasis on craftsmanship is crucial, particularly since Ponoko and Shapeways are already offering 3D printing and laser-cut products. AESTHETICS: 2D I think that including crafts gives us a distinctive edge. It also facilitates cross-pollination by introducing digital technology into crafts workshops and vice versa. Finally, using local materials is also important to us; local sourcing is a high priority.

Let me zoom in on making money. Designers have to come up with new business models. Do you have ideas or examples from your experience with the _Downloadable Design_ platform?

At this stage, the designers are not there yet; they are just getting started. One designer came up with an interesting suggestion: as you download a product, say a chair, you receive more and more pixels. If people could stop a download half-way, they could get the design for free, but it would be incomplete or low-resolution. If they decide to download the whole product, they would have to pay for the privilege.

Another idea was to offer an interior design service, so customers could have their interiors custom-made to suit their individual needs, based on variable designs that would be available on the platform. They would pay for the customization rather than for the products. Rather than buying a ready-made cupboard, they

would pay to have the basic design adapted to their individual requirements. MASS CUSTOMIZATION

IN SO MANY CASES, YOUR HOUSE IS TOO SMALL OR TOO BIG FOR THE STANDARD SIZES. WHAT IF YOU COULD ADAPT ALL THESE MEASUREMENTS TO SUIT YOUR SPACE?

I asked the designers to think of different stages, different levels or different services; to think of a way to create a need for their services. While this is the most obvious idea, it's not easy for a designer to conceive a product that generates demand for a service. It's easy to do that with something like a phone, which comes with software, but it becomes a real challenge when you're working with purely physical products. But there is another difficulty: customers have to get used to customization. Take the example of _Blueprint_, a physical blueprint of a home — or rather parts of a home — in blue Styrofoam which Jurgen Bey designed the Droog shop in New York. The idea was that people would buy the products but could specify the materials to their own liking. There's a display model of a complete fireplace in blue foam, with a chimney and everything. If somebody wants to have this fireplace in their home, they could have it that shape done in tiles or bricks. But people don't dare to buy it like that; they first want to see it for real, as a tangible object. They want to know what material it is made of, what it looks like, how it feels. We've learned that a project like that could only work if you produced an actual, physical specimen and offered that for sale.

Similarly, people don't want to make all their clothes by hand themselves; they want to try the garments on in the shop to see how they'll look. We've also discussed whether we would want to offer a separate category of designs: to expand what we offer, not only for download but also for sale. But what would be the point of a platform for downloadable design if you also

131

have a web shop? Not having a standard web shop is one of the important reasons why I'm working on this project, so we're not going to have one. However, the fact that this topic keeps cropping up is certainly a sign of things to come.

What do you feel it signifies? Is it just laziness on the part of the consumer?

No, it's a lack of confidence. Changing the colour of your sneakers at Nike ID is less of an issue.

I've done it once; it was quite fun.

But now try doing that for a whole cupboard or bookcase, a design that would become a physical object. Imagine that you could change all the parameters. Not just an option for customization, but a required part of the process. You would have to specify each and every aspect. So the question is, wouldn't people rather go to a shop and simply buy a cupboard?

It may have to do with lack of confidence. Also, not everyone is an expert in interior design. That's also why standard furniture exists. Not everyone starts out with an empty floor plan. All those consultants and home decoration centres are there to help people define their interior design preferences. This is a separate issue from the presumed lack of confidence; you could call it 'assisted design literacy': how to design your own world.

We would be willing to help people. All these design magazines offer plenty of advice on home decoration, and there does seem to be a demand for it. But then we need to consider the extent to which design can be open. I remember modular furniture in the 60s. People wanted to see examples, too, back in those days; they wanted to see a visual impression of the best way to combine those modules. These are investments that people make. Downloading something that's purely digital doesn't cost much.

And if you don't like it, it's not a big deal.

But with downloadable design, `DOWNLOADABLE DESIGN` people really need to take the next step. It means that they would have to go to a workshop to have the product made, or they would need to make it themselves. You say that it sounds like fun, but I doubt it would be fun for the majority of people out there; they wouldn't want to take the time. That even holds

true for me; I wouldn't want to do it either. I've got other things to do.

This trend, this movement, this development: how does it change the design profession?

Designers have always wanted to work for the general public. in the 1920s and '30s, it was products for the masses that they wanted to design. Designers gave directions for how to make things that were good for the masses, and the belief was that the masses needed to be educated. Then, in the 1960s, there was an emancipation of the masses. The re-industrialization led to incredible market segmentation, so the masses had more choices and could buy more. As a result, designers started to follow the preferences of the masses. When the market is saturated, it becomes segmented; it's a logical progression.

> IF YOU DOWNLOAD MUSIC, YOU CAN START LISTENING TO IT IMMEDIATELY. DESIGN IS DIFFERENT; YOU STILL NEED TO GO SOMEWHERE TO HAVE IT MADE, OR YOU HAVE TO MAKE IT YOURSELF.

After that, a counter-movement emerged, as evidenced by Memphis and Alchimia, who got their inspiration from the choices of the masses and used it to design highly exclusive products. The inspiration from the masses has always been there, always. However, design is always a top-down process. In the 1990s, some designers started to turn away from an overly designed environment; they reached a saturation point. They were interested in the fluidity of form. These designers would initiate a process, then stop the transformation at an interesting point and produce the result. It was presented as a free-form exercise, but it was very much directed by the designers.

132

New opportunities are emerging from the Internet and from digital fabrication, which means that the masses can start to participate in design.

That seems like a logical next step, at least from your perspective. But when I look at the products showcased on sites like Ponoko and Shapeways, I am concerned that the result will be a huge volume of unattractive and clunky design. This trend will not end well. `AESTHETICS: 2D`

You say this as an expert in design?

I say it as a human being. I am worried that this trend will spread like a virus. In my opinion, the internet has brought us a lot of ugly stuff. There have been a lot of beautiful things, too, but a lot of ugly ones. Leaving people to their own devices... I don't oppose it on principle, but it's not my thing.

The design world draws inspiration from these developments, but these trends are not all that's going on. Looking at what's going on in the design world, the designers we work with and the projects we work on, I see two things happening. On the one hand, there is the open source story, which is about trying to find possibilities for participation; that goal is in line with the principles we espouse.

The other side is a devotion to local sourcing, a type of anti-globalism. `MANIFESTOS` Many designers are concerned about the transparency of production processes and would like to see more use of local materials and local sources. That is part of our platform, too, since we want to encourage working with local sources and local workshops. Another important issue at the moment is sustainability, the concept of relying on renewable resources.

Designers are becoming entrepreneurs. By telling them to create their own way to make money, we relate to their sense of entrepreneurship. However, the concept of finding their own innovative ways to earn a profit has not yet been developed. This is a real challenge; they really have to make that mental shift towards entrepreneurial design.

On the one hand, there are designers like Tord Boontje, `DESIGNERS` who distributed the design of his chair as a file as early as the 1990s. These digital designs were the start of a growing trend, but the content was static. There wasn't much you could do with it, other than possibly choosing a different upholstery fabric; the idea was simply to distribute it as-is. It was essentially a predecessor of open design. As a designer today, I can imagine that I would have to get used to deciding what to give away for free and what to keep. I would define the parameters, but to what extent would I really have to relinquish control of my design? It is an interesting dynamic, and designers do need to maintain a creative focus on it.

Another issue that I've noticed is that designers do not really believe that consumers would download their designs. If you download music, then you have it and you can start listening to it immediately. Design is different; you still need to go somewhere to have it made, or you have to make it yourself. That's more onerous.

PEOPLE ARE TOO SCARED TO ADD THEIR OWN CONTRIBUTION TO A LAMP THEY BOUGHT FOR ABOUT 100 EUROS.

133

The *Downloadable Design* platform is a learning process for us, too. We started it as an exploration of a concept, and we want to investigate it thoroughly. It is important for us that the platform is curated, that we have a certain amount of control over what is put on the platform. We are playing around with ideas for allowing people to upload things, but I'm still undecided about whether or not I want to do it. In any case, I would want uploads to be related to the designs being posted by our designers. Maybe people could upload how they made the products they downloaded, so it would remain within the parameters defined by the designer.

Open design as a new way of designing. What does that mean to you?

At Droog, we've been doing open design all along, right from the start. Our work has always been connected to projects or events. `EVENTS` We've always been interested in the interaction with consumers.

Consistently, one of the key elements in our work has been that consumers could personalize a design, that our designs had an element of fun, pleasure or interactive co-creation. CO-CREATION

A very good example is *do create*, a concept that we realized in collaboration with the KesselsKramer PR agency in 2000.[1] One of the projects was *do scratch* by Martí Guixé, a lamp that's covered in black paint. People were supposed to scrape patterns in the paint to create their own drawing. This lamp has been sitting around in the shop for seven, eight years, and nobody has ever bought one. People are too scared to add their own contribution to a lamp they bought for about 100 euros. Even when we added sample drawings that people could copy onto the lamp themselves, nobody would buy it. We only started selling the lamp when we had artists do the drawings. After that experience, we decided not to continue this product. This type of interactive design did not seem to work.

Then, in 2008, we did *Urban Play* in Amsterdam, which also involved a contribution by Martí Guixé.[2] It was a large cube built from blocks of autoclaved aerated concrete or AAC, a low-density, non-toxic material that can be carved very easily. The idea of this *Sculpture Me Point* was that everybody could add their own sculpture. Everybody chopped away from day one, but after six weeks the result was deplorable. So we ended up with two questions. A, are people willing to do something? And B, what happens when people actually do it; is the result interesting?

Did you do further research on co-creation involving interaction with users? What did it reveal?

One of the projects that started from the Droog Lab is a digital platform for co-creation invented by Jurgen Bey and Saskia van Drimmelen. That comes fairly close. It is about co-creation, CO-CREATION but it provides a platform for designers to work with other designers. Jurgen and Saskia moderate participation; only people they find interesting can get involved. It is extremely curated; they decide who gets in, who stays out, and who will be making something together, but they also allow room for people's individual development. We are also working on a different platform which is about 'upcycling' dead stock from producers. The aim here is to make dead stock accessible for designers. It's got nothing to

do with using digital technology; it is about all the material that would otherwise simply be thrown away. In point of fact, most of these discarded products get recycled. RECYCLING But the point here is that all those designs vanish into thin air. Thousands of shavers just disappear. A designer designed them; a certain amount of development went into them. Costs were incurred, and a lot of energy was spent. That's another development we're pursuing: we try to direct design towards re-designing what already exists.

CHINA, FOR INSTANCE, MIGHT BE COMING TO THE END OF ITS TENURE AS A CHEAP MANUFACTURER PRETTY SOON. THAT'S ONE OF THE REASONS WHY WE STARTED DOWNLOADABLE DESIGN: TO INVENT NEW SYSTEMS.

Again, this is about the creativity of designers. In some sense, it could be considered co-creation, since a designer is building on something created by another designer. The challenge here is whether it is allowed. Somebody designed it, but now it's dead stock that the company would rather throw away than have us picking it up and putting designers to work on it. There are very loose links to co-creation, to bottom-up design. More importantly, however, these are all developments that are part of what is happening now. So much more is going on now; the bottom-up part is only a small proportion of it.

You talked earlier about services, mentioning the example of interior design. The interesting thing is that you link the designer to the consumer directly, rather than through a middleman or organization.

That truly is a development that is happening right now. Take the fashion collective Painted, for example; they would love to make products for the user. The designers would prefer to make clothes for real

134

people, not averaged-out stuff in shops; they would much rather make things one-on-one, in direct contact with the user. And I think that this really what's going on in design at this very moment.

Distribution and the middle links in the production process are issues that IKEA has started addressing. We have first-hand experience with how much energy, money and time it costs. Everyone is trying to invent something to mitigate this problem, be it *Downloadable Design* or a designer who works directly for the customer. That's where everybody is looking for solutions at the moment. It has to do with the current system; the whole production chain is starting to fall apart. There are environmental questions, economic questions, questions about production in developing countries. Not long ago, everybody was starting to have their stuff made in developing countries, but people in those countries are starting to earn more. China, for instance, might be coming to the end of its tenure as a cheap manufacturer pretty soon. That's one of the reasons why we started *Downloadable Design*: to invent new systems.

Our other answer is a resolution of the dead stock issue. If we develop a system in which products are not thrown away, but instead are 'upcycled' and brought back into circulation, then we would not need to use so much new raw material; we could use what we already have. There are a few things that need to happen before people start adopting the concept, but we are interested in exploring systems to see how we could create new incentives for creativity, but also how we could start to fix the ecological and economic problems.

In the Droog Lab we are addressing yet another issue: the problem of globalization. TREND: GLOBALIZATION You see the same stuff everywhere; you get the same retail chains everywhere; you get shopping malls everywhere. High-rise buildings are springing up all over the place; food travels all over the planet with no consideration of what's in season. These examples are part of an incredible and very special aspect of globalization that makes people forget where things come from. People start to take everything for granted and lose touch with what is part of their own culture. That's why we set up this lab, as a system to develop creativity based on local conditions, based on how

people live and work. We want to develop creative ideas that come from talking to normal people – a taxi driver, a hair dresser – not graduates from an arts academy. GRASSROOTS INVENTION This approach allows us to get to the heart of the matter, achieving a comprehensive understanding of how creative ideas are viewed by the end users. The aim is for designers come back with so much inspiration that they are able to develop new ideas in a global context.

WE WANT TO DEVELOP CREATIVE IDEAS THAT COME FROM TALKING TO NORMAL PEOPLE – A TAXI DRIVER, A HAIRDRESSER – NOT GRADUATES FROM AN ARTS ACADEMY.

Led by Jurgen and Saskia, the Droog al Arab team came back from the Droog Lab project in Dubai with the idea for a platform for co-creation. CO-CREATION After seeing all these shopping malls, they have seen how the current system of mass production is a one-way street that leaves consumers in the dark about how things are produced. On their platform, they want to show how things are designed, especially how they are designed collaboratively, and they want to establish contact with customers and producers on that single platform. MASS CUSTOMIZATION

In another project being done in the suburbs of New York, the team led by Diller, Scofiodio + Renfro wants to bring new life to these emptying satellite towns by turning residents into entrepreneurs. An amateur chef might start a sideline as a restaurant owner, or a person might open an informal library because they have a lot of books. Our designers are not at all interested in downloadables and the like, but they are investigating what happens at that level and developing ways to react to it creatively. At that point, they step back let the residents do their own thing. It's such a fun project. Imagine going to visit a suburb, and discovering that one house has become a restaurant, another one a library, and another one a café. Imagine that somebody opened a cinema simply because they had a projector. All the fun things are available again, and people don't have to leave the neighbourhood to find them. It creates a renewed sense of community.

IMAGINE THAT SOMEBODY OPENED A CINEMA SIMPLY BECAUSE THEY HAD A PROJECTOR.

On the one hand, I am fascinated to see what those people are actually going to do. On the other hand, I am interested in how we are blurring the boundaries between public and private; essentially, we are asking people to fulfil a public role in their private home. Accepting that involvement could even have an influence on the architecture of these people's homes. What will houses look like if suburbs develop in that direction? If everybody, or at least a significant part of the population, becomes entrepreneurs, then their homes will look differently. Their private residence will include a public section.

136

That's exactly why I do these things. I always return to the challenge of inventing a system, a method of generating innovation, regardless of how it happens. *Downloadable Design*, innovating the designer, upcycling dead stock, working within the local context, whatever. For me, these are all parts of the same story, facets of one whole entity. Maybe, two months from now, I will have dreamed up something else, have had yet another idea.

Those are a few of the projects we are running at the moment. All these initiatives are born from the same motivation: a sense of curiosity about the user, and a drive to bring innovation to design in a different way, by developing fresh methods while never forgetting that design is also fun.

NOTES

1   www.droog.com/presentationsevents/do-create

2   www.droog.com/presentationsevents/detail

GOVERNED ADVERTISEMENT

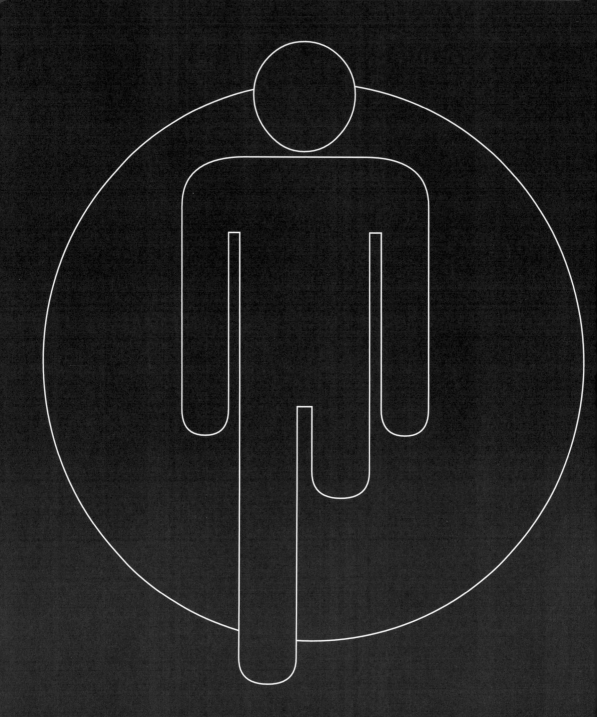

CO-CREATE YOUR HEALTH INSURANCE POLICY.

CREATION & CO: USER PARTICIPATION IN DESIGN

PIETER JAN STAPPERS & CO*

*FROUKJE SLEESWIJK VISSER & SANDRA KISTEMAKER

The roles of the designer, the client (or producer, or manufacturer) and the user are being shaken up in industrial practices that have, until now, been oriented mainly towards mass production. Stappers and his colleagues illustrate the contemporary occurrence of co-creation and co-design and describe the hybridization of the designer's role.

Pieter Jan Stappers is a full professor and chair of Design Techniques, and the director of the ID-StudioLab at the Faculty of Industrial Design Engineering at Delft University of Technology, The Netherlands. Froukje Sleeswijk Visser is an assistant professor at ID-StudioLab and the owner of design consultancy firm ContextQueen, Rotterdam. Sanne Kistemaker is a designer at the Muzus design group in The Hague. Together, they have developed the contextmapping method. Pieter Jan's perspective is positive; he believes that "open design promises to bridge the gap between designers and end-users, and where possible to reduce the industrial detour of centralized fabrication, distribution, sales and marketing."

http://studiolab.io.tudelft.nl

Open design has numerous aims; some of the most important ambitions include breaking down the barriers between designers and end-users, making it possible for non-designers become designers, AMATEURISSIMO and cutting out the middle-man by having end users fabricate the products they need. Inspiring examples have been presented in the domain of craftsmanship. New, craft-based industries are visibly taking off, either locally oriented or operating globally over the internet. However, the feasibility of open design for more complex products, such as washing machines, cars and jet planes.

The Creative Guy

As yet, it is unclear where the limitations of a user-centred approach to user involvement lie. Despite these complicating factors, the roles of designer, client, user and end user are being shaken up in these more complex areas of design and product development.[1] Traditional caricatures of the designer as 'the creative guy' and the user as a recipient, a 'passive, un-critical consumer' have been questioned and surpassed in a growing variety of ways.

One example mentioned frequently is the 'lead user approach',[2] in which select subgroups of dedicated, tech-savvy users contribute to the process of generating solutions, and develop new features for products. This presents a clear challenge to the traditional division of roles in the design process, but it only serves the needs of specific subgroups in the user populations. Other approaches, such as generative techniques and contextmapping[3], try to involve end users as experts in their own experience by taking them through a carefully orchestrated and supported process of fostering awareness, reflection and expression, in order to help them become competent partners within the design team. In commercial practice, the use of focus groups critiquing proposed new product designs, usability

THE OLD VIEW: (STRICTLY) SEPARATED ROLES

142

The traditional view of design identifies three roles: the user, who buys and will live with the product, the designer, who conceives the product, and the client, who manufactures and distributes the product.

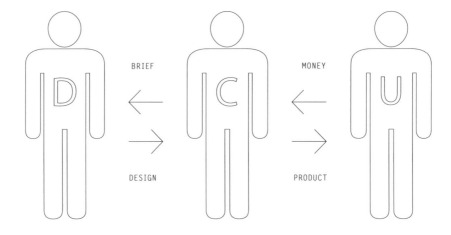

BRIEF

MONEY

DESIGN

PRODUCT

tests, or marketing consultations can also involve users in more active ways than have been practised so far. It is important to define the distinction between co-creation CO-CREATION and co-design; co-creation indicates a collaborative creative effort, either large or small, and often localized, while co-design refers to co-creation used in the course of the design process, preferably from beginning to end. In this article, we focus on contextmapping, a specific aspect of co-design, in which end users are assigned the role of expert informant, and are supported in that role through access to dedicated tools for observation, reflection and expression. The production of these tools and facilitation of the process have become design research activities which are carried out by professionals with a background in design and/or research.

The Traditional View in Transformation

The *traditional view* of design identifies three roles: the user, who buys and will live with the product, the *designer*, who conceives the product, and the *client*, who manufactures and distributes the product. Popular visual representations of these roles, as well as training materials used in several types of design education, show the connection as a chain of single, narrow links. In this view, the client takes the initiative. For instance, the client conducts market research, spots an opportunity in the market, gives a brief to the designer which specifies design requirements, and expects to receive a concept design in return. A number of trends are chipping away at this linear, unintegrated model from all sides. In co-creation, roles and responsibilities which had previously been thought of as separate are interacting, merging, or even being swapped back and forth between the parties; some roles are disappearing in the form in which we knew them, and new roles are appearing.

THE NEW VIEW

In the new view of co-creation, these roles and responsibilities are interacting, merging, or even being swapped back and forth between the parties; some roles are disappearing in the form in which we knew them, and new roles are appearing.

143

INFORMANT
USER
EXPERT
TESTER
CO-DESIGNER
CO-USER
EXPERT
CO-USER
RESEARCHER
CO-DESIGNER
PRODUCER
FACILITATOR
PROCESS MANAGER
ENTREPRENEUR
META-DESIGNER

There are several reasons for this shift. First, as our lives get more complex, people are more informed, and they need to be more informed.

Users are getting savvier

The internet has made it possible for users to be more informed, giving them opportunities to be involved and have a say in what is made for them.

`TREND: NETWORK SOCIETY`

Designers are getting savvier too

As the design process incorporates more and more areas of expertise from different parties, managing this process increasingly calls for research skills and a talent for facilitation. In some places, including our own school, design education is starting to include those vital skills in the curriculum; elsewhere, people with backgrounds in organizational management or social sciences are specializing in addressing those roles.

THE DESIGNER-CLIENT RELATIONSHIP IS NO LONGER AS SIMPLE AS A BRIEF STATING A CLEARLY DEFINED PROBLEM.

Design clients are diversifying

Some areas of human endeavour are adopting design perspectives. As a result, principles and practices of design are being used to address increasingly complex problems. Projects such as the design of hospitals, services, or policies generally involve multiple stakeholders and areas of expertise. As the structure of design processes shifts, design techniques are being recognized as supporting these very different people by facilitating shared, solution-oriented thinking. Referred to collectively as 'service design' or 'design thinking', such larger-scope problems are being claimed for the design profession (or at least the design procedures).

Partly as a result of these developments, the relationships between the parties are changing.

→ The designer–client relationship is no longer as simple as a brief stating a clearly defined problem and the concept design proposing a single solution. In the *Dashboard User Guide*, Stevens & Watson distinguish five degrees of how the client is served by the designer, ranging from prescribing (one concept to deliver on the brief), through menu (several concepts to choose from), co-creation `DIY` (collaboration as equals), and assistance (the client receiving design coaching and help), to DIY (the client does the design while the designer observes and interjects comments as needed).[4]

→ The client–user relationship is opening up in open design and meta-design. In open design, manufacturing options are becoming widespread and widely accessible, and resources for sharing design ideas are available (open movement). In meta-design,[5] products are made with sufficient adaptability to leave a number of final design choices to the user.

→ The designer–user relationship is opening up strongly throughout the entire design process. In several industries, competition on technology and price has saturated the market, and clients are taking a closer look at the user experiences and contexts of use in order to improve their products. Elsewhere[6] we called this the "contextual push", a force in product development that complements the classic forces of 'technology push' and 'market pull'. Users are being involved increasingly early in the design process, not just in the post-conceptualization phases (e.g. usability testing and concept testing), but also in the fuzzy front end of strategic planning, information gathering, and conceptualizing. The challenge here is not only the timing of when different players are involved, but also the responsibilities and powers granted to them. Frequently, users can participate in informing design, providing ideas for solutions, or evaluating proposed concepts; however, at this stage, they are rarely involved in deciding what will be made (as would be the case in fully fledged participatory design).

IN SMALL AND MEDIUM ENTERPRISES, THE SEPARATION HAS ALWAYS BEEN LESS CLEARLY DEFINED: INDIVIDUALS OFTEN TAKE ON SEVERAL ROLES IN THE PROCESS, WITH THE BENEFIT THAT SEVERAL VIEWPOINTS ARE MORE SMOOTHLY INTEGRATED THAN IN LARGER CORPORATIONS.

The list above shows how some of these developments are unfolding. The traditional view, with its clear separation of roles, seems too restricted to address the current complexities, but its influence has not yet been lifted from design-speak, from thinking, or from practice. In our experience, the separations between these roles are more entrenched in the larger industries, where roles are often separated over many specialized individuals or departments. In small and medium enterprises, the separation has always been less clearly defined: single individuals often take on several roles in the design process, with the benefit that several viewpoints are more smoothly integrated than in larger corporations.

Co-creation with Users in Industrial Practice

User involvement is progressively moving toward the front end of designing. The people controlling the design process are seeing that the user can be a source of valuable input, not just a channel for directing output.

To generalize somewhat, it would seem that the complaints department in many companies was the place that received most input from the users, in the form of returned products. In many cases, the product was returned not because of a product defect, but because the user could not figure out how to operate it, or discovered after purchase that the product completely failed to fulfil his expectations. In the 80s and 90s, consultations with users moved up

earlier and earlier, first advancing through sales and marketing, then usability testing, and finally concept evaluation. What happened in these three phases is that users were called in after the concept had been developed to test the products in practice, hopefully revealing any mistakes. This helped companies launch better products by eliminating problems earlier in the design process.

In the 90s and 00s, user involvement was solicited from the other end of the process, bringing in users in increasingly active ways for contextual informing, idea generation, and concept development. KNOWLEDGE Although the participatory design movement had shown that intensive collaboration with users can be effective throughout the process, progress in the industry in this half of the cycle has been slower and often limited to incidental involvement (short, local contributions).

Contextmapping: Informing Design

Contextmapping methods help users to observe and reflect on parts of their lives, and to use these reflections in making a 'map' that reflects the various facets of their experiences. This map provides the design team with information, inspiration and empathy, feeding further development of the concept design into a product.[7] The approach is built on four main principles:

→ Users are involved as the experts on their own experience.

→ The user's expertise can be coaxed into expression by applying appropriate techniques, which typically involve self-observation and reflection.

→ The information gathered on the context of use should be like a map: it should provide multifaceted, rich and supportive leads for the design team to explore the experiential context. This requires both empathy with the users (a concrete, holistic, feel for the context) and an understanding of the context (an abstract overview of what could be generalized to other users, other situations and future developments).
→ Facilitating this process requires a mixture of design competencies and research skills.

145

In a series of some 100 design research projects, ranging from individual student graduation projects to larger collaborations CO-CREATION in consortiums of academic researchers and industrial partners, these methods were developed to fit both user needs and industrial practice. In some cases, user participation has gone beyond informing the process, moving into the realm of idea and concept generation and development.

The client involved in this project offers a large range of hearing protectors for private users, for use in a range of situations: swimming, working, flying, making and listening to music, sleeping or riding a motorcycle. The focus of this project was to gain insight into the life, experience and context of amateur musicians.

DESPITE OUR HOPES AND AMBITIOUS RHETORIC, DESIGN IS OFTEN NOT AT THE FOREFRONT OF COMPANIES' ATTENTION.

146

The company did not have its own design department; most of the innovations were developed internally with people from the existing team, who came from different backgrounds. The CEO and other people responsible for innovations were highly involved and were part of the research and design team during the entire project. The initial study and the idea generation brainstorming sessions were conducted and facilitated by design agency Muzus, resulting in a concept that was further developed by a second, technical, design agency, and handed back to the company (so we already see several separate design agencies at work).

Process and Techniques
The techniques support designers, helping them to develop empathy for this user group, learn about their lives, understand their context and be able to step into their shoes. COMMUNITY The client already had longer-standing relations with users, but felt that the existing relationship had not led to new ideas for a

while. In the contextmapping study, seven musicians who played in amateur bands formed a fresh band and played their instruments in a three-hour session. The participants prepared themselves with a sensitizing package during the week before the test session. By taking part in creative assignments, explaining the artefacts and discussing the different topics, the user group of musicians painted a rich and detailed picture for the research team. Employees from the client company observed the session, took notes from their perspective and subsequently engaged in a discussion with the musicians. An immediate result of the session was the reassessment of several stereotypes; the design team went home with plenty of ideas to for further innovation.

Insights, Ideas and Concepts
Three substantial new insights emerged from the session and subsequent analysis. First, hearing protection is currently geared toward individual usage, but it has an adverse effect in a band: if one band member is using hearing protection, volume will be increased and all other members will suffer. Second, many musicians are ignorant of the risk of hearing damage, and are completely unaware of the decibel threshold for damage. This lack of awareness was new to the client. Third, this group is different from all user groups that this company serves. In contrast to, for instance, construction workers operating heavy machinery, these musicians actually *want* to hear the sound, even while they are protected from the full impact of it: they love their music and want to be able to experience it to the fullest.

Based upon these user insights, the client conferred with users and the research and design team to generate new ideas for innovative hearing protection that is appropriate to the context, experience and needs of amateur musicians. The resulting concepts covered several different levels: helping musicians become aware of the danger of high volumes; developing new ways of communicating with musicians in their familiar context and fitting their tone of voice; redesigning marketing for this specific user group; developing concepts for new innovative products.

Although this company had already had contact with their users over a longer period, they found that that they had often asked the same people for feedback over and over, only requesting confirmation of their own ideas and asking users to reflect on existing ideas. The experience of opening up, adding a fresh perspective and stepping into the shoes of a specific user group led to new directions for innovation at different levels.

Where Is This Going?

The traditional view is splitting at the seams. In many industries, the traditional separation of roles is recognized as no longer inevitable, effective or desired. However, the evolution to new forms of designing has by no means produced a stable and unified view of how the roles are distributed now. Moreover, these processes are not easy to implement. Despite our hopes and ambitious rhetoric, design is often not at the forefront of companies' attention due to such factors as budget constraints, insufficient awareness of what a design approach can contribute and should cost, and a lack of innovative user-driven attitudes. The same holds true for the newer trends of doing research within design, especially user research; the concept of opening up design processes to end-user participation HACKING DESIGN is often not even considered.

In our experiences with large and small industries, we see a variety of formats being used, combining ingredients in different constellations and using different degrees of separation or specialization, depending on the object of design. Moreover, we see a greater need to orchestrate these processes in the large design projects currently gaining attention under the label of 'service design'; some design professionals are shifting into this new role.

IN MANY INDUSTRIES, THE SEPARATION OF ROLES IS NO LONGER RECOGNIZED AS INEVITABLE, EFFECTIVE OR DESIRED.

Clients (or providers, from a user's perspective) need to become aware of what is possible, and consider how they can become more flexible to accommodate the new design paradigms. The paradox here is that this may be more difficult for the larger industries, which already include user participation in their research budgets, than it is for smaller companies, who have much smaller budgets, but often build a stronger relationship with their users. In large companies, different phases of the design process are often split up, connected only through formal documents that are too limited to convey the full richness of user contexts. These overly structured transitions cause valuable insights to be lost because they are not handed over effectively to the new team. On the other hand, smaller companies, who have a longer-standing relationship with users, are often not aware that their users' expertise can be brought to bear more effectively with the aid of appropriate methods. STANDARDS

THE ROLE OF DESIGNERS IS BECOMING MORE VARIED: PART CREATOR, PART RESEARCHER, PART FACILITATOR, PART PROCESS MANAGER.

147

The role of designers is becoming more varied: part creator, part researcher, part facilitator, part process manager. We see graduates of design schools specializing in these roles to varying extents. Users' roles are also changing. A side effect of co-creation CO-CREATION which we have often observed is that the participating users do not lose their awareness of their own expertise once it has been identified; indeed, they are eager to develop it further. In our own experience, we find that participants are eager to return months after their initial participation, having continued to develop the expertise that was awakened in the study.[8] Gawande recounts a series of similar participatory studies in the area of hospital hygiene, where various participating users discussed and suggested solutions.[9] One effect was that after the sessions, these users would take initiatives to change their work environment in ways that they had never done before in their traditional roles as nurses, cleaners, or doctors. Awakened expertise can lead to confidence, inspiring users to take increased responsibility and initiative. It is likely that this effect can be found in all areas of co-design and co-creation OPEN EVERYTHING in particular, and open design in general: the act of taking part in the creative process, and becoming aware of the expert within, gives people the confidence to take initiative.

NOTES

1 How these roles are labelled is a major headache in itself when reading or talking about design, and the various varieties reflect values in the field. For *user* one can read *customer, consumer* or *beneficiary*; for *designer*, read *design team, developer*; for *client*, read *provider* (from the user's perspective), *client*; for *product*, also read *service, system, experience*. The different labels are real and important, but dealing with the nuances in this Babylonian word game would go beyond the scope of this text.

2 Von Hippel, E, *Democratizing Innovation*. MIT Press, 2005.

3 Sanders, E & Stappers, P, 'Co-creation and the new landscapes of Design', *Codesign*, 4(1), 2008, p. 5-18.

4 Stevens, M & Watson, M, *Dashboard User Guide*. Institute without boundaries, Toronto, Canada, 2008. Available online at www.thedesigndashboard.com/contents/dashboard_userguide.pdf, accessed on 13 October 2010.

5 Fischer, G, Giaccardi, E, Eden, H, Sugimoto, M and Ye, Y, 'Beyond binary choices: Integrating individual and social creativity', *International Journal of Human Computer Studies*, 63:4-5, 2005, p. 482-512.

6 Sanders & Stappers, op.cit.

7 Sleeswijk Visser, F, Stappers, P, Van der Lugt, R, & Sanders, E, 'Contextmapping: Experiences from practice', *Codesign*, 1(2), 2005, p.119-149. Stappers, P, & Sleeswijk Visser, F, 'Contextmapping'. *GeoConnexion International*, July/August 2006, p. 22-24. Stappers, P, van Rijn, H, Kistemaker, S, Hennink, A, Sleeswijk Visser, F, 'Designing for other people's strengths and motivations: Three cases using context, visions, and experiential prototypes', *Advanced Engineering Informatics*, A Special Issue on Human-Centered Product Design and Development. Vol. 23, 2009, p. 174-183.

8 Sleeswijk Visser, F, Visser, V, 'Re-using users: Co-create and co-evaluate', *Personal and Ubiquitous Computing*, 10(2-3), 2005, p. 148-152.

9 Gawande, A, Better: *A surgeon's notes on performance*. Picador, 2007.

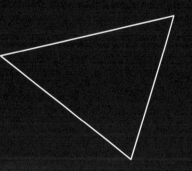

Rrod

Create & Publish Your Designs. Now!

DESIGN LITERACY: ORGANIZING SELF- ORGANIZATION

DICK RIJKEN

The position of knowledge and expertise is changing radically, particularly in relation to how design literacy is affected when confronted with digital tools and media. Dick Rijken analyses design literacy on three levels – strategic, tactical, and operational – and examines the requirements of open design for developing a design vision, design choices and design skills.

Dick Rijken is a professor of information technology and society at The Hague University of Applied Sciences and the director of STEIM, a design studio for artistic research on and development of instruments and tools for use in electronic music live performances, located in Amsterdam, The Netherlands. Dick defines open design as "the process of sharing design documents (drawings, models, specifications, flowcharts, manufacturing instructions, etc.) so that others can use and/or modify these designs and republish modified versions of them in such a way that the designs are publicly accessible, free of charge, and come with legal (copyright) clauses that enable all these kinds of use and re-use."

http://nl.linkedin.com/in/dickrijken

Life in this network society TREND: NETWORK SOCIETY is complex. We are involved in many different kinds of fluid relationships with friends, family, acquaintances, co-workers, project partners, companies, brands, websites, platforms, clubs, schools, and many other kinds of communities. More often than not, we maintain these relationships using digital media like Facebook, YouTube, Flickr, and plain old email. We connect, communicate and share like our lives depend on it - as, increasingly, they in fact do. SHARING

In his article, Paul Atkinson talks about the demise of the *grand narrative of modernist design*. While this is very true, it is not solely applicable to design; it applies similarly to all grand narratives, and to modernism in general. Where we were once infatuated by concepts like universal truth and linear progress, we now find ourselves in a chaotic maze of anecdotes and interconnected ideas. Linear progress has become perpetual change with no shared direction. Within that change, we are on a perpetual quest for personal meaning, no longer seeking truth. All this is not necessarily a bad thing, but it does make life difficult and unpredictable. If we can learn to improvise and to adapt, life can be deeply meaningful and rewarding. We are not there yet, though; there is still a lot to learn.

154

WE CONNECT, COMMUNICATE AND SHARE LIKE OUR LIVES DEPEND ON IT. AS, INCREASINGLY, THEY IN FACT DO.

This article deals with the changing position of knowledge KNOWLEDGE and expertise in open networks. Digital tools and media are generic infrastructures for creating, sharing and transforming information. They enable and facilitate personal learning on a massive scale. Anything that can be converted into a digital format can also be stored, shared and used by anyone, anywhere. This changes everything that has anything to do with ideas – and therefore also changes design. It changes how we design, it changes what we

design, it changes how we think about design, and it changes how we learn and teach design. Ultimately, it will also change who designs. Web 2.0, with the concept of user-generated content at its core, will not leave the design discipline untouched.

Fundamental Paradoxes

In order to understand what is happening to design, we need to understand two strongly related paradoxes that are fundamental features of networks: the paradox of identity, and the paradox of choice.

The paradox of identity arises from the fact that networks are made of nodes and links, i.e. identities and relationships. Nodes have their own unique identity, but that identity is meaningless without links to other nodes. We have become more independent from others through the development and actualization of our own unique individual self. But at the same time, we have become more dependent on others, since who we are depends to a large extent on who we relate to and interact with. We feel a need to stand out in a crowd, but we are nothing if not connected. TREND: NETWORK SOCIETY

We depend on fluid networks around us for our daily lives' activities. Parties are announced on and communicated through Facebook, and the fun is later shared SHARING through pictures on Flickr. We find jobs using LinkedIn, where we present our professional résumés, and ask people we've worked with in the past to write positive testimonials about us. We don't exist if we have no visible presence in the networks we want to be involved in. If you are what you act like, you better make sure you act like who you are – or who you want to be.

This makes the network society an essentially cultural place. This is true not just in the anthropological sense that everything we learn is seen as 'culture', but in a very instrumental sense as well: activities like 'expression' and 'reflection' that are at the core of art and related cultural activities give form to the networked life of an individual. And this brings us to the second paradox, the paradox of choice. We are the designers of our own lives through the choices we make, and there are more choices open to us now than ever before. At the same time, this freedom has a dark side to it: we *must* choose, whether we like it or not. MASS CUSTOMIZATION The freedom of choice that we have is also an inescapable obligation. With choice comes responsibility. The ability to reflect and give form to our lives within given constraints is just as important for an individual as reading, writing or arithmetic. In this context, we move from 'design as culture' to a culture of design, where design is part of our natural mode of being.

Atoms and Bits

There is help at our disposal. Digital tools, digital media and the vast resources on the internet collectively create a massive open and accessible infrastructure for individual and communal expression and reflection. In some domains, we have seen an explosive amount of activity (music production, digital photography) that has turned whole industries upside down. OPEN EVERYTHING Other domains are just getting warmed up. This is particularly true for three-dimensional objects. As different technologies for 3D printing are becoming affordable, Fab Labs ('fabrication laboratories', a concept developed at MIT's Center for Bits and Atoms) have spread from inner-city Boston to rural India, from South Africa to the far north of Norway. Activities in Fab Labs range widely, including technological empowerment; peer-to-peer, project-based technical training; local problem-solving; small-scale, high-tech business incubation; and grassroots research.

THERE IS A PRODUCTION INFRASTRUCTURE IN THE MAKING THAT WORKS WITH STANDARDIZED FORMATS FOR SPECIFYING 3D DESIGNS, SO THAT OUR IDEAS FOR OBJECTS CAN BE PUBLISHED, SHARED AND MODIFIED JUST AS EASILY AS VIDEO CLIPS ON YOUTUBE.

There is a production infrastructure in the making that works with standardized STANDARDS formats for specifying 3D designs, so that our ideas for objects can be published, shared and modified just as easily as video clips on YouTube. Do-It-Yourself is no longer a matter of wood and nails; DIY DIY is becoming more refined in terms of possible forms and construction concepts. In other fields, technological impulses like this have created an explosion of creativity among experts and amateurs alike. Accompanying that surge of creative expression, there is an awareness of the fact that technological facilitation is only meaningful at a very basic level. Anything that is fundamentally expressive or reflective derives its value from ideas and values that are embodied – and ideas and values come from people, not from technology. Again: anything is possible, but what do we want? Before we can rearrange atoms, we have to rearrange bits. Ideas! A richer palette of possible material forms requires a richer imagination than ever before. Buying a guitar does not make me a musician. Access to 3D design tools does not make me a designer.

Why Keep It Simple?

The concept of self-organization is an intriguing idea. Online media environments like YouTube, Flickr and Blogspot prove that well-designed (!) infrastructures ARCHITECTURE can indeed facilitate personal expression on a mind-boggling scale, but they have one thing in common: simplicity. The media formats are simple ('upload a picture here', 'this is a heading, type your text here'), and the media produced and shared by these tools are simple (a picture, a movie clip, a piece of text). But real life is not always that simple. As I've argued above, in networks, life can be annoyingly complex and most of us are not born with sufficient imaginative capacity to fully utilize the potential of the production technologies that are currently available. Most of us need help. When it comes to more complex media or artefacts, rolling out infrastructures and expecting self-organization to take care of the rest is simply not enough. Organizing self-organization is a lot of work, and does in fact involve a great deal of design and inspiration.

155

WE ARE DESIGNERS OF OUR OWN LIVES THROUGH THE CHOICES WE MAKE. THIS FREEDOM HAS A DARK SIDE TO IT: WE MUST CHOOSE, WHETHER WE LIKE IT OR NOT.

Traditional DIY stores know this very well. They don't just sell basic construction materials anymore, but increasingly also offer ready-made lifestyle products: lamps, furniture, various semi-manufactured products, and so on. What's more, they know that they need to help amateurs when it comes to making choices. Most websites for DIY stores DIY feature some form of assistance. Besides tips and suggestions from famous designers, there are online tools that help buyers figure out their personal preferences for interior design. I've even seen moodboard tools for interior decoration. For people who feel completely adrift in the sea of choices, there are style coaches to help buyers find out who they are and what choices to make.

Design Literacy

When it comes to more innovative or complex designs, inspiration and imagination are just as crucial as production technologies. This holds true for seasoned pros and enthusiastic amateurs. When motivated prosumers want to express their identities, they need different kinds of knowledge and skills, which together make up what we can call 'design literacy'. I suggest we conceptualize this at the following three levels:

Strategic vision
Know what you want, based on knowing who you are and what you want to achieve. This is about an awareness of personal goals and values. It can be very explicit, translated into formulated criteria, or very implicit, in which case there is an intuition that can be used to judge examples and design choices. Both approaches can work; more often than not, they co-exist in some form. Whatever it is that you're going to make, you have to feel its soul and formulate its mission. There is probably no better example here than Steve Jobs,

who has always had a very specific vision about using computing technology for personal goals, as opposed to serving the needs of businesses or governments. Apple was founded in 1979; over 30 years later, his vision has become a reality. Every product Apple has produced under Jobs' guidance was a conscious materialization of that vision. On a more intimate level, amateurs who want to redecorate their homes will be stifled rather than liberated by all the choices and possibilities if they do not have some kind of understanding of what kind of 'vibe' or 'atmosphere' they want in their house. They, too, need a vision. There is no other way.

Tactical choices
Be able to make choices that determine what it is that you are making. What you are making is ultimately a design that can be produced, in order to make the vision a reality. We are caught between heaven and earth here, and this is the true level where design takes place: crucial decisions are made on a conceptual level that will eventually determine the details of the end result. Choices about content, structure, behaviour and form are made and fixed. This is where professional design becomes a profession, and craftsmanship begins to play a role. The question is: how much professional expertise is needed? Can this be done by an amateur? AMATEURISSIMO It's hard to have to start from scratch. Tweaking something that's already close may be a better way to go. Open design to the rescue! If you see something you like, just download it and modify it to represent your vision. We'll return to that later.

Operational skills
Be able to use available production tools and infrastructures. This can range from knowing how to point and shoot with a digital camera or upload a video to YouTube to making a final mix of a song that sounds good on different speaker systems or specifying a design with 3D modelling software for a 3D printer.

These are the pillars of what we can call 'design literacy': the development of vision (strategic), the formulation of a design (tactical), and technical production (operational). There are interesting interactions between the three levels, however.

Ultimately, available production tools and infrastructure determine what can be made in the first place, so operational skills and tactical choices are often strongly aligned. There are also crucial links between tactical choices and strategic vision. If a 3D modelling tool is very user-friendly, very responsive, and well connected to the production tools (possibly through data standards), then the boundary between a sketch and a final design starts to blur, and users can work in a state of flow, where all three levels are active simultaneously.

ONLINE ENVIRONMENTS PROVE THAT WELL DESIGNED INFRASTRUCTURES CAN FACILITATE PERSONAL EXPRESSION ON A MIND-BOGGLING SCALE, BUT THEY HAVE ONE THING IN COMMON: SIMPLICITY.

The distinctions between the three kinds of literacy are epistemological: they involve different kinds of expertise. All three involve mentality, knowledge, and skills – three very familiar pedagogical concepts. Thus, design literacy can be learned, just like many other things, but there's more to it than learning to work the tools.

Becoming Literate

Professional designers DESIGNERS have all the necessary expertise. They have an important role to play in the large-scale development of design literacy. They can be heroes when their high-quality designs inspire eager amateurs. They can produce examples to be shared on online platforms that can be used, modified and re-distributed. They can explain how they work, e.g. as teachers in face-to-face courses and online videos. In working towards the advancement of design literacy, professionalism is still our starting point.

Going back to the three central concepts of design literacy mentioned above (vision, design, and production), there are interesting opportunities and challenges in the organization of design literacy:

Strategic vision
The development of a personal vision can be facilitated by presenting, explaining and discussing high-quality designs from professional designers. The development of vision can be a vulnerable and intuitive process, and seeing how pros do it (in a video interview, for instance) can be very helpful and inspiring. Formulating the right question is often the best way to try and find a solution. Inspiration is the keyword here: designers can be inspiring through what they make, but also through showing how they came up with the right vision to begin with.

Tactical choices
The formulation of a design can be facilitated by the same high-quality examples, when they are published in ways that allow for inspection, modification and sharing. Open design plays a crucial role in this. Online environments that feature collections of high-quality examples that can be analysed, used, modified, discussed and re-published hold immense potential. Users need to be able to inspect the internal structure of a design, and then modify and share it. Designers can produce these examples and share their methods and insights in interviews or debates, and design teachers can develop new pedagogical methods and formats. In the world of digital media, users make mashups, REMIX devising new combinations of chunks of information found elsewhere to create coherent new constructs. Open design allows for a similar approach to 3D objects, physical equivalents to mashups that can also be shared and discussed with others.

Operational skills
Technical production is the easiest skill, since all it requires is decent interface design for the relevant tools, supported by access to technical knowledge in the form of instruction manuals in print, video, or other formats. Many people can teach themselves how to do this and help each other using social media, such as forums or blogs.

157

Not everything can be done exclusively in the digital domain. There is definitely a need for face-to-face encounters with 'designer heroes', design teachers and fellow design amateurs. There is a potential here for existing cultural institutions like public libraries, archives and museums to organize the exchange of knowledge KNOWLEDGE between pros and amateurs, as well as but just as much between amateurs and other amateurs. They can become hotspots in the real world where amateurs go to work on their expertise. STEIM is an example of such a hotspot.

Design into the Future

The STEIM story below illustrates a shift in the focus of skilled professionals: from high-quality production to high-quality coaching and education in order to facilitate expression and reflection in a larger community of passionate amateurs. Such a significant shift does not happen out of the blue; it is a deliberate choice and it takes real work, based on an informed awareness of how our world is changing. REVOLUTION This new mentality is the ideal complement to the

exchange of information and ideas that is made possible through open design and new technological infrastructures. This calls for an ecosystem of people, institutions, relationships, tools and open infrastructures, where design becomes a natural activity for all those involved. Deliberate initiatives to foster design literacy need to address the three levels discussed above. Open design is essentially a highly social affair: amateur users will gather in online environments that help them by offering good examples in the form of available open designs, which are accompanied by interviews with heroes that explain how they navigate through all three levels of literacy. Heroes are attractors; people will flock around them, learn from them and from each other. Some parts of this ecosystem will grow and flourish autonomously, but others will need to be very consciously designed and planned in order to create a vibrant and living environment. It will help us find inspired ways to deal with tough issues like identity and choice in complex and unpredictable networks.

THE STEIM STORY

STEIM is a laboratory in Amsterdam that experiments with electronic musical instruments for live performance. This was a very specialized affair in the 80s and in the 90s. STEIM's instrument designers would develop personal instruments and user interfaces for musicians. They became world-famous for their expertise in connecting musical goals (strategic) to technical solutions (operational) through skilful design (tactical).

During the 90s, however, sensor technology and software became more widely available and more affordable. At the same time, the internet became a widely used platform for sharing knowledge and solutions among musicians. STEIM's core activity became a DIY craze. STEIM consistently supported this trend, being one of the first organizations to hack cheap Wii controllers

for musical applications and publishing electronic diagrams for its best-known musical instrument, the crackle box. But as this was happening, STEIM and its professionals had to reorient themselves to the changing situation.

Nowadays, STEIM is an important node in a world-wide knowledge network. There are more workshops than ever before. Moreover, starting in 2011, STEIM will offer a master's degree in 'Instruments and Interfaces' in collaboration with the Royal Conservatory in The Hague. It has become a vibrant hub for learning about DIY instrument design and meeting other people with similar interests. There is a strong co-creation culture. Musicians are challenged to develop their personal ideas about the kind of music they want to make (strategic vision), and STEIM helps them develop their

ideas, through co-design (tactical choices) and co-production by means of software configuration and the building of physical objects (operational skills).

Many people who visit STEIM don't just leave with an instrument; in their time there, they have learned how an instrument is made. And the instrument is just the beginning; there needs to be substantial time spent in learning to play it, as well as resisting the temptation to tweak it further. This represents a big risk at the tactical choice level: know when to stop modifying and start using a product! This is expertise that transcends the operational level. This is years and years of experience feeding into how musicians are currently coached and educated.

www.steim.org

EDUCATED ADVERTISEMENT

ADD STEPHEN HAWKING TO YOUR EXTENDED NETWORK

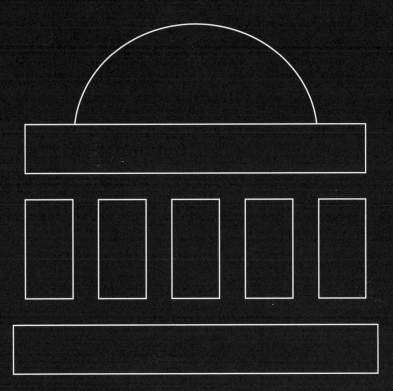

Universities of Openness

KNOWLEDGE WAS POWER, ONCE

TEACHING ATTITUDES, SKILLS, APPROACHES, STRUCTURE AND TOOLS

CAROLINE HUMMELS

Taking a critical look at current educational models, open design will involve a shift in the relationship between designers and potential users in terms of attitude, skills and approach. Caroline Hummels discusses the consequences of open design for the educational approach and for the structure and tools offered. She advocates an educational model that reflects the flexibility, openness, and continuous development of open design.

Caroline Hummels is Director of Education at the Department of Industrial Design, and associate professor on 'Aesthetics of Interaction in the Design of Intelligent Products and Systems' at Eindhoven University of Technology, The Netherlands. For Caroline, "open design is a specific approach to design, in which a group of intrinsically motivated people from various backgrounds develop design opportunities and solutions together in an open community, based on respect for each other's skills and expertise. Open design requires a flexible and open platform that assumes open access, sharing, active participation, responsibility, commitment to do good work for its own sake, respect, change, learning and ever evolving knowledge and skills."

http://id-dock.com/pages/overig/caro/caro.htm

Does training for open design require a different style of education? Current initiatives like Linux, VOICED and Fab Lab show the beauty of open platforms for sharing and learning, without requiring its contributors to follow specialized AMATEURISSIMO education. Despite this innate advantage, an educational model that is slanted specifically towards open design is needed. This chapter discusses how we can shape that model in such a way that it enables designers to blossom in an open structure. Although I focus on design education, the model can also be applied to other fields of expertise.

The Aim and Focus of Open Design

So why do we need a specific education style to facilitate open design? In fact, we don't. I do, however, believe that education should reflect upon its own paradigms, and envision what types of designers society will need in the future. Open design is one of the reasons to look critically at current educational models. Society is always changing. REVOLUTION What that means right now, for example, is that we have to be able to deal creatively and flexibly with large amounts of constantly evolving information. It also means that we currently have to find answers to large societal questions, now that we have reached the limits of our financial and environmental ecologies, among other frameworks. Open design addresses and works with these overall trends. TRENDS

Open design assumes open access, sharing, change, learning and ever-evolving knowledge and skills. It is an open and flexible platform instead of a closed one. Consequently, open design emerges from the New Science paradigm of quantum physics, relativity and self-organizing structures, developed by such scientists as Einstein, Bohr and Prigogine.[1] Where Newton's classical-scientific view is essentially simple and closed – it can be modelled through time-reversible laws and all complexities can be reduced to simplicities – Prigogine's reality is multiple, temporal and complex. It is open and admissible to change.

Design education based on a New Science paradigm requires a transformative curriculum, according to Doll[2]. In such a transformative curriculum, teachers discard the God's-eye view, uniform curricula and tests that are considered objective and predictive. On the contrary, they emphasize and support a variety of positions, procedures and interpretations. Design education for open design could benefit from theories like Constructivism, where learning is the learner's active construction of meaning in context.

OPEN DESIGN IS BASED ON A LIBERTARIAN RELATIONSHIP BETWEEN DESIGNERS AND POTENTIAL USERS, AND NOT ON A RATIONAL ONE IN WHICH THE DESIGNER IS SEEN AS SUPERIOR.

It is possible to postulate what educating for open design could look like, based on a constructivist learning model. The educational model for open design described below addresses attitudes and skills, approaches, and structure and tools. The figures in the text exemplify these topics by showcasing the educational model we use in the Department of Industrial Design at Eindhoven University of Technology.

Learning the Attitudes and Skills for Open Design

In his book *The Craftsman*,[3] Richard Sennett describes the importance of a craftsman's intrinsic motivation, commitment to doing good work for its own sake, and an ongoing pursuit of mastery in his or her craft. This attitude is the basis for the success of open communities like Linux, where the reward system is based on the quality of the outcome, social appraisal within the group (peer review) and the personal development of the contributors. The success of open communities like Linux depends on a set of attitudes, skills and activities that foster learning from experience, developing skills through doing, curiosity, ambiguity, imagination, opening up, questioning, collaborating, open-ended conversation, experimentation, and intimacy. It is these attitudes, skills and activities that will also determine the success of open design.

I therefore consider it essential that design education focus on forming self-directed and life-long learners, who are intrinsically motivated and who take responsibility for developing their own competencies and delivering high-quality work. Design students should learn to trust their senses and their intuition, and to embrace ambiguity, open-endedness and experimentation, as explained in the next section on approaches to open design. Moreover, design students should develop the attitude geared towards collaboration, `CO-CREATION` preferably supported by methods, tools and structures that foster collaboration (as explained in the last section on structure and tools for open design). It is not only designers who are participating in open design; in principle, everyone can participate. The key aspect is that everyone contributes their own expertise, while respecting and building on the expertise of others. This is especially true when addressing larger societal questions and designing systems where expertise is needed from a range of fields, including design, social sciences and engineering. `KNOWLEDGE`

Blurring Boundaries

Open design implies that the boundary between designers and users is blurring, at least with respect to motivation, initiative and needs. So what does this mean for the interaction between designers and potential users? On the basis of my organizational classification,[4] open design is based on a libertarian relationship between designers and potential users, and not on a rational one in which the designer is seen as superior. Neither is it based on an integrating relationship, in which the designer looks after the interest of the majority of potential users. The libertarian approach emphasizes the freedom and personal responsibility of every individual. This means that the designer is no longer placed above users when determining what is right for them; rather, the designer is part of a larger community.[5]

To be clear, this does not imply that everyone now becomes a designer, as IKEA and many others are implying. `WYS ≠ WYG` The design profession is still something that requires many years of education and practice, like any other profession. It does mean, however, that potential users now add their own experience and specific competencies to the mix.

Based on the aforementioned, I consider it essential for current design education to teach students to cooperate with other experts, respecting their expertise and simultaneously reflecting on their own competencies. This means, for example, that design students need to learn to work as part of multi-disciplinary teams, collaborating with students from other departments and schools, both on the same level and on different levels, e.g. students from a regional training centre, a university of applied sciences and a university of technology working together on projects. Moreover, design students need to learn to collaborate intensively with potential users, not as objective researchers that perform one or several user studies, not merely as facilitators that run co-design sessions, but also as subjective participants in an intensive process in which they themselves are part of the solution.

The Approach to Open Design

Due to the flexibility, open-endedness and often innovative character of open design, students should have first-hand experience with the fact that design decisions are always conditional; such decisions are always based on insufficient information, are but taken to the best of their and the community's experience and knowledge at that point. They can use two strategies to generate information to support these decisions, which reciprocally provide focus: design making (synthesizing and concretizing) and design thinking (analysing and abstracting).

Since open design depends highly on different people and expertise, including the element provided by potential users, tangible solutions that can be experienced are essential throughout the design process to validate ideas and to guide further developments. `STANDARDS` Moreover, design-making opens up new solution spaces that go beyond imagination, especially in group settings and when focusing on innovative, disruptive products which lack a well-established frame of reference for users or the market. It recalls the adage 'quality through quantity'.

I consequently advocate that design students learn to use a highly iterative process of generating dozens of solutions and testing them *in situ*, in their proper context. The Reflective Transformative Design Process[6] offers such a flexible and open process that

165

THE EDUCATIONAL MODEL

The Reflective Transformative Design Process has two vertical drives for gathering information in decision-making and two horizontal strategies which generate information.

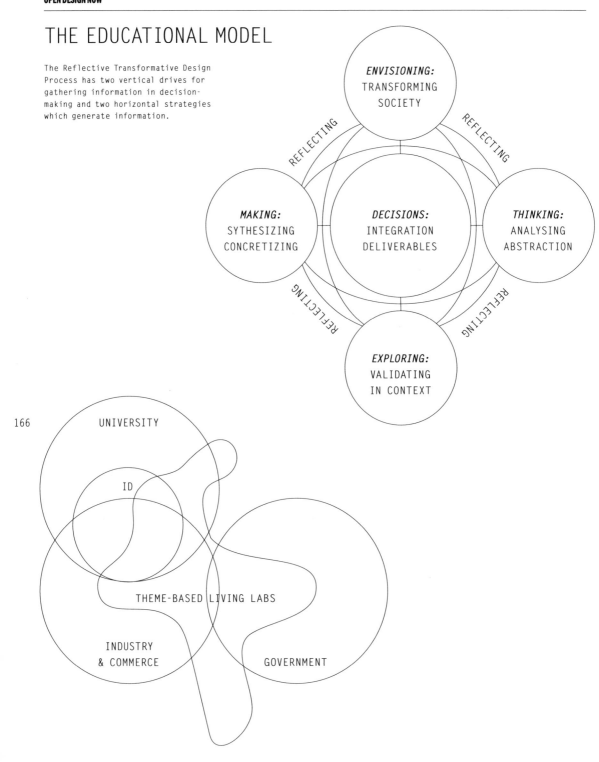

ENVISIONING:
TRANSFORMING
SOCIETY

REFLECTING

REFLECTING

MAKING:
SYTHESIZING
CONCRETIZING

DECISIONS:
INTEGRATION
DELIVERABLES

THINKING:
ANALYSING
ABSTRACTION

REFLECTING

REFLECTING

EXPLORING:
VALIDATING
IN CONTEXT

166

UNIVERSITY

ID

THEME-BASED LIVING LABS

INDUSTRY
& COMMERCE

GOVERNMENT

Thematic 'living labs' are used as carriers for joint education, research and valorization. Each theme has its own space that is used as education/design studio, research lab, library, workshop and test bed, with satellite test beds in the city. This approach is intended to create an open and flexible organization, demanding more responsibility and engagement from all participants.

it regards the act of designing not only as thought, but as a generator of knowledge. The process supports developing a vision of social and societal transformation, exploring solutions *in situ* with others, as well as offering moments of reflection.

Structures and Tools for Open Design

Open design requires a place to co-operate. That said, a hybrid design environment would both take advantage of a digital space that is always available all over the world, while making use of the intensity of collaborating in a physical workspace, making things, exchanging ideas and knowledge, and testing designs in context with potential users. A beautiful example of such a hybrid community is Beppe Grillo's blog,[7] which enables people to share digitally COMMUNITY and to meet each other all over the world. What does this mean for design education? Faculties, departments and schools have to think both physically and virtually about workspaces that enhance collaboration. CO-CREATION At the Department of Industrial Design here at Eindhoven University of Technology, we have structured our workspaces thematically to provide areas in which students can work together, share expertise and learn from each other. In addition to a supportive structure, open design would benefit from tools that support designing and sharing, for a variety of contributors. Design education can support students in exploring these tools through methods such as participatory design, co-design or rapid prototyping equipment at Fab Labs. Universities and schools can also develop open design tools and methods, such as Skin 2.0,[8] the Fab@home printers or design tools developed by former ID students at Studio Ludens.

Conclusions

Open design not only forces designers to think about their profession, role, attitude and competencies, but also challenges design educators to scrutinize their educational system. In this article I have discussed what open design means for the designer's attitude, skills and approach as well as for the educational structure and tools offered. Since we have stressed the flexibility, open-endedness and often innovative character of open design, the educational model for open design will also be flexible and open, and will need continuous development and testing with all parties involved to become a truly open design system.

NOTES

1   Doll, W. 'Prigogine: A New Sense of Order, A New Curriculum' in
     Theory into Practice, Beyond the Measured Curriculum 25(1),
     1986, p. 10-16.

2   Idem.

3   Sennett, R. *The Craftsman*. London, Penguin Books, 2009.

4   De Geus, M. *Organisatietheorie in de politieke filosofie*. Delft:
     Eburon, 1989. Cited in: *Hummels, G, Vluchtige arbeid: Ethiek en
     een proces van organisatie-ontwikkeling*. Doctoral dissertation,
     University of Twente, Faculty of Philosophy and Social Sciences,
     Enschede, The Netherlands, 1996.

5   Hummels, C. *Gestural design tools: prototypes, experiments and
     scenarios*. Doctoral dissertation, Delft University of Technology,
     2000. URL: http://id-dock.com/pages/overig/caro/publications/
     thesis/00Humthesis.pdf, accessed on 16 January, 2011.

6   Hummels, C and Frens, J. 'The reflective transformative design
     process', CHI 2009, 4-9 April 2009, Boston, Massachusetts, USA,
     ACM, p. 2655-2658.

7   www.beppegrillo.it/en/

8   Saakes, D. *Shape does matter: designing materials in products*.
     Doctoral dissertation, Delft University of Technology, 2010.

167

VERSION ZERO

lyc
funn
foreu
lilbe

LEARNING BY DOING

MUSHON ZER-AVIV

Mushon Zer-Aviv describes his efforts to teach open source design as an attempt to investigate why collaborative work combined with individual autonomy has not been common practice in design, as it is in open source software development. He discusses whether what worked for code might just as easily be transferred to design: the physical object as binary structure.

Mushon Zer-Aviv is a designer, educator and media activist based in New York Tel Aviv. His work involves media in public space and public space in media. He explores the borders of collaborative models as they are redrawn through politics, design and networks. He has been teaching new media research at NYU and open source design at Parsons The New School for Design and at the Bezalel Academy of Art & Design, Jerusalem.

Mushon defines open design as follows: "Design is a top-down visionary practice attempting to define systems. Hacking is a bottom-up visionary practice attempting to introduce rapture and creative disturbance into these designed systems. Open design is a journey to discover the best of both worlds."

www.mushon.com

I have been teaching open source design since 2008, in an attempt to figure out whether it can even exist. This article is an opportunity for me to reflect on and share my latest failures and successes in teaching what has yet to be learned.

I was first exposed to the open source world as a user of some free software; it was only later that I was introduced to the idealistic arguments about Freedoms, ACTIVISM as a more abstract principle. This combination of collaborative work and individual autonomy intrigued me. Coders were developing appealing political structures that were fostering creativity, collaboratively. I envied that degree of creative freedom; as a designer, I live in fear of 'design by committee'.

DON'T DESIGNERS KNOW HOW GREAT FREE COLLABORATION CAN BE? ARE THEY TOO AFRAID OF TRYING? DO THEY JUST NEED A HELPING HAND? OR IS THE PROBLEM THAT WHAT WORKS FOR CODE JUST DOESN'T REALLY TRANSLATE INTO THE DESIGN PROCESS?

172

Inspired by these initiatives, I started my own open source project, co-founding ShiftSpace.org; I took part as a designer, collaborating with Dan Phiffer, a coder. It was my enthusiasm about open development that inspired me, but I was surprised to find that this excitement was not shared by my fellow designers. Don't designers know how great free collaboration OPEN EVERYTHING can be? Are they too afraid of trying? Do they just need a helping hand? Or is the problem that what works for code just doesn't really translate into the design process?

I set out to answer these questions, but trawling through online resources did not yield enough satisfactory writing on the subject. Many discussions confused sharing with collaboration, CO-CREATION or were trying to advocate the use of open graphics software for purely ideological reasons. These arguments did not convince me; I was fairly sure that the ideological stance of coders could not be the only element that makes 'Free Software' such a desirable practice. Similarly, there is no intrinsic sociable instinct that leads coders to one another. The networked collaborative model of Free Software for coding is pragmatically the best way to go; any other way just makes much less sense. In this context, ideological reasons are secondary to simple pragmatism.

An Open Design Lab, with My Students as Lab Rats

It might be that we just haven't found the right way to transcend the design process; it's not as if we've tried all that hard yet. Art and design schools still nurture the image of the genius DESIGNERS as an individual artist. Originality is rewarded as a higher standard than communication, and copying is considered a sin. I figured the classroom would be the first place to start, so I proposed a class for the Parsons School for Design entitled *Open Source Design*. I assumed that our exploration of design based on Free Software methods should probably start with interface design, since interface is an integral part of most of the software we use. My hope was that I would be able to convince my students to contribute their design skills to some projects – have them get hands-on experience working on real projects while actually making some actual (and much-needed) contributions to Free Software.

To drive home the point about collaboration (and to scare off any students who might not be ready for the bumpy ride), I decided to kick off the first class with some bold statements:

"In this class, we're going to explore the possibilities of Open Source Design while learning HTML, CSS & WordPress theming. However, I should warn you that I don't have much experience in HTML & CSS, and I will practically be learning WordPress for the first time along with you guys."

You can imagine the looks on their faces. Luckily for me, only some of them left as soon as the class was over. My approach to this class was different than what I had done in previous classes I had taught. Rather than teach the students to use the technology, we learned how to figure things out on our own. Rather than memorizing every HTML element and what it might be good for, we learned to use Firefox and the Firebug extension to inspect the source code of every site. Open source made sense immediately when the students could read the HTML code `KNOWLEDGE` of any page like an open book. Unlike in other classes, the students were encouraged to copy, to analyse, to understand and to implement code and design patterns they found on the web. `HACKING`

To look at grid-based design, we used the Blueprint `BLUEPRINTS` CSS framework; for WordPress, we used the Sandbox and Thematic framework themes. In both cases, the students based their work on previous design decisions coded into these frameworks and explored ways of modifying the code or design to fit their needs. We were using design foundations that were strong, but at the same time easy to modify. It made sense to the students; they understood why the concept of openness might actually be relevant for them.

Teaching vs Learning

Like many other design educators, teaching is one of the ways that I can stay up to date. I am required to constantly keep myself informed, constantly learning and make sure I actually understand new subjects enough to teach them. That is also a benefit of being involved in open source initiatives. The professional exchange between coders facilitates a sustainable peer-to-peer learning environment – and one that extends beyond the structures of institutional education. To extrapolate, if I learn by teaching students and geeks learn by teaching each other, maybe my students can learn that way too.

The first assignment in my class was 'The Tutorial'. Students were required to create a (non-digital) tutorial on something they already knew how to do, preferably a topic that others might not be familiar with. They exchanged tutorials in class; over the following week, all the students had to follow the guidelines provided by their peers and report to

the class on their experiences. The students wrote tutorials on such topics as 'How to curve a football', 'A recipe for banana bread', 'DIY 3D glasses', 'Finding an Apartment in NY (Without Paying a Broker)' and 'How to Sell Multiple Pairs of Shoes'. A tutorial is an involved interactive design task, even when the tutorial is not digital. It also provided a framework for the semester that was constructed around knowledge sharing, documentation and peer learning.

ART AND DESIGN SCHOOLS STILL NURTURE THE IMAGE OF THE GENIUS. ORIGINALITY IS REWARDED AS A HIGHER STANDARD THAN COMMUNICATION, AND COPYING IS CONSIDERED A SIN.

Tutorial hunting has become a substantial part of the semester, as tutorials become a major source of pooled knowledge. We used a class mailing list where students could submit technical questions and ask for creative feedback. I encouraged them to post their code and questions on the blog and refer their peers to the relevant blog post from the mailing list. However, in many cases, a code snippet was not enough to get the full picture, reproduce the problem and help solve it; we needed to share the full code repository. I was concerned that getting the students on a version control system would be pushing them just a bit beyond the geekdom level that design students could handle in one semester, but it became unavoidable. I set them up on a centralized Subversion code repository, so every student would get every code update downloaded directly to their computers. They shared all the code by definition and could modify each other's work when needed. `SHARING`

This worked well, but it had an unacceptable side effect: at the end of each semester, the class code repositories created in that semester would be left abandoned. Symbolically, each class became an abandoned open source project. Obviously, that was not the message I wanted to leave the students with. I recently gave up on the Subversion system, which used centralized version control, and got my students on Git and the Github.com 'social coding' site. On Github, the students publish their code in public and other users (not just the other students in the class, but also other users) can easily fork, merge and comment on the code. When the semester ended, the students maintained control of their own repositories, beyond the context of the class.

Pragmatic, Not Altruistic

By that point in the semester, I have managed to convince the students why free and open source content available online is relevant to them and will advance their creative work. But that was the easy part; I have not yet managed to convince them why they should contribute too, why they should give back to the commons. MANIFESTOS

I initially set up the final assignment of the semester as an arbitrary task: "Find an open source project, and contribute to it as a designer." I was naïve, to say the least, and this ill-conceived task failed miserably. My students didn't really understand the projects they chose, and the geek-talk on the mailing lists was incomprehensible jargon to them. The communities they approached did not have a frame of reference to appreciate the students' contributions and were suspicious of the students' motives. The first semester of the Open Source Design class ended in disappointment; it was clear we were on the wrong track.

In the following semester, I understood that assigning an arbitrary contribution was the wrong way to go. I had a smaller class that time around, and we chose to work together twice during the semester. First, we took part in the WordPress 2.7 icon design challenge. Later, the students chose to help some of their friends get their portfolios up online using the Indexhibit system. They wrote tutorials, they recorded screen-capture videos, they wrote code examples and style comments. Finally, they posted their contributions on the class blog and on the Indexhibit forums. Back then, the documentation available for Indexhibit was lacking and the students' work was well received.

The second attempt had worked much better than the first one, but I knew its success had a lot to do with the qualities and personalities of the students in class. They enjoyed working together but at its core, the Indexhibit documentation was still a relatively altruistic contribution to a project that they were not actually planning to use after the class ended. If they were not going to benefit from their own contributions, why should they contribute again once they were no longer required to for a group assignment?

In the following semesters, I guided students to write the kind of tutorials they would have liked to find for themselves. Their tutorials focused on CSS, WordPress, Github... environments they used for their own benefit, in their own work. They not only covered the technical side of the technologies they documented; they also looked at the design aspects. At the end of the semester, the blog featured valuable, peer-reviewed and tested tutorials that benefited the students who had already completed the class. Months and years after each of these semesters ended, these publicly available contributions constantly receive thank-you comments from random users on the web. And still, it was not enough yet.

Toward a Collaborative Design Process

As far as knowledge sharing is involved, the tutorial approach has indeed proved itself. However, sharing technology and design tips is not collaboration. In this context, sharing has been happening *post mortem* to the creative act. To really challenge the design process and discover whether design can enjoy the benefits of the networked production REVOLUTION revolution, I needed to focus my efforts on design collaboration.

Writing a wiki and coding software both benefit from a highly collaboration-friendly technology: text. Both types of content generation use a vocabulary predefined by language, which levels the playing field for the various contributors. It poses implicit prerequisites (literacy) and it funnels the contributions through a finite list of the syntax options standardized by language. For better or worse, both visual and behavioural languages are not confined within such rigid structures. STANDARDS Ironically, it is the openness of these languages that makes networked collaboration harder.

In the last few decades, interface design emerged as an important cultural practice. There have been many attempts recently to coordinate and standardize this new language. The critical discussion of interface linguistics does not happen in the academic arena, it happens in the blogosphere. These interface linguists document design patterns and evaluate best practices for following them. Many of them are advocating semantic content and structured data, claiming such approaches would support efforts to index and process this content. The aim here is to serve artificial systems that are not intelligent enough to derive the meaning without external assistance. At the same time, these index-based and component-based approaches help structure the creative process as well. We see it in Wikipedia, where the way that articles are structured helps to focus and process the collaborative act. We see it in the structure of Cascading Style Sheets (CSS), where design decisions propagate through the document's structure. And we see it in interaction modules, where code libraries encapsulate a single action which can still be modified externally through APIs.

extend them, then break them; some might call it developing a design guide. We will try to evaluate the legibility and readability of our messages; some might call it usability testing. We will try to discover a new collaborative paradigm for the design process; some might call it 'Open Source Design'.

175

THE CRITICAL DISCUSSION OF INTERFACE LINGUISTICS DOES NOT HAPPEN IN THE ACADEMIC ARENA, IT HAPPENS IN THE BLOGOSPHERE.

The next frontier for the academic collaborative design lab that my students and I have been leading would have to involve the linguistics of interaction design. We will start drafting characters, then words and then sentences; some might call it building a structured visual language. We will try to define a syntax, then rearrange it and try again; some might call it designing modular systems. We will try to set standards, then

THE TRIBE
THE CROWD
THE SWARM

 GroupThink.

OPEN DESIGN FOR GOVERNMENT

BERT MULDER

Governmental institutions are challenged to use design and open design as a strategic tool. Bert Mulder addresses issues of participation and quality, and suggests how a government could develop a system that would include information, tools, methods and a set of values to reap the benefits of open design for citizen involvement.

Bert Mulder is an associate professor of Information, Technology and Society and the director of the eSociety Instituut at The Hague University of Applied Sciences in The Netherlands. He also advises government ministries, large cities and large and small organizations in business, healthcare, arts and culture and non-profit areas on the development of long-term internet strategies. Bert also acts as a consultant and concept developer for new services and systems that use information and communication technology. According to Bert, "open design is the design of products, systems or services through the use of publicly shared design information and processes. The philosophy is similar to open source."

http://nl.linkedin.com/in/bertmulder

Open design for government is a challenge. Not only is open design itself a relatively recent concept, but design and government generally do not interact easily. We do not often talk about governments designing things; we say that governments institute policy and procedures, develop urban planning and create services. Even in a recent Dutch initiative with the grand name of The Hague, *Design and Government* the tagline reads 'design for public space, architecture and visual communication'. When design for government is discussed at all, design is mostly seen as functional.

But design will become an increasingly necessary and strategic tool for government at all levels. That is why exploring the relationship between open design and government is not only interesting, but also timely and necessary.

TODAY'S SOCIETY REQUIRES US NOT ONLY TO CREATE A WIDER RANGE OF DIVERSE SOLUTIONS, BUT ALSO TO DO SO FASTER AND BETTER.

Exploring the possibilities of open design for government requires delicacy. Much of open design thinking seems to be in the 'hype' phase of Gartner's hype cycle, where arguments for and against reflect hopes and expectations rather than reality, simply because there is little or no experience on which to base tangible forecasts. This article takes a somewhat analytical approach, outlining several qualities of open design and government and identifying potential challenges. It describes a plan and proposes developments that would stimulate open design in the public sector. Essentially, this article tries to envision what open design would be like as a structural and strategic tool for government.

The Importance of Design

The first reason to consider open design for government is the increasing importance of design across the board. This increase is occurring because our increasingly complex society requires more design. TREND Where supermarkets in the 1960s stocked 1000 products, today's supermarkets carry between 20,000 and 40,000 items. All these products need to be created, produced, marketed, bought and used. This process is why design has grown from 'nice to have' to 'need to have': we need to create more products and services to sustain our society, and to present them in a way that is meaningful to us.

But design is also becoming more important for another reason. Today's society requires us not only to create a wider range of diverse solutions, but also to do so faster and better. New challenges require fundamentally new solutions; simply extrapolating the past will no longer suffice. And because solutions will have to survive into a future different from today, the ability to design well becomes more important. We need to shape society with the future in mind, REVOLUTION not relying on a past that increasingly has little bearing on the problems we face today; we need to realize better and more sustainable solutions using imagination, innovation and our talent for creativity and creation.

Why Government is Involved in Design

Future-driven thinking is what makes design fundamentally important for government. To face the challenges that the future will hold, the government needs to develop and integrate design competencies into its processes. Analysis and simple extrapolation governed by political processes will have to give way to imagination and more original creation, buildings more sustainable solutions. The development of social innovation serves as an example: design professionals are creating novel solutions in social contexts. SOCIAL DESIGN This approach involves a more strategic use of design by the government than the simply functional use of design in public space, architecture and visual communication.

A second reason why design capability becomes essential for government is the new complexity of the networked society: government policies and services are increasingly developed in networks that link

180

many different partners. The complexity of a context involving many different stakeholders and regulatory frameworks makes it essential to have a central concept to bind it all together. These considerations also mean that any development in the design field will potentially have relevant applications in the public sector. Clearly, the development of open design for government purposes is an important trend.

Open Design: Requirements and Domains

Current discussions of open design often refer to two related developments: open production and open design. Design(ing) with reference to the ongoing revolution that is triggered by the ubiquitous availability of digital design and production tools and facilities and that reverses the distribution of design disciplines. It portrays design as an open discipline, in which designs are shared and innovation of a large diversity of products is a collaborative and world spanning process.[1] Neither happens by itself and each requires very specific conditions. Analyzing those general requirements will make it possible to achieve a more precise indication of what preconditions would be needed to facilitate open design for government.

DIY `DIY` is a good example of how open design gets started. To really take off, do-it-yourself production requires access to appropriate materials, tools and techniques to empower enthusiastic amateurs. For instance, DIY projects around the house require a power drill, easily available wood and fastening techniques that unskilled workers can use. This is how amateurs start designing and making things in any field; every professional started somewhere. In the same way, open design emerges in parallel with the availability of user-friendly and accessible information, methods, concepts, values and tools that allow non-professionals to create their designs. Homebrew electronics materials are available in electronics stores, and the corresponding plans can be obtained from electronics magazines or websites. When all these resources are available, more people may be encouraged and empowered to create their own designs.

Both DIY production and open design empower the user by putting professional tools in the hands of the masses. Those tools are usually available on different levels. At the simplest level, professional solutions

are provided as easy-to-use templates `TEMPLATE CULTURE` that users can re-use and apply without significant modification. At the intermediate level, tools are available as design templates or generative code that users can modify to create their own designs. `BLUEPRINTS` At the highest level, skilled amateurs may access and use advanced design tools used by professionals. When open design for government becomes a reality, it will by necessity consist of a variety of ready-to-use solutions, design templates and advanced tools. Open design should be distinguished from other recent design developments in which users have been more intimately involved in the design process, such as participatory design, co-design or social innovation. In open design, many users are able to design on their own. They are not users involved in a design processes that is initiated and run by professional designers. Open design moves in two directions: outward, when individuals design and produce their own individual products, and inward, when people design solutions collaboratively. The latter faces the additional challenge of coordinating complex systems. Open design for government creates the conditions for many people to design solutions together – and that's exactly what governments do.

BOTH DIY PRODUCTION AND OPEN DESIGN EMPOWER THE USER BY PUTTING PROFESSIONAL TOOLS IN THE HANDS OF THE MASSES.

Open design for government may lead to different outcomes than are currently being achieved. These outcomes may include harvesting novel ideas from a larger audience, such as in crowdsourcing; improving the quality of a design; promoting participation and loyalty; or facilitating the creation or composition of actual services. Open design may be used for all or any of these, but will have to be adapted to the desired outcome. There are two roles that open design could fulfil in the private sector. First, it could serve the government in its interactions with the people, as a civic resource that gives citizens the ability to take part in the processes of governing. Second, it could serve the government internally to support and contribute to existing government processes supporting government agendas. Again, it could be used in both directions, inward and outward, but the way open design is used would have to be adapted to the desired outcome. The tools for open design themselves are not affected either way, but supporting a pre-existing agenda means obeying pre-existing procedural constraints, which means that open design is not solely reserved for citizens.

When Open Design Meets Government

When open design meets government, design must adapt to the constraints of government in order for the two to interact. In the same way that architects or industrial designers have a basic understanding of building materials, the forces of physics, and the requirements of production, design in the public sector is subject to its own specific constraints. What would open designers need to operate in a government context?

182

Open design and government might have been made for each other. After all, doesn't the government work for all of us, and wouldn't it be much better if we all contributed? In some sense, democracy at large might be seen as a form of 'design' where society is run 'by the people, for the people': all of the people are involved in designing better futures for each other. However, the structure of the democratic process as it stands now (whether representative or direct) hardly involves citizens in the process of designing new solutions. MASS CUSTOMIZATION The government seems to have its own requirements. So how could the characteristics of open design fit those requirements?

Open design for government will follow government activities. The government is involved in setting policies and providing services in such domains as economics, infrastructure and urban design, welfare and healthcare, culture, education and public safety. These are the subjects of government, and open design for government will have to produce useful solutions in those areas in order to be successful.

The government's agenda mirrors society's needs. Running a country or a city involves a finite number of activities; one might assume that open design

DESIGN FOR GOVERNMENT

Open design moves in two directions: outward, when individuals design and produce their own individual products, and inward, when people design solutions collaboratively. The latter faces the additional challenge of coordinating complex systems. Open design for government creates the conditions for many people to design solutions together – and that's exactly what governments do. The challenges of open design: when open design meets government, it meets the same challenges that the government faces: participation, quality and complexity.

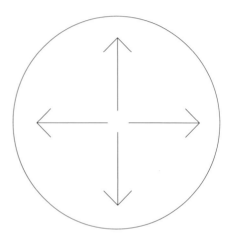

Outwards: distributed tools, individual designing, individual solutions.

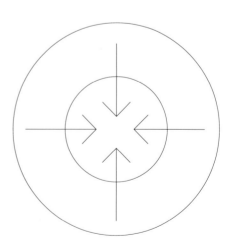

Inwards: distributed tools, collective designing, collective solutions.

would focus specifically on those activities. It can be compared to having a family, which also involves making a finite number of decisions in consensus: we really only need to sit down together a few times a year to deliberate such matters as buying an expensive household appliance, deciding where to go on holiday, choosing where to move or what school would be best for our children. While the process of open design may involve more people in the discussion, it will not increase the number of issues on the agenda, nor make dramatic changes to its structure.

Public administration works for the public good. Accordingly, open design for government will have to balance the wants and needs of many different citizens while dealing with power, politics and the manufacture of consent. That is why open design does not mean designing individual solutions for individual cases; rather, the process will have to take into account the balance of power between different stakeholders. One of the important elements in that process is fair representation: open design for government cannot be a process taken on solely by the strong and able; it must also involve the weak and underrepresented. SOCIAL DESIGN

Open design for government needs to support a deep and empathic sense of the needs of 'users'. The best solutions never consider such concepts as 'society', 'citizens' or 'the public' to be a generic class. One neighbourhood is not the next, one side of town is not identical to the other, and one city does not face precisely the same challenges as another. The same holds true from one generation to the next, and no group in society can be considered a carbon copy of another. Either the open participants, or the process in which they are involved, needs to have the ability to recognize and honour these distinctive qualities and let them ring through in the solutions that are created through open design. In order for open design for government to be effective, it has to be sensitive to the rhythm of government. Policy and development processes have their own dynamic and may take many years to synchronize. To achieve maximum effect, any contribution needs to play its role at the right time in the policy cycle or development process. It will be a major challenge to integrate a complex process of open design, with its own dynamics, without disrupting the necessary tempo and quality of decision-making.

Participation

Open design implicitly assumes that many people will participate once tools and materials become available. However, participation is more complex than that. Participation in today's political process is a challenge in itself, but participation in online activities is also uneven. On large-scale, multi-user communities and online media sharing sites, user contributions are characterized by participation inequality. Only 0.16% of all YouTube users actually contribute video content; approximately 0.12% of Flickr users contribute their own photos. It's called the 1% law: only 1% of users contribute, while 9% post comments, and 90% are silent observers.

DOESN'T THE
GOVERNMENT WORK
FOR ALL OF US, AND
WOULDN'T IT BE MUCH
BETTER IF WE ALL
CONTRIBUTED?

What's more, the online communities on those sites are not representative of average web users; actual participation is probably lower if the subset is extended to include all websites on the internet. In itself, the 1% law does not have to be a disadvantage. It closely resembles the state of political participation: only 3% of the Dutch population is actively involved in a political organization; of those, about 30% are active in local politics: about 1% of the population. Early findings on the reality of online political participation show that it tends to be biased, and, just as in real life, the active participants are always the same group of people. Preliminary research on e-petitions for the German Parliament shows this. The online audience is a different group from the people who participated in real life (in this case younger), but online political participants seem to belong to a separate group anyway: highly educated white males. In open source software development, participation is a major challenge. Projects have a hard time finding enough people who are sufficiently qualified and motivated, and an even harder time keeping those people involved. The current successful examples, such as Linux and Apache, draw their contributors from the 1.5 billion users on the global internet – and only about 1600 programmers among those 1.5 billion users are actual contributors. Scaled down to the level of small cities or neighbourhoods, that level of participation presents a major challenge. Although there are more than 120 million blogs on the internet, it is hard or even impossible to find one good blogger at the level of a single neighbourhood. There is simply too little news content and too few people able and willing to write daily or weekly posts. In the Netherlands, the number of contributors to the Dutch version of Wikipedia is too small to maintain good-quality content. Open design for government may be a good idea, but finding enough people to sustain it will be a challenge.

TO REALLY PARTICIPATE
IN A PROCESS
OF OPEN DESIGN
FOR GOVERNMENT,
PARTICIPANTS WOULD
AT LEAST NEED ACCESS
TO INFORMATION ON
ASPECTS LIKE THE
FINANCIAL, REGULATORY
AND POLITICAL
CONSEQUENCES OF THEIR
DESIGN EFFORT.

Another widespread assumption is that there is a correlation between civic participation and the democratic quality of society. A related assumption is that finding ways to increase online participation will, in turn, contribute to the democratic quality of society. Research does not support that assumption; rather, it shows that the relationship between participation and democratic quality may be more complex.

Quality

One of the challenges of open design for government is quality. Decision-making at a government level is not about individual and small-scale projects, nor is it about short-term, localized projects. Any contributions to the process would have to create the kind of quality that supports large-scale, long-term projects, answering to regulatory, financial and political constraints. Of course such an argument may be focusing too much on the design outcome: the real result of open design for government might be a greater sense of participation, transparency and increased loyalty.

Involving more people does not create better design, most of which comes from individual designers or small teams. In fact, involving more people may be detrimental to the quality of the result. Of course a larger group may produce more unexpected and useful ideas – that is one of the ways that crowdsourcing produces results. CROWDSOURCING However, turning ideas into a good design requires a completely different process. An illustration may be seen in online petitioning. First results show that e-petitions often fail to contribute serious new policy ideas, though they may increase the people's feeling of participation and transparency.

Good design requires experience and knowledge of many different aspects of materials, production, marketing and user needs. Design for government is its own domain requiring its own skills. For social innovation, where designers operate in a social context, professional designers estimate that about 5% of their colleagues possess the necessary skills to deal with new and different complexities. Open design for government invites untrained and unskilled participants; the open design process must empower them in a way that compensates for their lack of experience. In open design for government, projects may be active in a wide variety of domains and bring complex challenges on different levels. Open design is simple where challenges and solutions are straightforward and the aim of the process is participation. But when real complexity comes into play, creating the right prerequisites for open design becomes more of a challenge – it will require more extensive information, better tools, more refined methods and deeper shared values.

The Ecology: Information, Tools, Methods and Values

Open design relies on participants who have been empowered with the right information, the right tools, fitting methods and shared values. When done well, these create a constructive balance between the complexity of the design task and the abilities and motivation of the prospective participants. To really participate in a process of open design for government, participants would at least need access to information on aspects like the financial, regulatory and political consequences of their design effort. Then they would need tools to work with that information: visualize it, analyse it, integrate it. They would need methods to support the design process and the manufacture of consent. All of this would be active within a framework of values and concepts that is needed to design appropriate solutions.

NEW DIGITAL TOOLS ALLOW USERS TO CREATE MASHUPS THAT SHOW THE POLICIES AND REGULATIONS CURRENTLY IN EFFECT ON EVERY PIECE OF LAND AND PROPERTY.

The field of urban design shows the complexity and the power of such an ecology of information, tools and methods. In that field, basic information is becoming available now that datasets of geographic and policy information are open to citizens. This trend is apparent in the DataGov projects in several countries, including the US, UK, Australia and the Netherlands. New digital tools allow users to create mashups that show the policies and regulations currently in effect on every piece of land and property.

After Hurricanes Katrina and Rita, Louisiana was in urgent need of immediate community redevelopment, which had to be implemented far more quickly than usual. The Louisiana Speaks Regional Plan was a key part of the response. One of the design tools used in the project was the Louisiana Speaks Pattern Book, a resource used to inspire and empower all those rebuilding their communities. It contained an extensive analysis of Louisianan quality in buildings, communities and regions and provided design patterns for new houses and communities, formulated as easy-to-understand examples with the aim of inspiring better, higher-quality projects. The design patterns incorporated the complexity of historical analysis, the qualities specific to the region and the possible modern interpretations in such a way that it was easier for designers to create quick solutions while retaining good quality.

These efforts were based on another generative model, which aims to bring about a '21st-century correction' of the American urban landscape. Called Smartcode, it outlines the best physical attributes of regions, communities and individual buildings and specifically embodies the views of the New Urbanism movement. It addresses all levels of design, from regional planning and the shape of communities down to individual buildings. Smartcode also outlines a design method in which local citizens are actively involved in calibrating the general design code for use in local circumstances. All this shows that, in urban planning, the general trend is increasingly facilitating the requirements for open design. As basic information becomes available, various tools are developed to use the data, followed by a design method that supports active involvement by citizens; finally, the code clearly describes its value systems. Of course, we may want to influence the trends to ensure that they suit the needs of a real open design for government – but the basic elements of the 'open ecology' are being developed.

This is just one example; there are many more, but it illustrates the necessary 'ecology' in which different components (information, tools, methods and values) may be necessary to support open design. The necessary support framework may be more readily apparent in urban planning, since it is already a design-based domain. When open design meets government, we should see a similar development in other domains like healthcare, welfare, public safety, economics and education. Creating the same ecology for policymaking in healthcare or public safety will require further development.

185

Fostering Open Design for Government

Open design is in its early stages and open design for government is a promise at best. What if we not only described the possible preconditions needed to facilitate open design for government, but also developed an agenda to stimulate it? Although some projects embrace new ways of working, such as crowdsourcing to involve citizens, that is far from open design for government. A much clearer practical agenda may help to harmonize relevant developments, creating synergy and better quality.

An agenda for development would require an investment on four fronts: further developing the core concept, outlining its possible implementations, identifying their components and stimulate experience in different projects. We need to ask ourselves what we really mean by 'open design for government', what it could be, what it should be and what it needs. Only a more operational view can provide the basis for a practical development agenda. Scientific studies are not the first priority; there is nothing to research yet. What is needed is a design effort to outline what open design for government might actually look like. We need scenarios, concept studies and small projects to refine possibilities and parameters. Such a clearer understanding of what open design actually means would allow us to gauge the current trends (such as open government data, new tools for visualization, new developments in design) and to determine whether they possess the right qualities to support a truly open design process.

We will see open design being used in government, partly because design is becoming more important, and partly because the tools and methods necessary for open design will become more readily available. Open design may serve a range of aims, from creating a sense of participation and harvesting new solutions, to genuinely inspiring better solutions for government challenges. However, in order to realize the potential this presents, we will need to make the move from dreams to reality, despite the serious challenges that arise in considering open design for government. As practical concepts are developed further, creating synergy between new and current developments may provide the parameters needed to support open design for government. Whether all of this will lead to higher-quality design for government will depend on the quality of the tools, methods and values that we come up with. Perhaps it is time to make use of the open design process in establishing open design for government.

LEAVE YOUR LAPTOP

TO YOUR GRAND CHILD

FROM BEST DESIGN TO JUST DESIGN

TOMMI LAITIO

Can open design contribute to the world's bigger problems, such as depletion and squandering of natural resources, population growth, consumerism and widespread poverty? In turn, can pooling knowledge and resources, re-evaluating the concept of time, and facilitating user participation help open design make a strong contribution to sustainability? Tommi Laitio investigates and reflects.

Tommi Laitio acts as a researcher for Finland's only independent think-tank, Demos Helsinki. Its aim is to develop democracy to suit the needs and capabilities of the people of the 21st century. The vision is essentially people-centric. At the heart of Demos Helsinki's work is extensive, high-quality research. It produces scenarios, recommendations and experiments that offer new insights into grasping the great challenges of the future. Central themes are well-being, democracy and citizen participation, future cities and low-carbon societies. For Tommi, "open design is a tool to solve problems that arise from systemic moral bankruptcy, building stronger communities along the way."

www.demos.fi/node/327

IN A WORLD OF
MATERIAL SCARCITY
AND COMPETENT PEOPLE,
THE RIGHT QUESTION
TO ASK WHEN DESIGNING
IS NOT WHO KNOWS BEST.
RATHER, WE SHOULD
BE ASKING WHAT IS JUST
AND FAIR.

The world's problems are rooted in moral bankruptcy that underlies all the systems in which we live and operate. Over 90% of the resources taken out of the ground today become waste within three months.[1] To avoid the catastrophic effects of climate change, we need to cut our carbon emissions to a tenth of the present level. Approximately 75% of the world's population live in countries where national consumption exceeds the planet's bio-capacity.[2] Worse yet, the world's population is expected to grow by 50% in the next forty years. That will make nine billion of us.

Consuming less will not be easy. In the developed world, the demand for new products, different lifestyles and more active forms of participation grows as people gain new skills, have more expendable time and money, and find themselves looking for meaning in their lives. Meanwhile, basic standards of living are far from being met in many parts of the world. While the developed countries are dealing with hedonistic angst, approximately 50,000 people die daily from poverty-related causes – most of them women and children. One billion people go to sleep hungry every day.

The world as it is, in all its flawed complexity, TREND is the ultimate design challenge of today. The issues that need to be tackled do not have a clearly identifiable owner or one simple solution. We've entered an era of co-existing versions of truth that may not be fully compatible, even to the point of being mutually exclusive. The ultimate problems of this time are results of the way we eat, interact with others, exercise

and consume. This is why they are also far too serious to be left entirely to professional designers.

This complex combination of problems calls for open design. So far, professional designers have dealt with material shortages by minimizing their negative impact on production and distribution. Classic approaches to market segmentation no longer function when factors like age or ethnicity no longer define ambitions and desires. Neither professional-led design nor classic approaches will be broad enough to solve pandemic problems like climate change and other worldwide anthropogenic issues, stemming from an absence of moral responsibility. The facts are clear: we need a full paradigm shift; minor tweaks to traditional methods will no longer suffice. REVOLUTION

The challenge that we all share is to create design that actually solves problems. SOCIAL DESIGN The questions to be answered become far clearer with this strategic focus. If design is to be used successfully in striving for a fairer place to live, a number of things will be needed, including more participatory tools for understanding the architecture of the problem, quicker ways to test alternative solutions, smarter methods of negotiation and selection, and flexibility in production and distribution.

A Tale of Two Worlds

For the first time in human history, more than half of the world's population lives in cities. According to the UN, in 2020 half of these city-dwellers will live in slums. Aspirations for urban lifestyles are inevitably going to clash. It is harder to build communities when everyone feels they belong to a minority.

Urban freedoms need to be pursued in ways that do not limit other people's freedoms. Strong local communities COMMUNITY are fundamental in assisting people in planning their lives, sharing resources and knowledge, developing a sense of home, solving the problems they face, feeling safe, having room to laugh and play as well as building lasting relationships with the people around them. Community structures necessitate government investments as well as new inventions in affordable communication, food production, public transport and housing. It is in cities that the world of tomorrow is being made, as they build resilience against global turmoil. Issues like local food production are being acknowledged in government programmes. However, in order to share their ideas and resources, people need to feel comfortable and safe. This poses a tremendous challenge, especially in societies where people are most affected by global injustice. When people are struggling to meet their most basic day-to-day needs, the motivation to search for solutions together is small. The same applies to marginalized groups, even in developed societies. When people consider themselves victims of circumstance, opening up to others takes several preparatory steps. Equality, good public spaces and education are fundamental preconditions for open design. The same applies to open design for public services – and equal societies are both happier and more cost-efficient.[3]

OPEN DESIGN IS PART OF A SHIFT FROM 'WOW DESIGN' TO 'WE DESIGN'.

Even if there are many developments that run parallel in developed and developing countries, there are also vast differences. Developing countries urgently need affordable, yet sustainable solutions using easy-access resources. Initiatives like the non-profit International Development Enterprises[4] in Nepal allow the local farmers to tap into global information without having to spend their limited resources on personal equipment. The cooperatives share phones so that they can check market prices and avoid being taken advantage of in negotiations. SOCIAL DESIGN Combining local trust networks and striving for sustainability calls for other, better solutions than poor copies of the systems in the developed world. It also tackles one of the pitfalls that growing economies need to navigate: the risk of spending a disproportionate percentage of increased national revenues on technology instead of health and education. Systems like free text messaging, reliable communication networks and easy-to-build recharging systems become crucial.

The same logic was used in the development of the Open Source Washing Machine[5] using solar power, loudspeakers or bicycle tires. The design work started from the available materials and actual needs of the local communities. This approach to design would make it possible for developing countries to become frontrunners in smart recycling.

Smarter Crowds

The greatest potential in open design lies in building from incentives. According to Michel Bauwens, open and peer-to-peer processes have a built-in drive to seek the most sustainable solution.[6] When the entire process is a negotiation of the common good, there will be an automatic push to search for a solution that can be applied to various situations. As people twist and turn the matter, analysing it from many different angles, the true nature of the problem becomes clearer. A crowd of people will always be able to subject a problem to more thorough scrutiny than an army of corporate anthropologists.

In a climate of adaptation and rapid prototyping, PRINTING we can test the functionality of various alternatives in a faster pace. This reduces the risk of betting everything on the wrong horse, as is often done in the traditional process. Open design is part of a shift from 'wow design' to 'we design'. Making that shift, however, requires broader access to places of experimentation and learning like Fab Labs.

The new dividing line is the underlying motives of the people involved: whether things are done for benefit (altruistic motives) or for profit (selfish motives). Legislation and education play a key role in the ongoing change. As Michel Bauwens has pointed out, true for-benefit design leaves room for new people.[7] New people notice undiscovered errors and contribute new resources and new ideas. A good example of design for benefit is Whirlwind,[8] which has in the last 30 years provided thousands and thousands of wheelchairs to developing countries. Product development collaboration CO-CREATION between developing and developed countries has guaranteed that the chairs can handle the rough circumstances. The drawings are protected by a Creative Commons license. The biggest success is the RoughRider wheelchair, produced by local manufacturers and already used by 25,000 disabled people in developing countries.

By pooling knowledge and resources, individuals can actually turn the supply chain around. Inspiring examples can be found in the field of architecture. Take Loppukiri,[9] a home for the elderly in Helsinki,

DESIGN AGENCIES FUNCTIONING AS A COOPERATIVE OR A SOCIAL ENTERPRISE

	STRONG COMMUNITY	DESIGN PROCESS	PRODUCTION AND DISTRIBUTION
GOAL	IDENTIFY PROBLEMS AND SKILLS, CREATE URGENCY	BRING CONCERNS, IDEAS AND RESOURCES TOGETHER, TEST AND CREATE SOLUTIONS	SHARE THE GOOD
REQUIREMENTS	TRUST, FREEDOM, EDUCATION, GOOD PUBLIC SPACE	TOOLS, RESOURCES, KNOWLEDGE AND PEOPLE, ENTHUSIASM	BRANDING, COMMUNICATION, STRONG COMMUNITY
SUSTAINABILITY	INCENTIVE TO SHARE AND POOL RESOURCES IS HIGHER	CREATIVE SEARCH FOR MATERIALS AND IDEAS	PEER-TO-PEER DISTRIBUTION NETWORKS, LOCAL PRINTING
ROLE OF GOVERNMENT	INVESTMENTS IN EQUALITY (EDUCATION, LITERATURE, PUBLIC SPACE, ETC.)	NOTIONS OF SUSTAINABILITY AND COMMUNITY IN DESIGN EDUCATION	TRANSPORT, INFRASTRUCTURE, LEGISLATION
ROLE OF DESIGNERS	LISTEN, FACILITATE	TRAIN, PACKAGE, TRANSLATE	SHARE
RESULT	IDENTIFIED AND PRIORITIZED CONCERNS	SOLUTIONS, EMOTIONAL BONDS	TOOLS FOR BETTER LIVING, STRONG, RESILIENT COMMUNITY

194

Finland. Disappointed by the options for assisted living currently on the market, a group of pensioners pooled their funds and selected an architect to work with them on building residential facilities that would meet their specific needs. The Loppukiri cooperative did not limit their design process to their physical surroundings; they also designed structured activities and living arrangements in consultation with numerous professionals. The people in this community split domestic chores, cook lunch for each other and eat together. All in all, they have efficiently solved one of the greatest challenges of aging: loneliness and social isolation. The co-designed architecture of the building supports this community-based ethos and the members are keen to share their lessons with others.

As the example demonstrates, crowds do not make the professional irrelevant. The same approach could be adapted to other groups with special needs. The role of the designer would increasingly shift toward the roles of a trainer, translator and integrator. In order to tap into available resources and the in-depth knowledge held by the group, the designer needs to adapt to their needs and desires. Pooling a number of designers to tackle a bigger community challenge might be a way to win the trust of a new client. In a world where the crowds control the resources, the need for value-driven design grows. This clearly represents a potential growth market for design agencies functioning as a cooperative or a social enterprise.

Time Is Money

Open design requires a re-evaluation of the concept of time. People are willing to contribute more time to shared initiatives when they have a sense of the common good. True happiness comes from feeling needed, valuable, wanted, confident and competent. Open design at its best allows people with skills, experience, knowledge and enthusiasm to contribute their time and energy to building something together – and the desire is there. The recent economic turmoil and an increasingly well-educated population also add potential momentum OPEN EVERYTHING to the open design movement.

Super-diversity makes it all the more difficult to apply clear distinctions between experts and amateurs.

The strategy towards inclusion and trust often acts outside the global monetary world. It means valuing people's contributions based on the assumption that every individual can have equal value. This is where innovations such as time banks[10], the Design Quotient proposed by design agency IDEO, and hyperlocal currencies[11] come in. When people earn credits by participating in a design process, CROWDSOURCING we give a useful and important reminder that citizens have both the right and the responsibility to take part in shaping their world. Structured participation can accelerate the positive cycle; for instance, each person' contributions could be tracked in the form of hourly credits, which could then be traded for help from someone else. Systems that foster healthy co-dependency, such as time banks, remind us that everyone has something valuable to share: social skills, technical excellence, catering for a session, or translation. Tools like the School of Everything[12] – local social media for bringing people together to learn from each other – make it possible to provide a clearer impression of what a community actually can do.

Open design towards sustainable local happiness seems to take a major time investment. Luckily, time is something we have in abundance. The age of 'useless people' looks very different in different parts of the world. In Central Africa and the Middle East, the number of young people clearly outnumbers the number of elderly people; in sharp contrast, Japan has nearly five pensioners to every young person. Although many people from both groups will remain in or enter the labour market, the number of people who have nothing meaningful to do is still growing. Whether this time is directed into private endeavours or put to use for the common good is crucial to the well-being of our communities, as well as for the global resource potential. This means serious rethinking, especially in cultures where individual value has been closely linked to gainful employment.

Design for Better Living

Participation in the process is also a strong driver for sustainability. Taking part in the creative process associates the final result more strongly with an experience. Recent studies have shown without a doubt that product consumption has a lower impact on personal happiness than experiences. The sense of ownership generated by participation creates a

195

MAP OF FREE TIME ZONES IN 2050

The age of 'useless people', the young (15-24 years old) and the elderly
(older than 65), looks very different in different parts of the world. In
Central Africa and the Middle East, the number of young people clearly
outnumbers the number of elderly people; in sharp contrast, Japan has nearly
five pensioners to every young person.

196

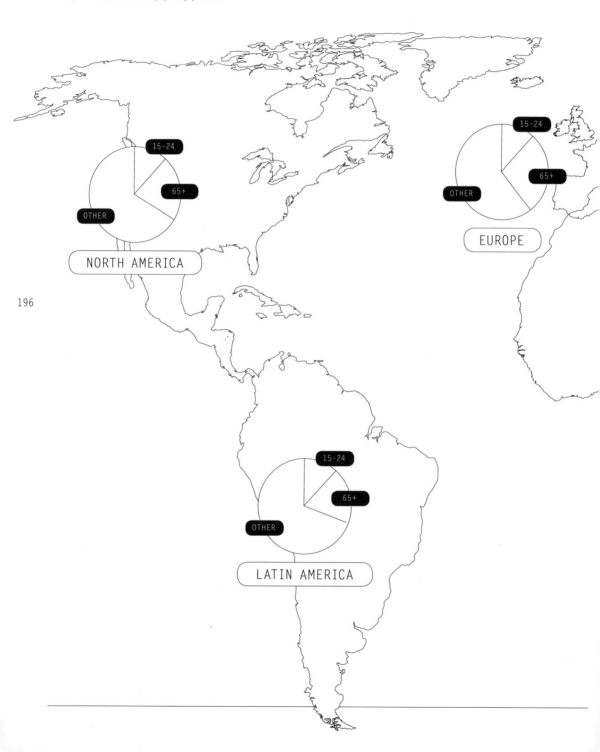

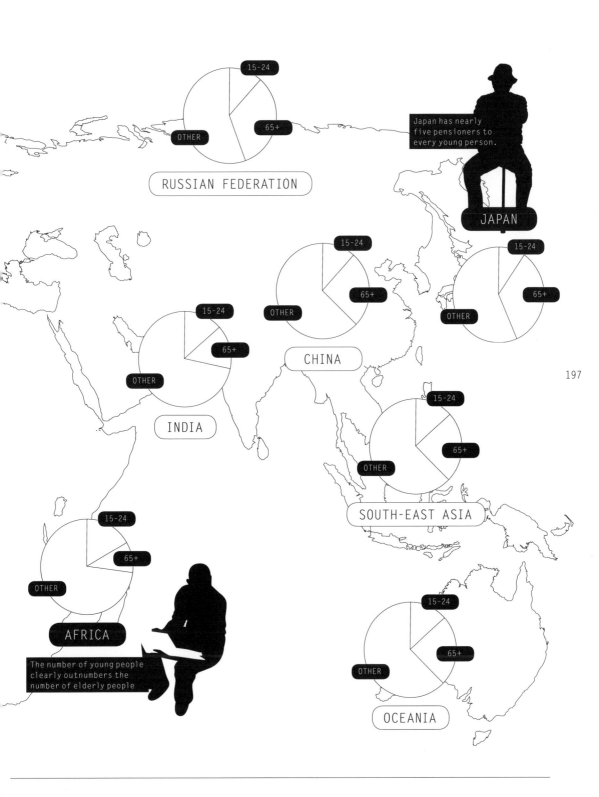

RUSSIAN FEDERATION

15-24
65+
OTHER

Japan has nearly five pensioners to every young person.

JAPAN

CHINA

15-24
65+
OTHER

INDIA

15-24
65+
OTHER

SOUTH-EAST ASIA

15-24
65+
OTHER

AFRICA

15-24
65+
OTHER

The number of young people clearly outnumbers the number of elderly people

OCEANIA

15-24
65+
OTHER

197

stronger emotional bond, both between the object and its owner, and between the object and the people in the owner's network. Objects with an experiential dimension transform into tangible memories, whereas pure objects are subject to material degradation and devaluation. In addition, if we assume shared ownership of the solution as well as the end product, we need more people to be involved in deciding how to handle disposal.

Design stemming from a desire to serve the common good is really about giving people tools to live fuller and better lives and creating objects with a longer shelf life. Inspiring examples of the potential already exist. For instance, Open Source Ecology[13] is a project of strengthening self-sufficiency in food production. Sharing the instructions on how to turn a Toyota Corolla into an eCorolla[14] allows people to improve something they already own. REMIX The Open Prosthetics Project[15] shares the peer-to-peer learning curve with all the physically disabled people of the world. The Factor e Farm in Missouri[16] explores ways to create an off-grid community relying on scrap metal and labour. By putting the results out in the open for everyone to see and adapt for their own use, communities of people can learn from each other. Through copying, prototyping, improving and formatting, the common good can grow. Motives are crucial here: if a person's intrinsic motives for participating are about solving problems in their own community, the right strategy for growth is sharing the methods openly.

It is difficult to say whether open design leads to better services and products. What it certainly does accomplish is building stronger communities. COMMUNITY It allows people to get to know the people around them while doing something meaningful. It builds bonds and healthy, reciprocal dependencies as people exchange services, equipment and time. As people join in, design is rooted in the DNA of their lives and they keep the end products longer. Open design also builds support for peer-to-peer politics.

Open design is a crucial tool for discovering 'Us' again. When successful, it challenges the traditional preconceptions about knowledge, professionalism and democracy. Open design shakes up the current balance of power. It will therefore not come as a

surprise that many of the remarks warning against the purported dangers of open design – lower quality, poorer aesthetics, more junk, things that will not work – express the same complaints echoed in every democratization process in history, all the way back to the French Revolution.

The right question to ask is not which process will lead to the best design. The fundamental question is far simpler: what is right and just?

NOTES

1   Chapman, J. *Emotionally Durable Design: Objects, Experiences and Empathy*. Earthscan Ltd, 2005.

2   http://wwf.panda.org/about_our_earth/all_publications/living_planet_report/, accessed on 16 January, 2011.

3   Wilkinson, R and Pickett, K, *The Spirit Level: Why More Equal Societies Almost Always Do Better*. Allen Lane, 2009.

4   www.ideorg.org

5   www.oswash.org

6   Michel Bauwens, TEDxBrussels, 2009. Video available online at www.youtube.com/watch?v=DGjQSki0uyg, accessed 29 November 2010.

7   Bauwens, M, ' To the Finland Station'. Available online at http://p2pfoundation.net/To_the_Finland_Station, accessed 29 November 2010.

8   www.whirlwindwheelchair.org

9   www.loppukiri.fi

10 www.timebank.org.uk

11 As used on the Dutch island of Texel, for example.

12 http://schoolofeverything.com

13 http://openfarmtech.org

14 http://ecars-now.wikidot.com/cars:electric-toyota-corolla:c-guide, accessed on 16 January, 2011.

15 www.openprosthetics.org

16 http://openfarmtech.org/wiki/Factor_e_Farm, accessed on 16 January, 2011

RECYCLED ADVERTISEMENT

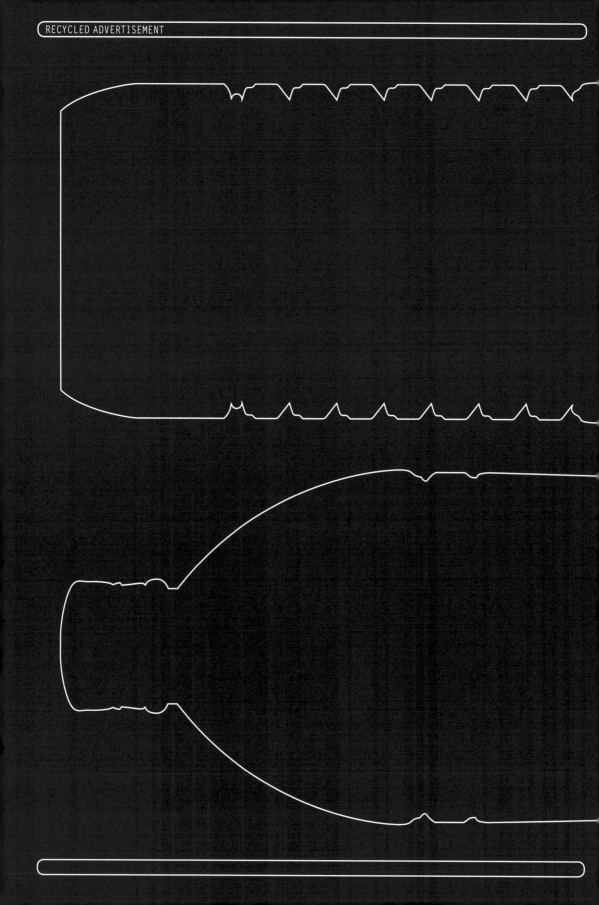

DIY = GOOD.
DIWAMS =
BETTER. Do it With
Already
Made Stuff

CRITICAL
MAKING

MATT
RATTO

Open design can be employed to develop a critical perspective on the current institutions, practices and norms of society, and to reconnect materiality and morality. Matt Ratto introduces 'critical making' as processes of material and conceptual exploration and creation of novel understandings by the makers themselves, and he illustrates these processes with examples from teaching and research.

Matt Ratto is an assistant professor and the director of the Critical Making Lab in the Faculty of Information at the University of Toronto, Canada, where he studies hands-on productive work as a reflective activity. According to Matt, "open design is a shorthand term for a shift in the institutions, practices and tools of design, a shift that is indicative of a re-democratization of making as a key human activity. The main value of open design is not just that more people are able to be engaged in constructive material activity, but that by being thus engaged, the wider population potentially develops critical material literacies that encourage greater insight into the social and environmental values of built objects."

www.criticalmaking.com

As noted by other authors in this collection, open design practices, communities, and technologies signal shifting relations in the world of design – between experts and novices, between proprietary and open access to information, and between producers and consumers of media and technologies – to name just a few. TREND: NETWORK SOCIETY

In addition to these more obvious shifts, open design also encourages an increasingly critical perspective on the current institutions, practices and norms of technologically mediated society. Open design, particularly in regards to digital hardware and software heralds new possibilities for artists, scholars and interested citizens to engage more fully in a simultaneously conceptual and material critique of technologies and information systems in society. Rather than just bemoaning the restrictions placed on users by institutionalized technological systems, engaged makers have the increasing ability and opportunity to constitute and construct alternatives. Such alternatives do not always replace the existing systems, nor are they often intended to. Instead, these material interventions provide insubstantiations of how the relationship between society and technology might be otherwise constructed. Again, this is particularly true for complex hardware and software solutions OPEN EVERYTHING that have traditionally been seen to require proprietary and closed development in order to ensure success.

Commons-based Peer Production

For example, the many open hardware and software cell phone projects, such as the tuxPhone project started in 2005, provided conceptual and material guidance for the increasingly open development of cell phone operating systems and applications. If nothing else, such projects demonstrated the institutional and legal hindrances to such open developments, revealing that the problems in creating open alternatives were not just technical in character. WYS ≠ WYG While the technical processes and results of projects like tuxPhone provided various kinds of guidance as to future handheld projects and the availability of open hardware alternatives, another important result of this project involved increasing the visibility of the institutional, organizational and legal arrangements that linked cell phone hardware and handset manufacturers to the telephony service providers – arrangements that made opening up the application and operating system development environments tricky at best. In point of fact, it ultimately took market leaders with a lot of pull – Apple and Google – to begin to untie the closely coupled linkages between cell phone applications, operating systems, hardware, and service agreements, and, in doing so, provide transformative competition in the cell phone market. ARCHITECTURE Both Apple and Google have done so in very different ways and for their own ends. However, Apple and Google's process and the technical and social choices that they have made are differently open and understood differently by those designers and makers who followed the open cell phone projects, compared to those who did not experience the open cell phone developments as they unfolded.

OPEN DESIGN HERALDS NEW POSSIBILITIES FOR ARTISTS, SCHOLARS AND INTERESTED CITIZENS TO ENGAGE IN A SIMULTANEOUSLY CONCEPTUAL AND MATERIAL CRITIQUE OF TECHNOLOGIES AND INFORMATION SYSTEMS IN SOCIETY.

Yochai Benkler, writing about open source and open content development initiatives, has described these communities and practices as 'commons-based peer production'[1] – a somewhat more inclusive term than the narrower 'user-generated content' that is currently in vogue. DOWNLOADABLE DESIGN One claim he makes is that these practices can result in different products and services than those currently produced through proprietary market forces. For Benkler, commons-based peer production can result in more than just open but substantively similar products and services. Instead, these practices can produce entirely novel results – and more importantly, they can serve audiences and needs that are under-addressed by the marketplace.

The above example demonstrates that open design potentially provides more than just another way of designing and creating novel products and services. Instead, and I repeat the word 'potentially' here, open design, when embedded in practices of socio-technical reflection and critique, provides the possibility for truly innovative thinking and making, the result of which is not just more of the same, but includes novel and more comprehensive understandings as to the relationships between social life and technical work. In our own scholarship and teaching, we call such potentials 'critical making'.

Critical Making

The term 'critical making' is intended to highlight the interwoven material and conceptual work that making involves. As a teaching and research strategy, critical making shares an emphasis on 'values' with both critical design and other critical practices – such as the critical technical practice[2] from which it derives, as well as value-sensitive design[3] and values-in-design.[4] I take the exploration of values in society and their implementation and concretization within technical artefacts as my starting point, choosing to explore these through a series of processes that attempt to connect humanistic practices of conceptual and scholarly exploration to design methodologies including storyboarding, brainstorming and bodystorming, and prototyping.

I call this work 'critical making' in order to highlight the reconnection of two modes of engagement with the world that are typically held separate: critical thinking, traditionally understood as conceptually and linguistically based, and physical 'making', goal-based material work. I see this as a necessary integration for a variety of reasons: first, as a way of overcoming the 'brittle' and overly structural sense of technologies that often exists in critical social science literature; second, as a way of creating shared experiences with technologies that provide joint resources for transforming the socio-technical imagination; and third, as a site for overcoming problematic disciplinary divides within technoscience.

While similar in practice to critical design and the other perspectives listed above, critical making has somewhat adjacent goals. As defined by Tony Dunne:

> Critical design is related to haute couture, concept cars, design propaganda, and visions of the future, but its purpose is not to present the dreams of industry, attract new business, anticipate new trends or test the market. Its purpose is to stimulate discussion and debate amongst designers, industry and the public about the aesthetic quality of our electronically mediated existence.[5]

Critical making, on the other hand, is less about the aesthetics AESTHETICS: 2D and politics of design work, and focuses instead on making practices themselves as processes of material and conceptual exploration. The ultimate goal of critical making experiences is not the evocative or pedagogical object intended to be experienced by others, but rather the creation of novel understandings by the makers themselves. Neither objects nor services are the currency of critical making. For me, it is the making experience that must be shared. Therefore, critical making is dependent on open design technologies and processes that allow the distribution and sharing of technical work and its results. BLUEPRINTS In this way, critical making relies on a constructionist[6] methodology that emphasizes the materiality of knowledge making and sharing. The 'objects' of critical making are intended to be shared making experiences, curated through both material and textual instructions. Such curated 'making experiences' have long been the domain of technical and scientific education; any toy store can provide myriad examples, and electronic 'kits' are currently experiencing a renewed enthusiasm. DIY What differentiates critical making is its attention to the interwoven social and technical aspects of modern life – what theorists call the socio-technical[7] – rather than being primarily about technical expertise or functional knowledge about the natural world.

These are fine-edged distinctions and might cause some readers to wonder why it is necessary to define yet another term for yet another design-based methodology. In point of fact, much of the ongoing scholarly and technical work associated with critical making was initiated by discomfort around the

205

dissonance of the term – why in fact does 'critical thinking' seem such a common-sense term, while 'critical making' seems odd to most of us? I believe this stems from a continuing separation in Western society between 'thinking', which is understood as happening primarily in the mind or at most through the mediation of language, and 'making', which is understood as an a-conceptual, a-linguistic, and habitual form of interaction with the world.

Makers – and that involves most of us in one way or another – understand the fallacy of this position. The phrase 'critical making' is therefore intended to signal a deep research commitment to the co-constructed nature of our socio-technical world.

Critical Making Lab and Method

The Critical Making Lab at the University of Toronto is sponsored by the Faculty of Information, and by the Canada Foundation for Innovation and the Social Sciences and Humanities Research Council. It was established as a research, teaching and infrastructure project. Our main focus is the material semiotics of digital information.[8] AESTHETICS: 3D In the lab, we explore how addressing information as both symbolic and material object reveals intriguing connections and contradictions in the role of information in individual, cultural and institutional practice. We work to unpack the complexity of information through critical making experiences that link conceptual and physical exploration. These experiences may be curated for pedagogical or for research purposes, but each tends to consist of the following interactive and non-linear steps: a comprehensive review of existing scholarly literature on a socio-technical topic; the development of a metaphorically connected making experience, typically using the 'kit' form; the definition of instructions to assist participants in making a technical artefact as well as following a conceptual argument; holding a workshop with stakeholders using the kit and instructions; recording and analysing the results.

Critical Making Teaching

The first critical making course was held at the Faculty of Information in 2008. In the winter of this year, we taught a master's level course that used making to explore critical information issues such as intellectual property, privacy, questions of embodiment, and

so forth. In this course, we made use of the Arduino software and hardware development environment due to its open source nature and its active and supportive artist and designer communities. We explicitly chose to use a physical computing platform rather than a mainly software-based development for two initial reasons. First, the material, hands-on nature of the Arduino called attention to the physicality of information, an important aspect of our teaching and research goals. When working in the primarily textual world of software development, it is less obvious that material work is going on. The Arduino makes such work part of the development process, and the 'push-back' of the physical electronics – the resistance of reality to our attempts to contain it – is therefore more present. Second, the movement to the material world often seems to be accompanied by a less functionalist, more emotional and embodied reaction to the topics under construction/discussion. Together, the 'push-back' of the material and the embodied and affectual nature of students' responses to it can engender a more invested and involved participant. These aspects of 'constructionist' pedagogy have been previously noted by science and mathematics educators.[9]

However, a third reason to use more material forms of development emerged during initial experiences. The 'making material' of digital interactions and experiences soon turned out to be an evocative strategy for unpacking the social and technical dimensions of information technologies. For example, one assignment given to the students was to build a 'physical rights management' (PRM) system, a digital system that managed physical objects in similar ways to how digital rights management systems manage digital resources. We had initially devised this assignment simply as a way of 'de-normalizing' DRM practices by changing their context and making them unfamiliar – a sort of surrealist move of de-familiarization. The students took us at our word, looked closely at how DRM systems controlled digital resources and created often dramatic analogues (literally) of such control mechanisms.

For instance, one group of students built a model of a photocopy machine that used RFID cards to set permissions on the physical copying of books and journals. If these permissions were not followed, the

206

system would automatically send a message to the appropriate (imaginary) authorities and display a message to the photocopy machine user to stay where they were until the police arrived. In the following year, students constructed an alternative PRM system, one that placed the control mechanism in the book itself. In this version, the books used a light sensor to detect when they were being photo-copied. If permissions on copying were breached, the book would 'self-destruct' by popping a balloon containing ink. GRASSROOTS INVENTION

THE ULTIMATE GOAL OF CRITICAL MAKING EXPERIENCES IS NOT THE EVOCATIVE OR PEDAGOGICAL OBJECT INTENDED TO BE EXPERIENCED BY OTHERS, BUT RATHER THE CREATION OF NOVEL UNDERSTANDINGS BY THE MAKERS THEMSELVES.

The absurdity of these modes of control was not lost on the students, who explicitly designed and built their systems based on an analysis of equally absurd methods that they had picked out from existing DRM systems. KNOWLEDGE Following this assignment, students remarked that previously they had understood in an abstract way how DRM influenced the use and creation of media. However, by constructing their own PRM system and having to make decisions about how it might function, they not only felt that they increased their knowledge, but they also became more invested and in a sense responsible for the adoption and use of DRM. In previous work on critical making, we have called this the movement from 'caring about' an issue to 'caring for' an issue.[10]

The course has since been taught in 2009 and will be taught again in 2010. However, teaching a course which is simultaneously technical, social, conceptual

and material is not an easy task, particularly when that course is located within a social sciences faculty rather than one of design or engineering. Such faculties are not set up to handle simple requirements such as sinks in classrooms, or ventilation for soldering irons. The material nature of critical making as pedagogy is demonstrative of why such methods are not more integrated outside of traditional disciplines. However, open design tools and processes provide some of the infrastructure necessary to do this work.

Critical Making Research
In addition to the pedagogical goals outlined above, we are also engaged in critical making as a research strategy. This typically involves curating critical making experiences in order to engender insight and perspective on socio-technical phenomena for stakeholders and other participants. Here we draw upon ethnographically informed research methodologies such as action research[11] and more explicitly on the methods and perspectives associated with cultural probes.[12] Past research that we have undertaken using critical making has addressed the role of materiality in social research[13] and current projects address the socio-technical implications of bio-sensors and the labour and organizational dimensions of digital desktop fabrication. As in the teaching strategies described above, open design tools and processes are essential to the development of critical making as research.

Conclusion and Future Work
Critical making is an intensely trans-disciplinary process, one that requires research skills from humanities and social science disciplines and a familiarity with a wide range of scholarly literatures. At the same time, critical making requires some technical expertise on the part of the researcher, who must curate a technical experience for participants with little or no technical background. AMATEURISSIMO

As a teaching and a research method, critical making is thus dependent on open design methods, tools and communities. To put it most simply, the expertise necessary to create prototypes and engage in processes of software and hardware construction must be open and available in order to allow for the kinds of critically engaged practices described above. Note that this is not about replacing or

207

reproducing designers or design expertise. 'Critical makers' (understood broadly) emerge from a variety of disciplinary contexts and only some of them are interested or engaged in the kinds of tasks associated with design.

Equally, critical making requires institutional resources such as space, equipment and access to expertise that is not typical of the humanities or social sciences. We have been lucky to be located in a supportive faculty, university and funding context that is interested in methodological innovation and in trans-disciplinary research. However, problems still arise, with critical making being seen as either too technical for humanities and social science researchers and students, or, on the other hand, as not being technical enough for the development of novel technological skills and products. Open design methods and tools provide some guidance and support in this regard, but more work is necessary to establish making as an intrinsic part of social research.

Ultimately, we see the integration of socio-technical critique and material making as a necessary part of what Latour has called the development of a 'cautious Prometheus'.[14] In his keynote address to the Design History Society, Latour lays out a model for acknowledging the interconnectedness of semiotic and material life. He also details design's role in helping us move from considering material things as given, natural and uncontested objects, e.g. 'matters of fact', to thinking of them as being intrinsically political, contentious and open to discussion and debate. He also acknowledges the necessity of this transition for political and ecological reasons, but notes that this move is far from over. Latour raises the issue:

> How can we draw together matters of concern so as to offer to political disputes an overview, or at least a view, of the difficulties that will entangle us every time we must modify the practical details of our material existence?[15]

Open design is a necessary part of this development, but not just because it democratizes or 'opens' design to the masses. Rather than replacing professional design expertise and skill, our sense is that by encouraging and supporting design methodologies

for non-traditional design ends – such as the socio-technical critique that is the main goal of critical making – open design helps bring about a kind of socio-technical literacy that is necessary to reconnect materiality and morality. This, ultimately, may be the most important consequence of open design.

NOTES

1 Benkler, Y. 'Freedom in the Commons: Towards a Political Economy of Information', *Duke Law Journal*, 52(6), 2003, p. 1245-1277.

2 Agre, P. 'Toward a Critical Technical Practice: Lessons Learned in Trying to Reform AI', in Bowker, G, Gasser, L, Star, L and Turner, B, eds, *Bridging the Great Divide: Social Science, Technical Systems, and Cooperative Work*. Erlbaum, 1997. Dourish, P, Finlay, J, Sengers, P, & Wright, P, 'Reflective HCI: Towards a critical technical practice', in *CHI'04 extended abstracts on Human factors in computing systems*, 2004, p. 1727-1728.

3 Friedman, B. 'Value-sensitive design', *interactions*, 3(6), p.16-23. DOI:10.1145/242485.242493.

4 Flanagan, M, Howe, D, & Nissenbaum, H, *Embodying Values in Technology: Theory and Practice*. 2005 (draft).

5 Dunne, A, & Raby, F, *Design Noir: The Secret Life of Electronic Objects*. Birkhäuser Basel, 2001.

6 Papert, S. *Mindstorms: Children, Computers, and Powerful Ideas* (2nd ed.). Basic Books, 1993.

7 Law, J. *After method: mess in social science research*. Routledge, 2004.

8 Haraway, D. Simians, *Cyborgs, and Women: The Reinvention of Nature* (1st ed.). Routledge, 1990. Hayles, N, 'The Materiality of Informatics', *Configurations*, 1(1), 1993, p. 147-170. Hayles, N, *How we became posthuman: virtual bodies in cybernetics, literature, and informatics*. University of Chicago Press, 1999. Kirschenbaum, M, Mechanisms: *New Media and the Forensic Imagination*. The MIT Press, 2008.

9 Lamberty, K. 'Designing, playing, and learning: sustaining student engagement with a constructionist design tool for craft and math', in *Proceedings of the 6th international conference on Learning sciences*, 2004, p. 652. Lamberty, K. 'Creating mathematical artifacts: extending children's engagement with math beyond the classroom', in Proceedings of the 7th international conference on Interaction design and children, 2008 p. 226-233.

10 Ratto, M. 'Critical Making: conceptual and material studies in technology and social life', paper for Hybrid Design Practice workshop, Ubicomp 2009, Orlando, Florida.

11 Lewin, K. 'Action research and minority problems', *J Soc.*

Issues 2(4), 1946, p. 34-46. *Argyris, C, Putnam, R, & Smith, D,*
Action Science: Concepts, methods and skills for research and
intervention. San Francisco: Jossey-Bass, 1985.

12 Gaver, B, Dunne, T, & Pacenti, E, 'Design: Cultural probes',
    interactions, 6(1), p. 21-29. DOI:10.1145/291224.291235.

13 Ratto, M, Hockema, S, 'Flwr Pwr: Tending the Walled Garden', in
    Dekker, A & Wolfsberger A (eds) *Walled Garden*, Virtueel Platform,
    The Netherlands, 2009.Ratto, op.cit.

14 Latour, B, 'A Cautious Prometheus? A Few Steps toward a Philosophy
    of Design', Keynote lecture for the Networks of Design* meeting
    of the Design History Society, Falmouth, Cornwall, 3rd September
    2008.

15 Idem (p.12).

GLOCALIZED ADVERTISEMENT

Your local flavor.

WikiCoke

CASES

CO-WORKING
DESIGNING FOR COLLABORATIVE CONSUMPTION

MICHELLE THORNE

The 20th century was the unfortunate era of hyper-consumerism. You know the stats: basically, the world is ending, and we, the insatiable consumers of the world, are at fault. Traditionally, there are two solutions for what to do with all the junk we buy and collect. You can dispose of it, or you can store it. Yet both options bring their own set of troubles, be it overflowing landfills or premium rent on storage.

As Bruce Sterling says, every moment devoted to stumbling over and tending to your piled debris are precious hours in our mortal lives, and time not spent with family, friends, your community, yourself. The things you own end up owning you.[1] So, with all this doom and gloom, is there any reasonable way to take action? Can we even make ACTIVISM a difference? There is one clear advantage we have in our generation: the power of the network.

We can leverage our networks. Unlike any generation that came before, we can provide and share infrastructure better thanks to network technology. We can buy, build, and collaborate locally and efficiently. We can shop smarter, share better, and use our networks, both online and off, to reduce waste, improve the economy and environment, and spare our bank accounts, and even have a good time and make new friends doing it. COMMUNITY

That's Collaborative Consumption

Think about co-working spaces, for example. You can rent a desk and share office infrastructure together with fellow digital nomads. No one, besides the people who actually run the space, have to own any of the equipment, and even they can lease or rent it from other companies. A huge advantage of a co-working space is that it makes it easy and attractive to share these resources, and by doing so, they make it more efficient (and let's be honest, more fun and social) for all of the people working here.

Let's think about other types of resources. Who needs to actually own a moving van? Not many folks. That's why services like Robben & Wientjes, a moving truck rental company in Berlin, are successful. The same holds true for platforms like the US-based car sharing service Zipcar, or airbnb and Couchsurfing – or even the Bahn bikes, Mitfahrgelegenheit, and stuff-sharing sites like NeighborGoods.[2] All of the many, many sites out there now make it easy to offer, find, and share goods and services: flexibly, agilely, and socially. SHARE

Here's another example: the common household drill. Do you own a drill? If so, can you even remember the last time you used it? Did you know that on average, a household drill is used a total of just 5-10 min its entire lifetime? That gives you what, like 20 holes max? Is that really an efficient object to purchase, maintain, and care for? *What if instead of all that time it spent idling on the shelf, it could be generating value, either by renting it out for cash or just helping out a neighboUr?*

Products like household drills, or moving vans, or a bike in a city you're visiting aren't necessarily desirable to own. Instead, isn't it just better to access them? Aren't the rights to use and access more important than owning it? This is a mantra for our times, for the century of collaborative consumption: *Wealth as a whole consists in using things rather than in owning them.*[3]

Design Challenges

Here are a few design challenges for collaborative consumption:

Create open layers. Think about interoperability across key components. How can you use open standards to enable remixing, modification, and improvements across products? REMIX How can open layers be applied to motors, power cords, outlets, connectors, joints, nibs for maximal customization and range of use?

Build modularity. Similarly, shared objects should be easy to repair REPAIR and modify. You shouldn't have to throw away your entire phone because it's scratched. Building modularity means fostering generativity.

Value added through usage. I think this is one of the most powerful design challenges. Think about an object that doesn't depreciate with use, but is instead improved by it. One example is a baseball mitt. When

214

you first buy it, it's very stiff and hard to catch a ball with. Over time, with use, it becomes more flexible and a better product. That's just on the physical layer. What about value added on a data layer? Think about how objects can learn from behaviours the more they're used. Like by collecting more data points. Or where the user contributes metadata, like marginalia, reviews, and fact-checking for books.

Personalize shared objects. Are you familiar with these phones that hold multiple SIM cards? Those are really common in places like Africa where one device is used by multiple people. Each person inserts their own SIM card and all their address books and personal settings are ready for them. The personalization follows the user, not the device. Can we apply this to other devices and services? Cars, printers, refrigerator, coffee machines, or even drills?

Diversify libraries. Libraries are not just for books. Think about other ways to pool resources, be it for commercial or community aims. You could have libraries of tools, or libraries of electronics, cooking appliances, moving boxes, jewellery and accessories, holiday decorations, toys, you name it. BLUEPRINTS It has huge potential. There are many business opportunities here, as well as many challenges to be solved by creative and adventurous people.

Let's break the mould. Don't design for the dump. RECYCLING Don't design for 20th-century hyperconsumption. Design for things to last, to be shared, and to be part of the future: a future of collaborative consumption.

→ HTTP://COWORKING.COM

NOTES

1   *Fight Club.* Dir. David Fincher. Perf. Brad Pitt. Fox 2000 Pictures. 1999.

2   Botsman, R and Rogers, R. *What's Mine is Yours: The Rise of Collaborative Consumption.* Harper Business: New York, 2010.

3   Aristotle, *Rhetoric.* Book I, Chapter 5, 1361a, trans. W. Rhys Roberts. Princeton University Press: Princeton 1984, available online http://www2.iastate.edu/~honeyl/Rhetoric/rhet1-5.html, accessed 14 January 2010.

DESIGNSMASH
AN OPEN DESIGN BUSINESS MODEL

ENLAI HOOI

It is still somehow an unusual thought that open design might be considered a viable, possibly even beneficial, strategy for business. The product design industry has been slow to move on the issue of open intellectual property, despite the fact that intellectual property is one of the safest fields for an open structure. While many people have the facility to copy software and download music, it is somewhat less common for people to have access to rapid manufacturing services, workshops, specific components and materials.

In truth, there should be no reason for preventing people with the resources to produce such objects from doing so. They tend to be the people most invested in how the processes of production relate to the quality of the object. They offer excellent and necessary critical feedback. DesignSmash is a company that produces and sells products based on Creative Commons CREATIVE COMMONS licences that allow the legal reproduction of designs. The feedback and design changes offered by the community of people invested in our open design project are an essential part of our business plan. Regular events EVENTS take place where designers come together in a collaborative design session, a charette, and 'smash out' products in the middle of a party. The products are laser-cut on the spot and presented to the audience at the end of the night.

While the design objects are not always fully refined after the four-hour design charette, the value of the object becomes clear. Importantly, the release of the design file over the internet allows other designers to comment on and modify the work of the original designer. The development process is user-driven. The potential revenue lost by DIY DIY is negligible compared to the benefits of the feedback and promotion received from allowing others to get involved in the design work. For a start-up company with limited resources, this interaction is essential.

The events offer the designer exposure and the chance to learn, produce, collaborate and dance within the

215

space of an evening. Some of these designs are picked up as products. If they are produced by DesignSmash, 12.5% of the product's profits go to the designer. This is significantly more than the industry standard; clearly, the designer will benefit from this arrangement. A further 12.5% of profits are reserved for future open design initiatives and open design education.

Customers decide whether or not to purchase a product based on an assessment of its value. When the cost of a product is below a certain threshold, i.e. low enough to be purchased without interfering with the buyer's lifestyle, the values of the brand have significantly more influence on whether or not the customer buys the product. Open design, local manufacture, the designer's story: all these aspects accumulate as mutually beneficial factors in the value equation that accompanies the product. DesignSmash has a clear position on this matter: why not? Why not give the designer a greater portion of the profits? Why not allow people to learn from the objects being produced? Why not re-invest in the design community? Why not? It will certainly be good for business.

216 → HTTP://DESIGN-SMASH.COM

DIWAMS
DO IT WITH ALREADY MADE STUFF

PAULO HARTMANN

As the environmental crisis grows ever more urgent, an awareness of ecological values is spreading. Overtly eco-friendly trends run rampant in corporate communications and marketing, plastering buzzwords like 'sustainability' all over every conceivable campaign and industry. Despite the hype, the growing eco-consciousness is a truly interesting movement that deserves attention for its simplicity, as well as the reutilization processes it inspires. DIY is good, but DIWAMS – 'Do It With Already Made Stuff' – is infinitely better.

Some Brazilian co-design pioneers have been promoting DIWAMS methodology for quite some time. Augusto Cintrangulo is a good example.[1] His Volcano project creates toys, musical instruments and games from wear-resistant and long-lasting packaging, delaying its entry into the garbage cycle. RECYCLING In addition, this post-consumer packaging project includes workshops where children and adults learn how to build the products. Thanks to Augusto's innovative, well-designed building process, no glue or stamps are used in the assembly of most of the planes, animals, cars and toy figures.

After creating tons of toys and a fully developed methodology with this innovative process, Augusto has now created a new project, *Banco Sinuoso* (Winding Bench),[2] built from the unused pieces of MDF spares from furniture manufacturers that use FSC-certified wood. Banco Sinuoso recently won bronze at the Prêmio Senai-SP Excellence Design Awards, exhibiting at the Senai-SP Design Show 2010 hosted by FIESP, the São Paulo Federation of Industries, and Senai-SP, the São Paulo branch of the National Service for Industrial Training. Banco Sinuoso is a modular system that can be used in public spaces. The modules are made from FSC-certified wood and finished with a water-based varnish.[3]

Another Brazilian eco-designer who has successfully applied the DIWAMS concept is Eduardo Pereira de Carvalho, a businessman that built the flotation system for his boat from 2040 recycled RECYCLING PET bottles.[4] Both designers view the educational layer of their projects as an intrinsic and crucial aspect, and frequently give workshops and lectures in local communities.

It would seem that DIY DIY culture and open source are not the only trends that will guide the following Industrial Revolution. The DIWAMS concept, 'Do It With Already Made Stuff', REMIX deserves due consideration here as well. DIWAMS design not only adds new recyclable material – which is a basic principle these days, almost mandatory – but also emphasizes re-using what is already there.

NOTES

1   www.volcano.tk, http://volcanoecodesign.vilabol.uol.com.br

2   www.designenatureza.com.br/catalogo09

3   www.principemarcenaria.com.br/Produto.aspx?cod=4
     http://premiodesign.sp.senai.br/PDF/catalogo.pdf

4   www.projetomegapet.com.br/
     www.treehugger.com/files/2005/09/wip_eduardo_de.php

FAIRPHONE
ANSWERING THE CALL OF A GENERATION

JENS MIDDEL

Suppose you want to make people aware of grave human rights abuses in a faraway country. Suppose you also want to convince them to take action against those abuses. And suppose, finally, that you want to interest even groups who aren't particularly idealistic. How do you pull it off? FairPhone is an answer to this question – and open design plays a crucial role.

To create and promote the world's first fair mobile phone, together. One that can easily compete with today's best and most sharp-looking phones. This is FairPhone's SOCIAL DESIGN objective – or better said: it's the common goal of the people visiting this interactive online community. Here, men and women from all over the planet pool their design skills, KNOWLEDGE campaign ideas and social concerns. In the process of trying to make a fair mobile phone, participants eventually realize that they'll need certain key minerals for the phone's production – and that phone brands have so far refused to reveal where these minerals came from, or are clearly retrieving them from African mines where working conditions are deplorable. TREND: SCARCITY OF RESOURCES FairPhone will facilitate both the participants' search for better mines and their petition to phone brands to contract those better mines.

The Call for Interaction
The keyword in FairPhone is 'together'. It is, after all, a community of people participating in a co-creation CO-CREATION process. It is not a traditional process, though; there is no-one hovering over the contributors, deciding who responds to whom or who does what. The only top-down coordination on the project is that the initiative presents 'challenges': specific design and campaign problems for visitors to solve. Contributors can choose for themselves which ideas and designs they send in, and have permission to freely use other people's entries as building blocks – just as their ideas and designs in turn might form the basis of other, future contributions. FairPhone is interactive, co-creational, peer-to-peer CO-CREATION and open. According to its founders, this is exactly what makes the project so

217

attractive to so many people – even the ones who usually aren't interested in taking part in idealistic initiatives.

The Call for Freedom

The founders in question are: *Waag Society*, a foundation that develops creative technology for cultural innovation; *NiZA, an NGO,* that fights for equal rights and fair distribution of wealth; *Schrijf-Schrijf*, a company specializing in creative communication concepts and text products.

Their basic assumption is that men and women in today's society may be more individualistic than ever, but are nevertheless social and creative creatures at heart. People still want to belong; they just want to choose a community for themselves, be free to decide when or where to participate in it and make a unique, individual contribution to the group's goals. They also want their participation to be challenging: to let their interaction with others stimulate their own personal development.

The Call for Justice

218

FairPhone taps into this modern mentality: by creating an internet community `COMMUNITY` that people can enter and leave at will; by inviting and enabling each person to use their own creative talents in completing a collective project; and by posting design and campaign challenges online, inviting participants to comment and build on each other's ideas. FairPhone also appeals to idealists, because it follows consumers' growing call for corporate responsibility and transparent production lines. The project is not primarily about developing a prototype of the first fair mobile phone. Rather, it is about bringing people together, inspiring all telephone brands to 'go fair' and fighting injustice the most effective way possible: together, as a collective.

→ HTTP://FAIRPHONE.COM

FIFTY DOLLAR LEG PROSTHESIS
INTERCONTINENTAL COLLABORATION ON PROSTHETIC DESIGN

ALEX SCHAUB, DEANNA HERST, TOMMY 'IMOT' SURYA, IRENE 'IRA' AGRIVINA

If you plan to produce a $50 below-knee prosthesis for a developing country like Indonesia, where would you start? Is it even possible, considering that a below-knee prosthesis in the Western world costs $4,000? Waag Society's Fab Lab Amsterdam in the Netherlands and the House of Natural Fiber, a media and art laboratory in Yogyakarta, Indonesia are working on a collaborative project aimed at finding answers to these questions.

The House of Natural Fiber (HONF) has initiated a number of projects in the surrounding area, ranging from arts and design to education and public services. In line with its consistent focus on interactivity between people and environments, HONF selects and structures its projects based on the needs of local communities. `SOCIAL DESIGN` One of these projects includes research on production and fabrication processes in relation to such fields as robotics, open source, and scientists (e.g. microbiologists). One of the partner organizations that benefit from the support provided by HONF is Yakkum, a rehabilitation centre for disabled people. HONF has been collaborating with Yakkum for almost 9 years, working as a non-official mediator and facilitator through workshops in the field of arts and empowerment. The collaboration with Yakkum confronted HONF with its biggest challenge in the context of fabrication processes. Yakkum produces prosthetics and orthotics for people with physical disabilities, particularly in Yogyakarta and other urban areas in Indonesia. However, these medical aids are expensive to produce, and take far too much time; one prosthesis is finished every two weeks. The situation is particularly problematic since there are many patients who urgently need prostheses, and most of them come from poor families. The aim of the $50 prosthesis project was to enable Yakkum to provide prostheses for two people a day using Fab Lab technology.

The first step in this collaborative process took place in May 2009, when Fab Lab Amsterdam invited HONF to an introductory prosthetics workshop for an initial exchange of experiences between users and designers. CO-CREATION The workshop covered methods, techniques and materials and included expert input from Hugh Herr, director of the Biomechatronics Research Group at MIT, and Marcel Conradi, director of the De Hoogstraat Rehabilitation Centre in Utrecht. End-user evaluation was provided by Appie Rietveld, initiator of Korter maar Krachtig,[1] a Dutch support and advocacy group for people dealing with limb loss.

A second prosthetics workshop in January 2010 aimed to define design parameters for adjustability, to devise inexpensive, efficient methods for production, and to explore the use of local materials – using local bamboo instead of aluminium reduces production costs considerably. TREND: SCARCITY OF RESOURCES Some very useful insights emerged, such as the discovery that the patent of the 'pyramid adapter', a crucial part of the prosthesis, is expired, which allowed the collaborating partners to re-engineer it.

The next step was to test a first bamboo prototype and to make it adjustable. Most prosthesis users currently depend on orthopaedists for every minor adjustment of their prostheses, but that could theoretically be avoided. Many users do not realize that they already have a lot of first-hand knowledge about their own prosthesis, since they wear them 24/7; they are the experts on their own prosthetics use. Children generally need to have their prosthetic legs recalibrated by a doctor every six months. In Indonesia, this costs a lot of time and money. An adjustable leg would enable end users to adjust their prosthetic legs themselves by feeling and experiencing the fit, measuring the prosthesis and adapting it.

Walking on different surfaces also requires adaptation of the leg. The roll-off curve of a foot changes drastically when walking on different surfaces. The majority of prostheses on the market are designed for just one standard surface. An adjustable prosthesis would enable users to manage aspects like the roll-off curve, the angle of the foot or the height of the prosthesis themselves. In Indonesia, prosthesis alignment is mainly done manually. To facilitate the process, the collaboration team started to develop tools, such as a cheap alignment laser device and a portable 3D scanner. As DIY DIY kits, these tools could improve accuracy while remaining affordable and accessible. Besides using digital fabrication resources, the team embraced open innovation principles, drawing

knowledge from the expert users in Yakkum, the designers from HONF and Fab Lab Amsterdam, academic advisors such as Professor Bert Otten (Center for Human Movement Sciences, NeuroMechanics, University of Groningen) and specialized manufacturers like Kamer Orthopedie in Amsterdam. Input from all the parties will be used in the process of developing and designing the adjustable leg. The concrete results of the $50 prosthesis project so far also include key design insights. For instance, adjustability allows end users to take a crucial step toward independence, and the visual design of the prosthesis is important to end users. In addition, knowledge transfer during production is important for empowerment and self-reliance. In terms of production, the team gathered knowledge KNOWLEDGE on how to user thermoforming to produce quality limb sockets quickly.

The next steps will address specific, tangible end-user needs and preferences. What do users need in order to adjust the prosthesis effectively? How would they like the design to look and feel? The aim is to develop a process or method for design based on the parameters defined in consultation with 'expert users': adjustability, open innovation and digital fabrication. To this end, a Fab Lab will be set up in Yogyakarta with a special Prosthetics section. The collaborative team working on the $50 prosthesis project will not stop there. In the future, they plan to research options for using intelligent materials to enhance the experience and effectiveness for the end user. Another goal is to explore the use of embodied cognition. Professor Bert Otten expects the process of prosthetic design to be guided by the team's increased insight into the development of embodied cognition in amputees as they learn to walk with the leg prosthesis. Their improved sense of dynamic balance can be observed best from the way they move and how they intuitively adjust the prosthesis. No technical insight or expertise should be needed to adjust the prosthesis optimally, as long as the design is based on embodied cognition.

→ HTTP://BLOG.WAAG.ORG/?P=2454

NOTES

1   The name of this Dutch foundation translates as 'shorter but powerful'. http://www.kortermaarkrachtig.com

219

FORM FOLLOWS USER
PARTICIPATORY DESIGN, THE OPEN FORM AND ART EDUCATION

DEANNA HERST

Participatory design has changed the role of the designer: from an author of finished products, like books or furniture, into a developer of frameworks or structures of 'open works', like Wikipedia.

Where users have traditionally been guided by physical forms created by the designer (e.g. reading a book), in 'open works' they now share responsibility for the design (e.g. co-creating a chair), in a process directed by the designer. Within the context of participatory design, the concept of 'user follows form' appears to have been supplanted by the opposite approach: 'form follows user'. In this scenario, the designer creates a framework that encourages the user to complete the form or product. What are the ramifications of this role-shifting for art and design education?

The 'form follows user' paradigm represents a shift towards the classical (modernist) notion of artistic authorship, traditionally defined by the 'genius' of the artist/designer. DESIGNERS This perspective is especially relevant in art and design education, where authorship is legitimized from an artistic point of view and students are trained to become 'authors' by developing their individual aesthetics and signature. Within the context of participatory design, the challenge for art academies is to find and develop new ways to define the artistic signature in participatory authorship and to implement these methods within the educational program. Which areas need to be explored for graphic designers, product designers and other design professions?

From a functionalist point of view, a commonly applied property of participatory design is 'usabililty': 'a method for improving ease-of-use during the design process'.[1] Usability concerns user accessibility and implies a corresponding experience and equal resonance for every user. For art academies, however it is equally important, if not more important so, to also identify aesthetic parameters, complementing the functional properties of the designed object.

Within the context of new kinds of authorship, fields such as participatory aesthetics or creative strategies for involving users will need to be explored further. A starting point could be the exploration of the 'open form'. In *The Poetics of the Open Work*, Umberto Eco describes the artistic use of the open form as follows:

> The author offers ... the addressee a work to be completed. He does not know the exact fashion in which his work will be concluded, but he is aware that once completed the work in question will still be his own. ... At the end of the interpretative dialogue, a form which is his form will have been organized. [...] The author is the one who proposed a number of possibilities which had already been rationally organized, oriented, and endowed with specifications for proper development.[2]

This quote pinpoints the role and position of a designer in a participatory situation. For art and design students, the awareness of creative responsibility for the 'open form' is an essential point of departure: how do you design rules for the user? A possible next step could be the exploration of participatory strategies derived from other disciplines, for instance storytelling. Anthropologist Marilyn Strathern has identified an effective participatory strategy: 'In some Papua New Guinean traditions [...] people are told half a story, and have to find the other half from within themselves – or from someone else'.[3] This approach is comparable to the Surrealist model of the *cadavre equis*; both offer a structure that, by its form, triggers its users. In these examples, form follows user, but in the end it is the designer who issues the invitation.

NOTES

1   Nielsen, J, Ten Usability Heuristics. Available online at http://www.useit.com/papers/heuristic/heuristic_list.html, accessed on 19 October 2010.

2   Eco, U, The Poetics of the Open Work. Cambridge, Massachusetts, 1989.

3   Strathern, M, 'Imagined Collectivities and Multiple Authorship', in Ghosh, R (ed.) CODE: *Collaborative Ownership and the Digital Economy*. Cambridge, Massachusetts, MIT Press, 2005. E-book available online at http://mitpress-ebooks.mit.edu/product/code, accessed on 13 January 2011.

FRITZING
A COMMON LANGUAGE TO EXCHANGE IDEAS

ANDRÉ KNÖRIG, JONATHAN COHEN, RETO WETTACH

Fritzing is an open source project with the aim of supporting designers, artists and hobbyists (i.e. 'non-engineers') to work creatively with interactive electronics. As computer processing power moves away from the desktop and 'into the cloud', it becomes useful and important to ensure that this resource is made accessible to tinkerers all over the world.

Originally a research project, Fritzing is now actively used by more than 10,000 people to document their electronic prototypes, share them with others, teach electronics in the classroom, and create PCB layouts for professional manufacturing.

Fritzing's most important contribution to design is that it gives its practitioners a common, familiar 'language' in which to document and exchange their ideas. COMMUNITY At Fritzing, we call this the 'breadboard view'; it is simply an abstract, but clearly recognizable software version of the way many of our practitioners work in the real world: with a breadboard, chips, and wires. Because these images are easier to interpret than photographs, Fritzing sketches are now used on sites like Arduino.cc or Instructables.com – and in the project gallery at Fritzing.org. SHARE

Beyond facilitating the sharing of knowledge, a major goal of Fritzing is to enable production. In the case of electronics, this means designing and manufacturing printed circuit boards, a skill that has so far been reserved for professionals. Fritzing lets a beginner AMATEURISSIMO seamlessly translate a breadboard sketch into a PCB design (and schematic design, if needed), ready to be sent to a production house or made at home. Additionally, we are setting up our own fabrication service that will eventually make it possible for users to order designs created by other users.

Fritzing is almost as open as it gets, in every respect. The software itself is open source, uses open standards and file formats (SVG, XML), can be used within an ecology of other open tools (such as Arduino, Wiring and Inkscape), and offers open access through online learning materials (under CC licences). OPEN EVERYTHING

Building on this foundation, Fritzing encourages open sharing of knowledge, from basic electronics to complete documentation for completed projects. Openness is hardwired into the structure of Fritzing: there is a 'sharing' button in the software, and Fritzing include rich export options and an online project gallery. We are committing to bringing about a culture in which sharing is self-evident, simply because it is easy and useful for everybody.

In another context, we think of Fritzing as a tool for democratizing production. By putting the tools of the industry into the hands of the people, we hope to open up the discussion of our technological future. People should not take the outcomes of the industrial process for granted. Rather, they should participate critically in shaping our culture, by creating their own objects as alternatives.

→ HTTP://FRITZING.ORG

221

IDEO & OPENIDEO.COM
SOCIAL PROBLEM SOLVING
BY COLLABORATION

TOM HULME

Great innovation requires widespread collaboration. The strongest evidence of this correlation is the spike in innovation that occurred around the time of the Industrial Revolution, when people from diverse backgrounds began living and working together in cities for the first time. Solitary inventors could deliver amazing discoveries, then and now, but the world is growing far too complex for individuals to make breakthroughs at the societal level as often as before.

Widespread collaboration CO-CREATION among diverse individuals requires clarity – making everyone aware of the process, roles and motivations. It is often improved by taking a visual approach to problem-solving, because images and drawings transcend language and enable communication across cultures.

New Ways to Collaborate

222

At IDEO, we have long embraced the idea that innovation and collaboration go hand in hand. When we work with clients, we typically bring in outside experts and consumers for design research and testing. In recent years, emerging technologies – from digital video to social networks – have provided completely new means to collaborate. Establishing our own web-based community and hosting challenges online seemed a natural next step. When we couldn't find a platform that accommodated all of our criteria, we created our own.

OpenIDEO.com brings together creative people from all corners of the globe to solve design problems SOCIAL DESIGN for social good. The platform is unlike any other: it walks participants through the innovation process in three distinct phases; it encourages visual contributions; and it features an automated feedback tool called the Design Quotient. The DQ rewards both the quality and quantity of an individual's contributions. All contributions are valued – even simply applauding the efforts of others.

When developing the platform, we specifically focused on encouraging collaboration as much as possible.

For example, OpenIDEO.com invites users to build on one another's contributions. BLUEPRINTS It also enables comments on every type of contribution, no matter how small. These two features have already produced innovative ideas that traditional closed calls for final solutions would never have yielded.

In OpenIDEO.com's first six months, the site had 10,000 active users who completed four challenges. To date, IDEO has received more than 1,500 inspirations and 1,000 concepts. We have also begun collecting success stories of how OpenIDEO.com is creating impact in the world – the only metric that really matters.

→ HTTP://OPENIDEO.COM/

IKEA HACKERS: THE LAMPAN
OPPORTUNITIES FOR 'NEW' DESIGNERS BRING CHALLENGES FOR 'OLD' DESIGNERS

DANIEL SAAKES

At the beginning of the 20th century, when standardization successfully separated design from manufacturing, a new profession emerged: the industrial designer. Industrial designers cater to mass production by making trade-offs between engineering, human factors, design constraints and marketing. Today, new ways of manufacturing and distribution are emerging that can effectively scale mass manufacturing down to small series of products marketed over the internet, or even unique products manufactured at home.

With these modern methods of fabrication and distribution, end users will participate as designers, and producers will be able to make their own trade-offs. It would not be overstating the matter to say that the traditional skills of the industrial designer will change fundamentally.

As an experiment, I designed a lamp, in the form of an 'IKEA hack'. HACKING DESIGN IKEA hackers are people that repurpose IKEA products to create personalized objects. In contrast to 'everyday creativity',[1] they share their results online. Due to the standardization STANDARDS and global availability of IKEA products, hacks can be reproduced by other people anywhere in the world. I shared SHARE my lamp design online on the Instructables website, a popular place to share everyday knowledge and skills.

For me, sharing the design turned out to be more challenging than making the design. I was designing not only for users, but also for makers. I wanted to take into account the availability of materials and the level of expertise that my makers would have, with the aim of designing for optimal reproducibility. What, for instance, are globally available, safe ways of connecting electrical wires? WYS ≠ WYG Reading the online discussions and comments posted by people making the lamp made me realize my responsibility.

I was amazed by the amount of people willing to void warranty, who felt confident that they would successfully be able to reproduce a lamp design that they found on the internet. After all, DIY disasters cannot be returned to the store. Also, I was surprised to find that makers made my lamp exactly as I had designed. I had secretly hoped to see new solutions and adaptations to the posted design. REMIX Then again, it is possible that makers had no incentive to adapt the design, or no incentive to share designs online.[2]

Similar to the way that IKEA hacks adapt existing products, desktop manufacturing will give end users the tools to make professionally produced products tailored to their preferences, without the need for compromises aimed at satisfying a large market. DOWNLOADABLE Currently, the design software to cater these technologies remains in the realm of professionals. The challenge is in adapting the software to the end user's needs, ensuring design freedom and including validation of engineering and human factors; SketchChair.com is an example of how these parameters can be incorporated. Desktop manufacturing facilitate user confidence, allowing designers to benefit from many iterations and affordable prototyping.

The challenge for the industrial designer will thus be in metadesign: designing for the 'new' designer: the empowered end user. Traditional designers will design the tools and techniques to support end users, as the designers and makers of the products they need, want and desire.

→ HTTP://WWW.IKEAHACKERS.NET

223

NOTES

1   Wakkery, M. 'The Resourcefulness of Everyday Design'. Available
    online at www.sfu.ca/~rwakkary/papers/p163-wakkary.pdf,accessed on
2   Rosner, B. 'Learning from IKEA Hacking: 'I'm Not One to Decoupage
    a Tabletop and Call It a Day''. Available online at http://people.
    ischool.berkeley.edu/~daniela/research/note1500-rosner.pdf
→   www.sketchchair.com
→   www.instructables.com/id/Big-lamps-from-Ikea-lampan-lamps

INSTRUCTABLES RESTAURANT
OPEN DESIGN IN A
RESTAURANT SETTING

ARNE HENDRIKS

The Instructables Restaurant[1] is the world's first open source restaurant. If you like the food, the restaurant gives you the recipe. And if you love the chair, or any of its other products, the restaurant provides the instructions for how to make it yourself.

The complete menu and interior are based exclusively on the open-access recipes and instructions available online, which are shared by members COMMUNITY of Instructables.com, a web-based platform for users to create and share detailed instructions for their own DIY projects, known as 'instructables'.[2] Nothing in the restaurant has been designed by its proprietor or its chef; they just make what they find online.

The restaurant not only appropriates this information to create its content, *décor* and atmosphere, it also showcases it and passes it on. Everything you eat or use in the restaurant comes with full instructions on how to make it yourself. The members who originally uploaded the instructables that were chosen for use in the restaurant are credited on posters and flyers hanging in the restaurant, providing publicity for their instructable.

The online world enters the offline world
The Instructables Restaurant turns the online potential of shared ideas into reality, and opens up this reality to the criticism of consumers. It tests and is tested, adopting an online feedback system in which members can comment on each other's instructables and rate them. Customers are encouraged to give feedback on the food and interior through the Instructables website. The feedback is immediately passed on to the member who uploaded the relevant instructable. Unlike a popularity contest, however, the restaurant also offers options for actually improving the instructable and how it works in practice. The restaurant's appreciative attitude toward criticism creates an open space of trial and error for every item on the menu and product list, with increased quality as a possible outcome.

The restaurant attracts its customers from the general public, from people who have heard or read about the Instructables website, and from the website's 1.8 million members. Everybody who is a member is a potential author (read: chef or designer) of the restaurant. This effectively creates a community of at least 1.8 million people who love the place, and may even have the ambition to be featured in it. In the end, the concept for the Instructables Restaurant was turned into an instructable as well. Everybody is welcome to start a similar restaurant and offer suggestions to make it even better.

→ HTTP://INSTRUCTABLESRESTAURANT.COM

NOTES

1   The Instructables Restaurant is a concept proposed by Arne Hendriks and Bas van Abel and developed in cooperation with Waag Society and Fab Lab Amsterdam.

2   Launched in 2005, Instructables.com was founded by MIT graduate Eric Wilhelm, who continues to play an active role as CEO; his profile on the website states his commitment to 'making technology accessible through understanding'. This active online community isn't just about sharing how you do what you do, though. Besides posting their projects, registered users can also offer suggestions and comments on other people's projects, collaboratively improving the end result. From recipes and crafts to furniture and solar panels, Instructables offers a wide range of projects, and it just keeps getting better.

→   www.instructables.com/member/ewilhelm

224

MEDIALAB PRADO
A METHODOLOGY FOR COLLABORATIVE PROTOTYPING

LAURA FERNÁNDEZ

Medialab Prado, part of Madrid's municipal arts department, is aimed at the production, research and dissemination of digital culture and the area where art, science, technology and society intersect.[1] Medialab Prado has several on-going programmes, all of which are free and open to the general public; two of their initiatives are discussed here.

The Interactivos? programme, launched in 2006, is an open research and production platform for creative and educational uses of technology, facilitating collective creation using open hardware and open software tools. Its goal is to experiment with the use of electronics and software in art, design and education projects. The Visualizar programme, which started in 2007, explores the social, cultural and artistic implications of data culture and proposes methodologies to make them more understandable, opening up opportunities for participation and criticism.

Medialab Prado organizes international events EVENTS in the context of its programmes, using a hybrid form that combines production workshops, symposiums and final exhibitions to showcase the results. These initiatives take place in Medialab Prado's new facilities, which provide a versatile space for reflection, research and intensive collaboration.

In that space, several projects previously selected from the responses to an international open call for proposals are developed in interdisciplinary working groups, consisting of the author of the initial proposal and all the people who are interested in collaborating. Over a three-week period, the members of each working group work in consultation with expert advisors to develop prototypes; at the end of that period, the results are presented and displayed in an exhibition.

The process is open to the public from beginning to end. Participants are encouraged to prepare proper documentation for their projects, both during and

after the workshop, and to publish the results and source code under licences that grant access to and distribution of the knowledge produced by the working groups. Medialab-Prado offers a range of tools to facilitate knowledge KNOWLEDGE exchange on the projects, including forums, wikis, blogs and a code repository.

The methodology developed by Medialab Prado has been used to carry out fifteen workshops so far, in which 140 prototypes were developed by more than 900 participants.

Low-cost, DIY Methods of Digital Fabrication

During the Interactivos?'09 Garage Science workshop, a *RepRap*[2] machine (a self-replicating 3D printer for rapid prototyping) REPRODUCTION was built at Medialab-Prado by a team of nine people. Inspired by RepRap, Zach Hoeken Smith from NYC Resistor started the MakerBot project,[3] an iterative design process that resulted in a low-cost 3D printer which can easily be built from a kit. In January 2009, Medialab-Prado organized a workshop to build and start using a MakerBot, with the aim of gathering a local community that can continue working on those two projects.

Text Digitization Workshop

In May 2010, a digitization workshop was held with the aim of covering the full scope of activity related to text digitization using free and open technologies. Inspired by DIY Book Scanning,[4] this workshop was about digital mark-up, editing and publishing, as well as the promotion of digital content.

→ HTTP://MEDIALAB-PRADO.ES

NOTES

1   http://medialab-prado.es/article/que_es

2   http://reprap.org

3   http://makerbot.com

4   www.diybookscanner.org

225

OHANDA
OPEN SOURCE HARDWARE AND DESIGN ALLIANCE

JÜRGEN NEUMANN

OHANDA is an initiative to foster sustainable copyleft-style sharing of open hardware and design. Since its emergence from the GOSH!-Grounding Open Source Hardware summit at the Banff Centre in July 2009, one of the goals of the project has been to build a service for sharing open hardware designs which includes a certification model and a form of registration. OHANDA is in process, and the process is open.

Why can't we just use any copyleft license?
In short: copyleft ACTIVISM derives its legal basis from copyright, which cannot be effectively enforced in the physical world. The equivalent would be patents, but the process of patenting hardware to make it open would be slow and expensive. The proposed solution with OHANDA is a label in the sense of a trademark. The label will allow the developer to associate a copyleft licence with any kind of physical device through OHANDA, which would act as a registration authority. The label could be compared to other common certificates, such as organic food, fair trade or CE certificates shown on products.

How does it work?
The designer DESIGNERS applies the copyleft license to the product designs and documentation. This makes it possible to licence the work under his name without restricting its use to the point that it could no longer be considered open.

First, the designer signs up for a registered account (as a person or as an organization) and receives a unique producer ID. When the designer registers at OHANDA, he accepts the terms and conditions of using the OHANDA label. This means that the designer grants the Four Freedoms to the user (see below) and publishes the work under a copyleft licence. The designer then registers the product and receives a unique product ID. After doing so, the designer may apply the OHANDA label to the product. The OHANDA label and the unique OHANDA registration key (OKEY) are printed/engraved on each copy of the device. This ensures that the link to the documentation and to the contributors always travels with the physical device itself, providing *visible proof that it is open source hardware.* The OHANDA registration key on the product helps the user link the product back to the designer, the product description, design artefacts and the copyleft licence through the web-based service offered by OHANDA. Empowered by the Four Freedoms, the user may develop the product further, BLUEPRINTS register as a producer in his own right, share his design artefacts under a copyleft licence, and be associated with the derivatives of the product.

Four Freedoms
The four freedoms from Free Software Definition lay the foundation for sharing hardware through OHANDA. The adaptations below are made by just replacing the term 'program' with the term(s) 'device /& design'. This may not be the most understandable way of describing freedoms of sharing open hardware, but it describes the degree of openness that OHANDA stands for. By granting these four freedoms for all documentation attached to a product, sharing takes place on a sustainable basis.

Freedom 0. The freedom to use the device and/or design for any purpose, including making items based on it. REMIX

Freedom 1. The freedom to study how the device works and change it to make it to do what you wish. Access to the complete design is a precondition for this. WYS ≠ WYG

Freedom 2. The freedom to redistribute copies of the device and/or design. SHARE

Freedom 3. The freedom to improve the device and/or design, and release your improvements (and modified versions in general) to the public, so that the whole community benefits. Access to the complete design HACKING DESIGN is a precondition for this.

Who owns it?
Ideally? Nobody... and everybody. A legal entity is needed to register a trademark. This legal entity should either be a credible, pre-existing, not-for-profit organization, or a new non-profit organization with

enough transparency in its operational management that the ownership of this common asset does not become an issue. Distributing the ownership gradually among all those who share their hardware feels like the right thing to do, but it may turn out too complex to manage in the long run. OHANDA is still a work in progress; existing certification models are being studied in order to adopt best practices. In the meantime, the community COMMUNITY gathering around OHANDA will simply proceed without any legal entity or definitive registered trademark.

→ WWW.OHANDA.ORG

OPEN RE:SOURCE DESIGN
VISUALIZING COMPLETE MATERIAL FLOWS

SOENKE ZEHLE

In an era of algorithmic cultures, designers willing to take on the challenges of sustainability must be prepared to deal with complex eco-politics. At the same time, any mapping of possible sites of aesthetic intervention must begin by visualizing complete material flows.

Aided by the research of non-governmental organizations and a wave of liberal celebrity journalism, users know that mobile media use here is linked to resource conflicts TREND: SCARCITY OF RECOURSES somewhere else. The call to shift to renewables has triggered a new type of resource conflict, less about the conditions of extraction than about the terms of transnational trade, giving rise to a new geopolitics of resource access. In the race to create independent supply chains for these essential materials, industry and political leaders in Europe and the US now regret having placed potential mining areas under environmental protection and are likely to reopen extraction in the name of resource autonomy.

227

Any such efforts may not go unnoticed, however; electronics activists ACTIVISM are already using free mapping tools to visualize global supply chains and demonstrate that transparency in the area of resource extraction is in fact possible. Above and beyond corporate social responsibility initiatives that may or may not amount to more than a greenwashing of largely unchanged production processes, such maps call on corporations to take responsibility for what is happening across their supply chains rather than delegating such monitoring to their suppliers. Complex data visualizations challenge claims that brand management is the only corporate responsibility in the age of intellectual property, ensuring that designers creating new gadgets and user experience strategies are placed adjacent to indigenous communities struggling to protect the integrity of local environments or local militias fighting over the revenue streams of a local. New environmental governance regimes and regulatory frameworks (WEED, RohS) offer designers access to vast material databases that list toxicity, as well as use and disposal hazards, although corporate participation is not yet required by law. Moreover, these lists of declarable substances only cover materials present in the final product, failing to address job health and safety or the workers' right to know what they are handling. The design (and scope) of such databases have become an eco-political terrain, giving rise to a new brand of design-related data activism to expand the collection and integration of supply chain data.

Open Source Design

The effective management of environmental standards across transnational supply chains and production networks requires some acknowledgment of worker demands to know the substances they work with, potentially raising health and safety standards for workers and consumers across industries. Even so, consumer choice in the notoriously fragmented world of electronics manufacturing, for example, does not yet extend to devices that are truly sustainable. As corporate sustainability reports show, electronics companies have no idea how to monitor, let alone control complete supply and disposal chains, lagging far behind their peers in the automotive industries.

228

Consumers interested in fair production are allies of designers no longer interested in 'designing for the dump',[1] RECYCLING but consumer-designer alliances are rare, despite the enthusiasm over user-generated content and the emergence of 'produsers'. Activist networks (like Bricolabs) lead the way in applying the principle of openness to hardware design – encouraging users to extend their desire to create and participate to the design and production of the very technologies of creation and participation. This pursuit of 'open re:source design' is aided by the wave of open educational resources (OER) available to designers. Material available online ranges from online syllabi on design and environmental topics[2] to free software design tools and corresponding handbooks for self-study.[3]

These developments place designers at the core of a new series of ethico-aesthetic conflicts, giving them a key role to play in the negotiation of competing futures, perspectives, and timescales of sustainability. In theory, they are well-positioned to play a pivotal role. At the same time, they are engulfed by a tentacular creative industries framework that lauds creative

autonomy without providing much more than precarity compensation, while short product cycles and the volatile attention economy of real-time communications networks limit the potentially disruptive force of the call for sustainability. But 'open' re:source design means, above all, to raise the stakes of these questions.

→ HTTP://CO.XMLAB.ORG

NOTES

1 Annie Leonard, *The Story of Electronics*. Available online at: http://storyofstuff.org/electronics/, accessed 15 January 2011.

2 Such as MIT OpenCourseWare (http://ocw.mit.edu), OER Commons (www.oercommons.org) and others.

3 Such as Floss Manuals (http://en.flossmanuals.net).

OPEN STANDARDS
DESIGN FOR ADAPTATION: A NEW DESIGN VOCABULARY

THOMAS LOMMÉE

Over the last 20 years, we have been witnessing the early developments of a networked economy that is operated by its interconnected participants. Decentralized information streams and sources have altered people's attention scopes, ambitions and goals and stimulated a more critical and pro-active attitude. Rather than swallowing manicured advertising made up by professional PR departments, consumers are now informing, inspiring and instructing each other with home-grown content – using Twitter feeds, blogs and YouTube movies to communicate their skills, knowledge and ideas.

But the global mouth-to-mouth mechanism of the World Wide Web TREND: NETWORK SOCIETY not only initiated a dialogue among consumers, it also started a conversation between consumers and producers. This emerging dialogue is generating exciting new business models and rearranging current artistic practices.

On the one hand, it enables consumers to participate in the design process at various levels. Blogs facilitate product reviews and ratings, while easy access to online instructions stimulate consumers to personalize, adapt, repair REPAIRING or hack HACKING products. On the other hand, producers can now obtain a huge amount of feedback on their products by observing all these millions of small movements online and subsequently respond to them in their next product releases. Some producers are even actively involving the end user in the creative process by asking them to design new applications (e.g. Apple's app store) or to propose new uses for their products (e.g. the Roomba vacuum cleaner[1]).

Out of this creative dialogue, the need for a common design language, a kind of shared design vocabulary with its own specific rules, characteristics and outcomes, is slowly STANDARDS emerging. This vocabulary is manifesting itself through common agreements within the dimensioning, assembly and material cycles of the object. The concept of introducing a set of open standards is nothing new. Whenever a need for sharing has become apparent, open standards have always emerged as a means to generate more flexible and resilient models of exchange. The internet, for example, is entirely based on HTML coding, a common, free-of-charge text and image formatting language that allows everybody to create and share web pages; Wikipedia is nothing more than a common standard template that can be filled in, duplicated, shared and edited over and over again.

Despite the obvious advantages that these common standards and design protocols bring, there is considerable scepticism among designers to adopt and embrace them – probably because, until recently, a seemingly infinite amount of resources indicated little need for more flexible and open systems, and the hierarchical, top-down monologue of mass communication offered few opportunities for exchange. In addition, these open models also raise questions of accountability, profitability and formal expression. How do we credit the contributors? How do we generate money? Last but not least, how do we balance openness and protection, freedom and restriction? Since every standard by definition imposes a restriction, it limits our choices and obstructs our freedom to design and shape, and it disrupts our independent position as designers.

Nevertheless, the more we continue to share and exchange, the more the need for common platforms will surface within all aspects of our culture. This doesn't mean that one system will replace the other. Sometimes the commons will do a better job; other times the classical systems will prevail. Both open and closed systems will continue to exist, but it is the evolution of both in relation to the emergence of a networked society as well as the growing range of hybrids (closed systems with open components) that need to be closely observed and tried out.

Designing within certain common standards will require a different mindset from all stakeholders of the design process. In order to think 'within the box', in order to accept and embrace the new opportunities that emerge out of common restrictions, we need to acknowledge that we are part of a bigger whole, rather than being the whole itself. It requires us to give up the myth to create 'something new', something that 'hasn't been done before' and to replace it by a willingness to dissolve into bigger projects that just make common sense. This new mindset will severely damage the romantic ideal of the 'designer-creator' DESIGNERS and shift it towards the 'designer-collaborator'.

And, let's face it, that's quite a different perspective to work from. No designer of our generation wants to be a pixel; we all want to be the full-colour image.

NOTES

1   The Roomba is an autonomous robotic vacuum cleaner that comes with a serial interface. This interface is incompatible with standard PC/Mac serial ports and cables. It allows the user to monitor Roomba's many sensors and modify its behaviour. Programmers and roboticists create their own enhancements to Roomba, resulting in numerous 'Roomba hacks'. Some hacks are functional, others are purely fun. So far, Roombas have been converted into floor plotters, robots controlled by a Wii remote, 'hamster-powered' vehicles, etc.

PONOKO:
THE DISTRIBUTED MAKING SYSTEM

PETER TROXLER

Ponoko first saw the limelight of success on 17 September 2007 at TechCrunch40, a conference held in San Francisco to showcase 'forty of the hottest new start-ups from around the world' to a 600+ strong audience. The event unfolded under the auspices of an expert panel which included Chris Anderson, Ron Conway, Esther Dyson and Caterina Fake. Ponoko was one of those forty, together with the likes of App2You, Docstoc, Kaltura, Tripit, Trutap, and Viewdle.

Ponoko was the odd one out. Instead of keeping safely to the digital information realm, its promise was to link the digital to the physical world. Users upload designs to the Ponoko website and select the materials; Ponoko then makes and delivers the product or product parts – and users can post designs in the Ponoko showroom for people to view and buy. Lauded as 'the world's easiest making system', Ponoko combines digital designing with internet technology for distribution, relying on local manufacturing for production of the designs.

Ponoko's first designer community in Wellington, New Zealand COMMUNITY consisted of 19 hand-selected designers. At a family gathering on 19 July 2007, the 27 designs available ranged from bike lights, lampshades and jewellery, to tables, room dividers, a chess set, CD rack, artwork and an architectural model of well-known Wellington neighbourhood Brooklyn.

In the 24 hours after the TechCrunch40 talk, Ponoko's website got over one million hits; their name was all over the media outlets and tech blogs. 'I believe that everyone wants to be a designer. Ponoko is going to make that possible,' someone commented on Ponoko's company profile at Crunchbase.com. 'Currently, Ponoko has no decentralized manufacturing competitors,' the directory entry said. Indeed, the 3D-printing service Shapeways PRINTING registered their domain on Monday, 18 February 2008.

After TechCrunch40, Ponoko quickly moved into the US market. Their user base continues to be mainly in the

United States; its hotspots are the usual suspects: the Bay Area, New York, Austin, Philadelphia. 'We have a good strong user base here in New Zealand, but the vast majority are in the United States,' Ponoko founder Dave ten Have admitted in a recent interview.[1]

In its early days, Ponoko's manufacturing capabilities were limited to laser cutting. In 2009, they partnered with CNC-router manufacturer ShopBot to create the 100k-Garages initiative, a network of 180 machine shops ready to professionally cut AESTHETICS: 2D any 2D design. In September 2010, they teamed up with SparkFun to be able to add electronics to designs, and as of November they offer 3D printing in collaboration with CloudFab.

Ponoko employs five full-time staff in Wellington and three in Oakland. They have arrangements with local design studios Formulor in Berlin, RazorLAB in London, and Vectorealism in Milan. Ponoko's user community counts a few thousand designers; some products have even made it to reasonable success. Still, Dan ten Have declines to comment on the profitability of Ponoko, saying only, 'the lights are still on'. For Ponoko, the challenge remains to 'kick the scale side of things', and Dan is hinting at some 'very deliberate rinse and repeat'.

→ WWW.PONOKO.COM

NOTES

1   MacManus, R. 'From Ideation To Creation: Ponoko's Sci-Fi "Making System"', in *ReadWriteWeb*, 28 September 2010. Available online at: http://www.readwriteweb.com/archives/from_science_fiction_concept_to_real_product.php, accessed 4 October 2010.

REDESIGN ME
ONLINE CO-CREATION AND CO-DESIGN

MAXIM SCHRAM

Open design by online communities is becoming more common among companies that had previously been secretive about the products they create. Dutch tea manufacturer Pickwick, for example, used the online design and idea community RedesignMe.com to interact with an audience of external designers, marketers and consumers.

The goal was to collect input from stakeholders and lead users on the subject of innovative tea products. A challenge was presented to a community of about 3,500 people; the assignment was to 'create innovative tea concepts that match Pickwick's brand values'.

The exercise proved successful in terms of the number of ideas generated. 90 people participated actively over a period of six weeks, creating 198 tea-related concepts. The concepts ranged from new flavours to new packaging, as well as items to be sold or given away as a marketing gimmick.

Initially, 70 people created 125 concepts without further encouragement. Our research showed that the presence of community COMMUNITY managers from Pickwick positively influenced participation. Because many people received feedback directly from Pickwick, participation went up, inspiring participating users to send in one or two additional concepts.

In addition to creators, there were also commenters. Over 500 people commented on the challenge and the resulting concepts. Discussions between people led to numerous improvements in the concepts. Some ideas that only consisted of a short story from one user were converted into a 3D model by another user. Other concepts were perfected based on discussions between participants and Pickwick marketers.

By the end, the challenge had been viewed by over 20,000 people, most of which were passive readers ('lurkers'). Although only about 2% of the total number of readers actively participated in the challenge, it is

231

possible to state confidently that Pickwick generated significant publicity as the first Dutch producer of fast-moving consumer goods to participate in this level of online co-creation. CO-CREATION

The Pickwick Challenge paved the way for other food companies to take advantage of co-design through online communities. While co-creation does not guarantee that original concepts will be found, companies say it helps them step back and see the bigger picture in relation to their business.

WWW.REDESIGNME.COM

REPRAP
THE VIABILITY OF OPEN DESIGN

ERIK DE BRUIJN

The RepRap digital fabrication system can 3D print a large share of its own parts. In fact, it reproduces almost 90% of the really important mechanical parts that convey most knowledge. The other 10% is the hot end and the main electronic boards for motor control.

This allows for a decentralized community to independently produce physical parts based on digital designs that are shared via the internet. Apart from improving the device, dedicated collaboration infrastructure ARCHITECTURE was developed by user innovators. Examples of such infrastructure include Thingiverse, a web-based design sharing platform, and CloudSCAD, a web-based Solid 3D CAD Modeller.

While open source software development has been studied extensively, relatively little is known about the viability of the same development model for a physical object's design. To remedy this knowledge deficit, a case study and survey of the RepRap community was conducted (n=386).[1]

There is substantial adoption and development of open 3D printer technology, PRINTING even when compared to unit sales of the largest vendors in the 25-year-old industry. RepRap community members are spending between 145 and 182 full-time equivalents and have spent between 382,000 and 478,000 US dollars on innovation alone. At the RepRap project's six-month doubling interval, it is entirely feasible that its adoption and disruptive levels of innovation will exceed that of the incumbent industry.

Open design and open source software also share many similarities. Design information can be digitally encoded and transmitted much like software code. The motivation to develop or improve software or a physical object may be induced partly by the ability to benefit from its use. In the context of this study, another important similarity is that, both in open source software and open design, the tools to practice open source development are often user-developed as well.

Within the community, there is a higher incidence in modifications of hardware than in software, and, surprisingly, hardware modifications are expected to be relatively easier for others to replicate. The level of collaboration CO-CREATION is also higher for software than for hardware.

Open source physical design, also known as open design, differs from open source software in that it has an embodied manifestation. This has implications for dissemination of the related knowledge and the logistics of this manifestation that has led observers to think that open design is fundamentally different. Moreover, OSS differs from open design in terms of the maturity of its licenses.

Personal Fabrication

In the research, special attention is given to the role of the capability provided by digital fabrication, and their effect on the ability to collaborate. It affects the cost of development, production, reproduction REPRODUCTION and distribution of physically embodied innovations. While artefact-embodied tacit knowledge influences the locus of innovation, the implications of this 'embodiment' can be mitigated. Results from the survey indicate higher levels of sharing, collaboration and even a perceived higher replicability for hardware, when compared to software. This supports the notion that personal fabrication tools can play an important role to enable distributed activity in open design.

Through Thingiverse, 1,486 designs of physical objects have been shared in the last six months. Also, more than 10,000 objects were independently manufactured by its members' machines. While already substantial, this level activity exhibits similar exponential growth characteristics.

In offering its tools, infrastructure and incentives, the RepRap community uses the open source development methodology to design physical objects, achieving great success and promoting democratization of the process. The extensibility of this phenomenon has many implications. Obtaining the digital design for a product becomes increasingly attractive compared to having to acquire the physical object. BLUEPRINTS This is partly due to logistics of physical objects, involving lead-times and transport costs.

Many RepRap community members possess a fabrication capability that the average person does not have access to. While this does limit the present-day generality of the study's findings, there are many reasons to expect a high likelihood of personal access to digital fabrication in the near future. The rapid development and adoption of increasingly affordable, yet more powerful and valuable fabrication technologies and the anti-rival logic of open design allow user-dominant collaborative development to have significant implications for the provisioning of goods in society.

→ HTTP://REPRAP.ORG

NOTES

1   Erik de Bruijn conducted his study entitled 'On the viability
    of the Open Source Development model for the design of physical
    object: Lessons learned from the RepRap project' together
    with Jeroen de Jong (EIM and Erasmus University Rotterdam) and
    Eric von Hippel (MIT Sloan School of Management). Available
    online at http://thesis.erikdebruijn.nl/master/MScThesis-
    ErikDeBruijn-2010.pdf, accessed 19 November 2010.

233

SHAREABLE
OPEN DESIGN FOR
AN ACCESS ECONOMY

NEAL GORENFLO

Like any innovation, open design by itself is neither good nor bad. Its social value depends entirely on how it's used. It can be used for the common good, or it can be used to destroy the human and biological communities we depend on for survival.

The latter would not only be tragic, but boring. We deserve a better story than this! Our species has already accrued 2.5 years of ecological debt.[1] And the debt is mounting rapidly – this year we'll use an estimated 150% of the resources the earth can generate.[2] TREND: SCARCITY OF RECOURSES Despite this profligate level of resource use, a billion of our fellow passengers on Spaceship Earth live in extreme poverty. This is an EPIC FAIL!

So the question is: how can you help reverse ecological debt and raise a billion people out of poverty? This is a challenge worthy of your remarkable ingenuity. Sure, there's time to create that sculpture of Obi-Wan Kenobi with your 3D printer, but set aside some time for this EPIC WIN too! Don't you think our species has more exciting places to go than oblivion? Let's look at the problem at the level of products for a possible road map.

What's obvious is that we don't need more stuff. 99% of the stuff humans make becomes trash after just six months.[3] And most of our stuff is idle most of the time. For instance: Cars are idle an average of 22 hours a day; Power drills are used an average of 20 minutes total; Most lawn mowers are used 4 hours a year.[4]

Learning from Car-sharing
So what can we do about this? Car-sharing offers a clue. Duh, we should share! Car-sharing statistics show the positive change that could come from an access economy, one where products are services accessed on demand DOWNLOADABLE DESIGN by users. A 2010 study[5] of over 6,000 North American car-sharing members found that 51% joined who didn't have a car but wanted access to one. Almost a quarter of members shed a

car, 1,400 cars total. A 2004 UC Berkeley study of City Carshare[6] found that members drove 47% less after joining and saved 700,000 pounds of CO2 emissions. If you're wondering if car-sharing makes things worse by increasing access to cars, consider that the average ratio of users to cars in North American car-sharing systems is 1:24.[7] Compare this ownership in the US where cars outnumber drivers by 1.2 to one.[8] And more benefit is coming – car-sharing companies[9] are partnering with ride-sharing companies to increase the number of passengers per car rental.

I don't know of another innovation that increases access to a resource *and* decreases the environmental footprint. Our environmental and energy crises have some people thinking we must scrimp to survive. Sharing offers a better story – it suggests that we can live well and still reduce our footprint.

But the impact goes beyond material concerns. Research shows[10] that sharing makes us happy and can prolong life. SHARE In addition, the New Sharing Economy study[11] done by Shareable Magazine[12] and Latitude Research[13] showed that car-sharers share across dramatically more categories than non-car-sharers – 11 versus 8. Not only does sharing offer many benefits, it also begets more sharing. Now that's an elegant hack.

The news gets better - entrepreneurs are applying the car-sharing template TEMPLATE CULTURE to a wide range of assets that include parking spaces,[14] planes and boats,[15] camera lenses,[16] textbooks,[17] children's clothing,[18] handbags,[19] spare rooms[20] and houses,[21] office space,[22] household items,[23] and a lot more.[24] What's more, the New Sharing Economy study suggests there's a big future in sharing – 75% of participants felt that their sharing of material goods will increase in the next five years. Rachel Botsman,[25] author of *Collaborative Consumption*,[26] believes that the access economy could be as big as the Industrial Revolution. REVOLUTION

So I invite you to help build the access economy. Aside from that sculpture of Obi-Wan Kenobi, there may be no better use of your talent.

→ HTTP://SHAREABLE.NET/

NOTES

1   www.footprintnetwork.org/en/index.php/GFN/page/
    glossary/#ecologicaldebt

2   www.footprintnetwork.org/en/index.php/GFN/page/
    earth_overshoot_day

3   http://dangerousintersection.org/2010/08/24/beware-annie-
    leonards-depressing-presentation-about-all-of-our-stuff-unless-
    youre-ready-to-implement-big-changes/

4   www.amazon.co.uk/Whats-Mine-Yours-Collaborative-Consumption/dp/
    B003VIWNEO

5   www.carsharing.net/library/Martin-Shaheen-Lidicker-TRR-10-3437.
    pdf

6   www.citycarshare.org/pressrelease_01-12-04.do

7   Go To 2040 Regional Comprehensive Plan Strategy Analysis, http://
    bit.ly/ci4RHo

8   http://en.wikipedia.org/wiki/
    Passenger_vehicles_in_the_United_States" \l
    "Vehicle_and_population_ratios_.28millions.29_since_1960

9   www.zimride.com/zipcar

10 http://shareable.net/blog/
    seven-ways-that-sharing-can-make-you-happy-and-healthy

11 http://shareable.net/blog/the-new-sharing-economy

12 http://shareable.net

13 www.life-connected.com/

14 www.parkatmyhouse.com/uk/

15 http://sharezen.com/

16 www.borrowlenses.com/

17 www.chegg.com/

18 www.thredup.com/

19 www.bagborroworsteal.com/

20 www.couchsurfing.org/

21 www.airbnb.com/

22 http://en.wikipedia.org/wiki/Coworking

23 http://rentalic.com/

24 http://us.zilok.com/

25 www.rachelbotsman.com/

26 www.collaborativeconsumption.com/

THINGIVERSE
HOW THE INTERNET, SHARING AND DIGITAL FABRICATION ARE ENABLING A NEW WAVE OF OPEN SOURCE HARDWARE

ZACH SMITH

Thingiverse.com was started on a lazy Saturday afternoon in late October 2008. I was at the local hackerspace, NYC Resistor, with my friend Bre Pettis. As usual, we were tinkering with our RepRap machine and dreaming of the day when 3D printing would be ubiquitous. As we worked, we chatted about what it would be like if you had a 3D printer that could make you anything you wanted. We decided that one of the coolest things would be the ability to download designs from the internet that your 3D printer would then turn into real things.

We then asked ourselves what that would look like. HELLO WORLD We did some quick Googling and found that almost all the 3D model repositories on the internet were behind paywalls. We were shocked and appalled; the future of digital fabrication was supposed to free us from the tyranny of distribution costs as we applied the techniques of free software to hardware. Being people who prefer action to words, we set out to build a site that reflected what we wanted the future to be.

Thingiverse COMMUNITY was built from the ground up as a place for people to freely share their digital designs for physical objects. We built it to be as inclusive as possible. It will accept almost any digital file, so long as it is a design for a real, physical object. In fact, most of the early designs on the site are vector drawings for laser cutters. Later, we branched out with support for 3D models, electronics, and designs intended for CNC machines.

Once the rough framework was in place, we started adding features to encourage open design and collaboration. The first step was a licensing system that allowed users to very explicitly state the licence which the listed files were available under. Designers can choose from a number of licences, including Creative Commons, CREATIVE COMMONS GPL, LGPL, BSD,

235

and Public Domain. The licensing is even available in a machine-readable format on the page itself. We also wanted to encourage collaboration CO-CREATION by including a derivatives system that allowed people to upload modifications to a design. This feature was a hit because it allowed modified designs to easily give attribution, as well as creating a nice tree structure of all the derivative works available. This was a victory for both the designers and people who wanted to improve on designs that were already available. The designers got credit for the initial work, and the users were easily able to find the latest designs.

The result of this is that Thingiverse is now home to nearly 4,000 open source OPEN EVERYTHING objects. It has over 5,000 active users and nearly 1 million downloads across all of the design files. It is home to a huge variety of open source hardware projects. On Thingiverse, you can download open source bottle openers, statues, robots, toys, tools, and even 3D printers. REPRODUCTION It is the largest repository of open source hardware on the Internet and a wonderful place to share your things with the world.

236 → WWW.THINGIVERSE.COM

(UN)LIMITED DESIGN CONTEST
EXPERIMENTING WITH OPEN DESIGN

BAS VAN ABEL

Open design covers an extensive area and its contours are not yet clearly defined, making it difficult for designers to come to grips with the developments. One of the most tangible open design experiments was the (Un)limited Design Contest, which challenged the designers to try something out and experience for themselves what happens next. Alexander Rulkens (Studio Ludens),[1] Sylvie van de Loo (SEMdesign)[2] and Goof van Beek[3] share their experiences.

All designs that were submitted were made with digital manufacturing technology, using machines that turn digital designs into physical products. Digital manufacturing offers the designer many new possibilities. Professional designer Sylvie van de Loo used a computer-controlled laser cutter to create her *Fruit bowl 128*. DOWNLOADABLE DESIGN The bowl is constructed from 128 pieces cut out of cardboard. Her initial idea was to work out a prototype of the bowl in clay. As she was drawing the bowl in 3D on the computer with a friend, she began checking the possibilities for manufacturing the product digitally. For this, she went to the Fab Lab in Utrecht.

Sylvie: "I've been in the Fab Lab before, but I didn't see the potential for my own work at that time. I thought it was all a bit too technical; I felt that a creative approach was lacking. Now I'm discovering that the technique is an important source of inspiration to me." Sylvie took the advice to turn her bowl into a technical drawing program, which was capable of breaking the 3D form up into sectional planes with a specific width. This approach allows her to generate forms for different materials, which are then cut out with the laser cutter. AESTHETICS: 2D It is a fairly technical process, which has had an important influence on the creative process and was one of the deciding factors in the final form and appearance of the end product.

Sylvie: "Working with the laser cutter was really a revelation for me. What a cool machine! Anything is possible. You can form 3D layers out of 2D layers. It's very precise, and you can engrave the most beautiful forms with it. Because you yourself get to work with the prototyping technology, the process of making it is a valuable addition to the final design. If I hadn't had the chance to experiment with the machine, the definitive form and choice of material would never have occurred to me." HELLO WORLD

But still, designer Alexander Rulkens van Studio Ludens feels there is a great deal of room for improvement in how people gain access to the designing process and machines. ARCHITECTURE Alexander: "I think the Fab Lab concept can benefit from better interfaces to wield the great power that the technology can give." He didn't submit a product for the contest; instead, he submitted a software tool that enables everyone to create their own design easily.

Sharing for Yourself

It's clear that access to technology offers new possibilities, but what possibilities does sharing creative work offer the designer? Goof van Beek won the design contest in 2009; his design received extensive publicity. Goof: "It's fun when people come up and talk to you because they saw your design somewhere. I'm not sure if it really was the open nature of the design that gave the dress the amount of attention that it got, but it was a good first introduction to the reality outside the environs of my study. Meanwhile, I have been approached to take part in an exposition."

It could be that the conditions of the contest played a role in this: under the (Un)limited Designs terms, the design could be published and shared without prior approval from the DESIGNER designer. On the one hand, this made it possible for the designers to establish a name for themselves more quickly, and a company that finds the product interesting knows who to go and talk to. However, it also means that designers have given their permission for others to adapt the design and publish their derivative design. "It is a bit scary, but it also has its advantages," says Sylvie. "The bowl is finished as far as I'm concerned, and I think it's really great that someone else could pick it up and give it their own twist."

She isn't afraid this openness will stand in her way as a designer or harm her business interests. Sharing the design also associates her with the product as the original designer – and even if a design hasn't been explicitly shared, the designer still always runs the risk of ideas being stolen.

Alexander emphasizes that it's not just a business matter. Alexander: "The major benefit of sharing is the opportunity to get feedback on your thought and design process early on. You are opening yourself up to the knowledge of others, to different perspectives, which you need as a designer to come up with ideas that are relevant to society. The fact that your design is open to improvement ultimately means that it will be better suited to the people who are going to use it in their day-to-day lives."

Signature

But looking at the entries in the design contest, only three products were submitted in the 'fusion' category. It's a category that provides incentives for the re-use and re-interpretation of designs that had already been submitted. REMIX Sylvie and Goof both expect that this has to do with the importance of the designer's signature style, especially in a contest. Sylvie: "There is a difference between what you use from other designs as an inspiration for your own design, and basing your design entirely on somebody else's. Originality is important to a designer, and designers aren't used to explicitly recognizing others for contributing to their design. This makes us choose the safe way by inventing something new.' Goof: "It's strange that we don't consider improving somebody else's product a challenge, because I would really like to take a few designs in hand in my surroundings. I do know several designs that I think could be done better." Sylvie thinks that education has an important role in forming this attitude. Sylvie: "At the academy, we were encouraged to be original by creating work that is unique and distinguished. DESIGNERS I never saw anyone literally taking an existing design as a starting point for a personal interpretation or addition. Maybe we still consider ourselves too good to do that."

Alexander has a somewhat more radical view. He believes that open design will essentially change the role of the designer. Alexander: "Designers will have to start listening better in a world where the designer

237

doesn't make the design decisions, but rather facilitates the process of designing decisions." The meaning of a signature style is changing, as is the way in which we handle that signature style. Alexander: "We have to move towards a system where a person's contribution to a design can be measured and that person can be given proper credit for their efforts. This means that the designer has to let go of the feeling that "it was my idea".

It is not yet possible to draw hard and fast conclusions from the results of the (Un)limited Design Contest, `EVENTS` but it is clear that the designers will engage in the challenge. The most valuable aspect of this kind of experiment is that it enables us to explore certain aspects of open design. In the first edition of the contest, the question was still whether designers were willing to throw open their own design. The emphasis in the second edition was on compound products; the challenge for the third edition will probably be achieving a design dialogue between the contestants.

→ HTTP://UNLIMITEDDESIGNCONTEST.ORG

238

NOTES

1   www.studioludens.com

2   www.semdesign.nl

3   www.goofvanbeek.nl

(UN)LIMITED DESIGN CONTEST
OPENNESS IN VITRO

MARIA NEICU

Openness is no longer only seen in the context of open software; it has become a broadly applicable concept, carried by the digital in the analogue world. Design tools are in user's hands now, as access to software programs and machines (such as laser cutters or embroidery machines) is opened up in the new context of digital fabrication. Openness has been picking up momentum, but has not yet hit its high point.

Amateurs `AMATEURISSIMO` seem well-equipped to take on the stage of combining crafts with high-tech: they no longer expect professionals to tell them what is *right* and *wrong*. As design is being opened, experts have to re-legitimize their professions in the face of a high demand *"for other kinds of taste construction"*.[1] But *access* alone is not sufficient to achieve this goal. Access is only half-way to openness. If it never progresses beyond access, openness is just a popular bit of `OPEN EVERYTHING` rhetoric, an over-used *"fashionable label"*.[2] But what does it take to move further? The other part of the journey is collaboration – the only way to give amateurs the opportunity to make a change. This is the only way for openness to bring serious societal relevance to this profession. If both access and collaboration `CO-CREATION` were attained, then both amateurs and experts would reach a new mindset – one that thinks *beyond design*. A first initiative in this sense is the (Un)limited Design Contest. `EVENTS` Under the auspices of a design competition, the event provides a context for testing Openness *in vitro*:

Firstly, it provides Access: opportunities, tools and social recognition for the work of non-experts. Everyone that has an idea can bring it to life: participants are encouraged to create prototypes tailored to their subjectivity. Design becomes *invitational*.

Secondly, it re-connects design with crafts: Crafts are no longer about working only with *things*, physical objects, but also with entities of intangible value, like symbols, people and networks; these entities are starting to be considered more and more intellectually engaging. `KNOWLEDGE` As the status of artisanal work done by hand is upgraded by the addition of a symbolic capital, a new awareness is brought to bear on the artefacts around us, and especially on how we can act upon them. Open design causes a shift in our relationship with the stuff we use, bend, break, wear, consume and eventually throw away. It does justice to what these items are really worth. On the one hand, this brings back to us an ancestral sense of curiosity about the artefacts with which we fill our worlds; on the other hand, it demands that we re-think our responsibility in the way we interact with them.

And thirdly, the contest brings people together: experimenting to see whether "shared thinking" can actually happen. The (Un)limited Design Contest `SHARING` comes as a line of defence: an attempt to prove that openness can move beyond a transitory buzzword, and that collaboration `CO-CREATION` is possible, transforming design as a profession into a valuable part of future society. As shown by the (Un)limited Design Contest, the value of an object design is expressed in its potential for being taken beyond its original confines. The 'unfinished' nature of the script offers the intangible value of an open design. `BLUEPRINTS` The derivatives are not perceived as 'corrective' in this sense. The existence of derivatives does not mean that your original is incomplete or malfunctioning – on the contrary! When others are mixing, mashing and transforming your design script, they are offering their greatest compliment. It is the prize offered by the community: proof that your idea is valuable and considered worthy of further development. By improving your idea, the collaborators are actually approving it.

Adopt and Improve

In open design, adopting and improving is a way of cherishing. The moral is that nothing gets modified unless it is worthy of the time it will take to modify it or add innovations. Humans are limited in their creational power, so togetherness becomes a pre-requisite for socio-technological innovation: different life stories, mindsets and knowledge experiences are added by other participants, enriching each open design project. These initial efforts are only the beginning; this experiment has to be repeated. The first steps towards fruitful collaboration have already made. Design is fully engaged in the re-shaping process, and openness seems to be breeding a new design culture – a culture that is still under construction.

→ HTTP://UNLIMITEDDESIGNCONTEST.ORG

NOTES

1   Roel Klaassen, Premsela
2   Victor Leurs, Featuring-Amsterdam

239

OPEN ADVERTISEMENT

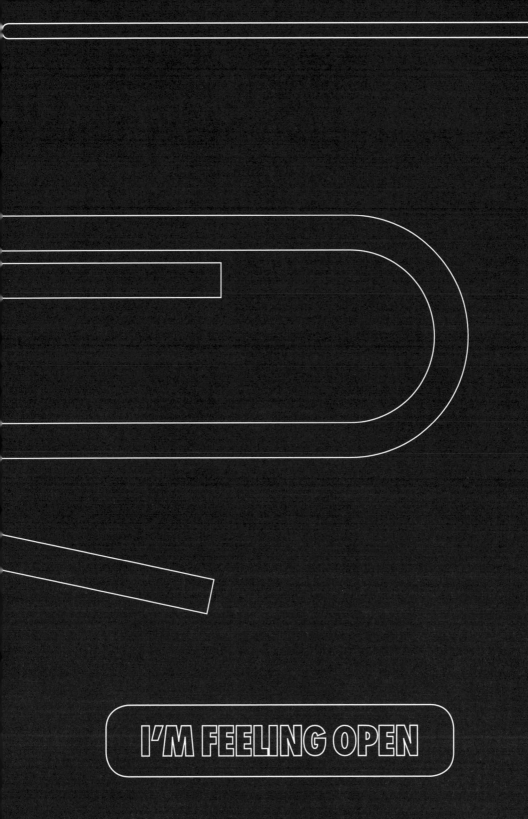

I'M FEELING OPEN

VISUAL INDEX

A

001 COPYLEFT FESTIVAL 2008: 'BE RIGHT, BE COPYLEFT'

002 COPYLEFT COMMIES FLAG

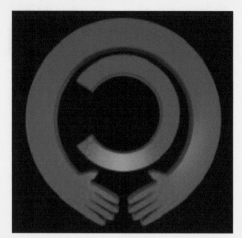

003 COPYLEFT IN GREECE

004 CREATIVE COMMIES

005 COPYLEFT ON INDYMEDIA → P.68

006 MYCREATIVITY CONVENTION, AMSTERDAM 2006

007 FUNDACIÓN COPYLEFT, MADRID

FundaciónCopyLeft

008 KIDNAPPING INTELLECTUAL PROPERTY

009 ANARCOPY

010 NO COPYRIGHT → P.100

ACTIVISM

Private forces put the commons under pressure. The digital public domain demands another approach to protection of the commons, and also inspires another type of activism. If the insurgents had had a digital network, the French Revolution might have been a Communist revolution. Is copyright a means to protect innovation or has it been perverted to a new apogee of class struggle between corporations and consumers? Let's prove the 'tragedy of the commons' wrong and wake up from consumer paradise. Everybody is an activist in light of today's ecological challenges.

011 COPYLEFT PIRATE SYMBOL

012 BITE ME APPLE BY PROEF AMSTERDAM

013 BOX CREATOR BY DAVID SJUNNESSON

014 CAT BUCKLE BY ZELDA BEAUCHAMPET

015 CUSHION LAMP BY MANI ZAMANI

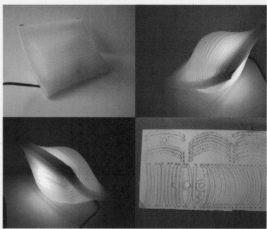

016 FISH BURNED INTO CHICKEN BY PROEF AMSTERDAM

017 EXPERIMENT BY FAB LAB BARCELONA

018 MODULAR NECKLACE, PONOKO JEWELRY DESIGN CHALLENGE → P.230

019 LANDSCAPE BY FAB LAB BARCELONA

020 ONE-PIECE BATHING SUIT BY ELISABETH DROOG

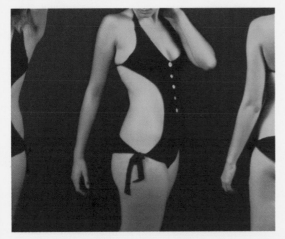

021 LASER-CUT OUTFIT BY KIRSTEN ENKELMANN

022 RASTER EXPERIMENT BY KOEN MOSTERT

AESTHETICS: 2D

2D layers make good parts for 3D objects. Based on the principles of modular design and architecture, a laser cutter makes it possible to produce all kinds of complex models and large objects. Community workshops make the technology available for everyone. It not only offers a lot of ingenious fun, but it is also deadly serious for supporting DIY prosthetic limbs in parts of the world where this is not offered by professional healthcare. Learning such a craft might become a necessity for us all in the near future of the repair economy.

A

023 3D-PRINTED GENERATIVE STRUCTURE

024 3D-PRINTED GENERATIVE STRUCTURE

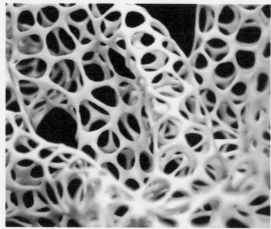

025 3D-PRINTED GENERATIVE STRUCTURE

026 3D-PRINTED GENERATIVE STRUCTURE

027 3D-PRINTED GENERATIVE STRUCTURE → P.36

028 3D-PRINTED GENERATIVE STRUCTURE

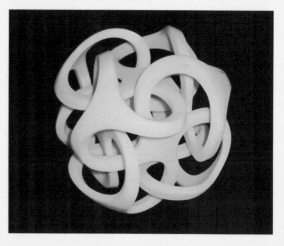

029 3D-PRINTED GENERATIVE STRUCTURE

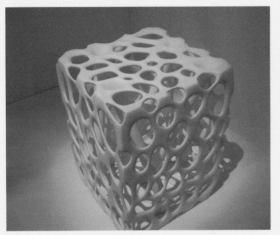

030 3D-PRINTED GENERATIVE STRUCTURE

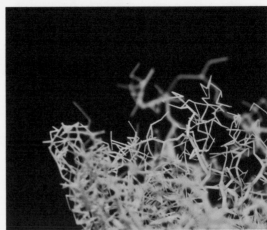

031 RING DESIGNED WITH GENERATIVE ALGORITHMS USING GENETIC CODES

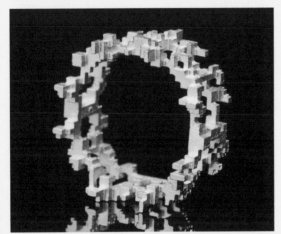

032 3D-PRINTED GENERATIVE STRUCTURE

033 3D-PRINTED SCIENTIFIC MODELS → P.220

AESTHETICS: 3D

Generative design often finds shape in frac-
tal-like objects produced by CNC milling
machines and 3D printers. Not just for
addicted fanatics, they are also useful in
case you need to replace a part of your
ancient vacuum cleaner you can't order anymore. 3D printers offer the ability to print
parts and assemblies made of several
materials with different mechanical and
physical properties in a single build process.
The technology generates its own aesthetics.
In a way it brings to mind the early days of
Flash, or, for that matter, embroidery.

034 BANNED PARODY OF CCTV GALA BY BEIJING LOCALS, CHINA

035 BANNED PARODY OF CCTV GALA BY BEIJING LOCALS, CHINA

036 YOU, AS TONY STARK, AS IRON MAN → P.17

037 ELF EARS

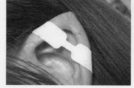

038 CHOOSE YOUR OWN KNITTING GRANDMA

AMATEURISSIMO

Isn't the distinction between professional and amateur strange? It takes more than average skill to engineer a drag racer. Amateur involvement ensures the survival of informal knowledge and is an important force in open design. The unrestrained and playful attitude levels complex technicalities with ease, finding its ultimate expression in amateurissimo, making the most baroque of DIY culture. As work and private life become increasingly intertwined, amateurissimo will make for a highly innovative market power, with YouTube as the engine that drives it.

039 CASE MODDING: YOUR PC BECOMES A CARTOON CHARACTER

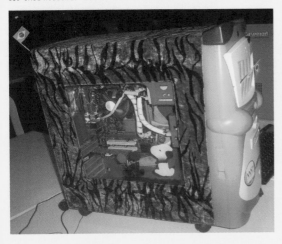

040 CASE MODDING: YOUR PC BECOMES A TOY CAR

041 ROBOFANATICS: THE MOBILE BAR ROBOT

042 ROBOFANATICS: INDIVIDUALITYBOT

043 PIMP MY WHEELS

044 PIMP MY GRILL

047 SHADES OF WOOD, BLUEPRINT DETAIL → P.91

048 SHADES OF WOOD, BLUEPRINT DETAIL

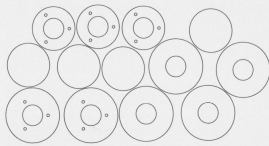

049 SHADES OF WOOD, BLUEPRINT DETAIL

050 SHADES OF WOOD, BLUEPRINT DETAIL

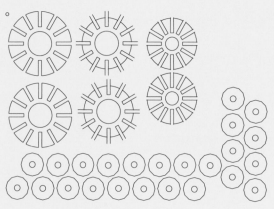

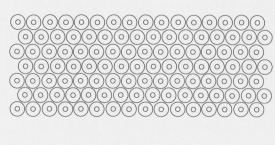

BLUEPRINTS

051 SHADES OF WOOD, INSTRUCTION

Blueprints are representations of objects-
to-be of the highest technical order.
Combining the technical drawing and the
instructions on how to execute that drawing,
the CAD file you send and squeeze into any
sort of printer can be regarded as such.
Blueprints and their derivatives form an
essential component of open design, as they
are the appearance of design in the form of
content-to-be-materialized. As such, they
are food for thought for IP lawyers who
embrace the open design ideology: blueprints
for all!

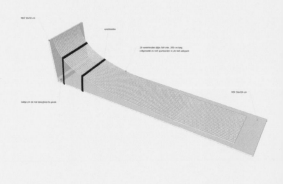

052 SHADES OF WOOD, DETAIL

053 SHADES OF WOOD, LAMP BY JORN VAN ECK AND OVERTREDERS-W

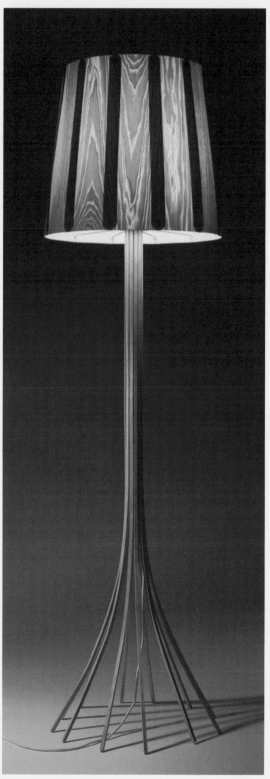

054 SHADES OF WOOD, DETAIL

055 SHADES OF WOOD, DETAIL

C

056 MAKING A COMPLEX STRUCTURE:

057 DON'T TRY THIS ALONE!

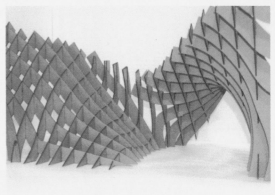

058 ALL YOU NEED IS PEOPLE, MARKERS AND... A FLIP CHART!

059 KIDS CO-CREATE ALL THE TIME

050 BARCAMP: USER-GENERATED CONFERENCES AKA 'UNCONFERENCES'

061 XINDANWEI ('NEW WORKING UNIT'), A FREEHAVEN FOR FREELANCERS

C

062 THIS BOOK WAS CO-CREATED FROM THE START → P.320

063 JSF: CO-CREATION IS NOT ALWAYS LOVE AND PEACE → P.140

064 FOR THOSE WHO THINK CO-CREATION LEADS TO NOTHING → P.164

065 CO-CREATING IS LIKE MAKING MUSIC

CO-CREATION

Were ancient community arts not about co-creation? Did farmers co-create by cultivating the commons? Has mass production taken away the mentality to co-create? Did the digital revolution restore the desire for it? Does the restoration of co-creation have the potential to change the world for the better? Do miners co-create, or bankers? Co-creation is a method for people to regain their ability to design their lives, their environments. This book is a testimonial to collaborative approaches: let co-creation expand into as many realms of life as it can.

066 DID FARMERS CULTIVATING THE COMMONS CO-CREATE?

C

067 INSTRUCTABLES.COM → P.224

COMMUNITY

Communities may be the opposite of consumers; consumers get everything mass-produced for them as individual entities, while communities take action, making more conscious choices. Groups tend to emancipate more easily than individuals and the internet is a powerful catalyzer. Since the rise of that network, the number and variety of communities has exploded, for better or for worse. Commercialization of online communities is mirrored by the revival of offline communities. Cooking together may form an important kind of collective agency.

068 INSTRUCTABLE: IKEA BIG LAMPS BY DANIEL SAAKES → P.223

069 INSTRUCTABLE: RECYCLED 55 GALLON BARREL CHAIR BY MONKEYBRAD

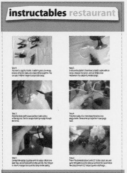

070 COMMUNITY SOUP

071 CROWD SOURCED CHEESE CAKE COMPETITION

072 INSTRUCTABLES RESTAURANT AT FAB 6

073 INSTRUCTABLES RESTAURANT: SETUP → P.224

074 CREATIVE COMMONS LICENCE: PUBLIC DOMAIN → P.66

074 CREATIVE COMMONS LICENCE: BY → P.4

076 CREATIVE COMMONS LICENCE: NON-COMMERCIAL (EUROPE) → P.4

077 CREATIVE COMMONS LICENCE: NON-COMMERCIAL (JAPAN) → P.4

078 CREATIVE COMMONS LICENCE: NON-COMMERCIAL (USA) → P.4

079 CREATIVE COMMONS LICENCE: NON-DERIVATIVE → P.66

080 CREATIVE COMMONS LICENCE: REMIX

081 CREATIVE COMMONS LICENCE: SHARE ALIKE → P.4

→ P.4

C

082 CREATIVE COMMONS LICENCE: SHARE

083 CREATIVE COMMONS LICENCE: ZERO

CREATIVE COMMONS

Creative Commons addresses problems and possibilities of the classic copyright in the digital era. All phases and steps in a design process that are not the physical making nor software can be covered in an open fashion by Creative Commons licences. All parts that can be regarded content – from the first sketch on a napkin until the final CAD file – can be released under four conditions to be recombined in six different licences.

084 LAWRENCE LESSIG

085 EARLY EXAMPLE OF CROWDSOURCING: THE OXFORD DICTIONARY

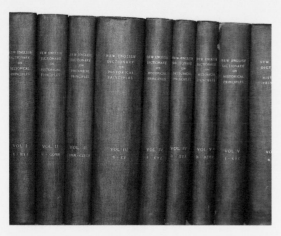

CROWDSOURCING

Crowdsourcing is a way for occasional communities to work together: rhizomatic collaboration. Individuals voluntarily taking on the role of a pixel in an image; part of a string of DNA coding for a remotely set function that creates or sustains the whole. In a networked gift economy, everyone is a potential sleeper cell. Collaborative efforts like these find themselves in a growing culture of individuals contributing to a world with a stronger social commons, essentially related to the type of social agency brought about by open design.

086 ONE FRAME OF FAME, ROEL WOUTERS, 2010

087 TEN THOUSAND CENTS, DRAWN BY 10000 ANONYMOUS ARTISTS, 2008

088 MECHANICAL TURK, A MARKETPLACE FOR WORK → P.52

Make Money
by working on HITs

HITs - *Human Intelligence Tasks* - are individual tasks that you work on. Find HITs now.

As a Mechanical Turk Worker you:

- Can work from home
- Choose your own work hours
- Get paid for doing good work

Find an interesting task → Work → Earn money

Find HITs Now

089 ACCESS TO A GLOBAL WORKFORCE 24/7

Get Results
from Mechanical Turk Workers

Ask workers to complete HITs - *Human Intelligence Tasks* - and get results using Mechanical Turk. Get started.

As a Mechanical Turk Requester you:

- Have access to a global, on-demand, 24 x 7 workforce
- Get thousands of HITs completed in minutes
- Pay only when you're satisfied with the results

Fund your account → Load your tasks → Get results

Get Started

C

090 A MILLION DOLLAR HOMEPAGE, ALEX TEW, 2005

091 GUERRILLA GARDENING → P.180

092 RED BLUE CHAIR. GERRIT T.H. RIETVELD (1918) – "RIETVELD PUBLISHED MANUALS ABOUT HOW TO MAKE HIS CHAIRS" → P.121

D

SPECIAL NOTE UNLIKE THE REST OF THE BOOK, THE IMAGE OF RIETVELD'S RED BLUE CHAIR (1918) MAY NOT BE COPIED (© GERRIT T.H. RIETVELD)

093 ROUGH AND READY, TORD BOONTJE (1998) – "IT WAS ESSENTIALLY A PREDECESSOR OF OPEN DESIGN" → P.133

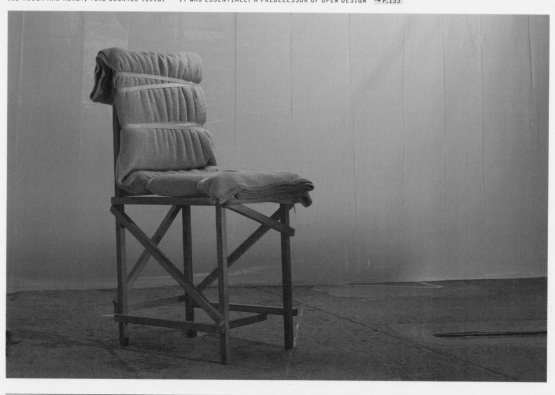

094 ARM CHAIR (2008) AND BONE CHAIR (2006) BY JORIS LAARMAN – "OPEN SOURCE VERSIONS OF MY WORK FOR EVERYONE. THAT IS MY GOAL" → P.125

095 HACK CHAIR, RONEN KADUSHIN (2009) – "THE CHAIR HAS CONFLICT IN IT. THERE IS SOME ANGER IN IT" → P.111

D

096 FIRST PORTABLE B&D DRILL, 1916 → P.26

097 DRILL FOR THE CONSUMER MARKET, 2010 → P.214

098 THE ARTS & CRAFTS MOVEMENT

099 IKEA PARODY

100 BUILDERS MARKET → P.156

DO IT YOURSELF

We find ourselves in the brief pocket of
the history of mankind in which DIY is a
choice, compared to thousands of years of
a DIY-by-default past and thousands more
of a DIY-by-default future, not to mention
the vast majority of people on the globe
at this very moment for which the term is
redundant. Like modern mass fabrication
technology has produced the term DIY,
modern peer fabrication technology
might make it disappear again. How about
knitting your own car tonight, or modding
your furniture in the microwave?

D

THE MAKER'S BILL OF RIGHTS

If you can't open it, you don't own it.

Ease of repair shall be a design ideal, **1**
not an afterthought.

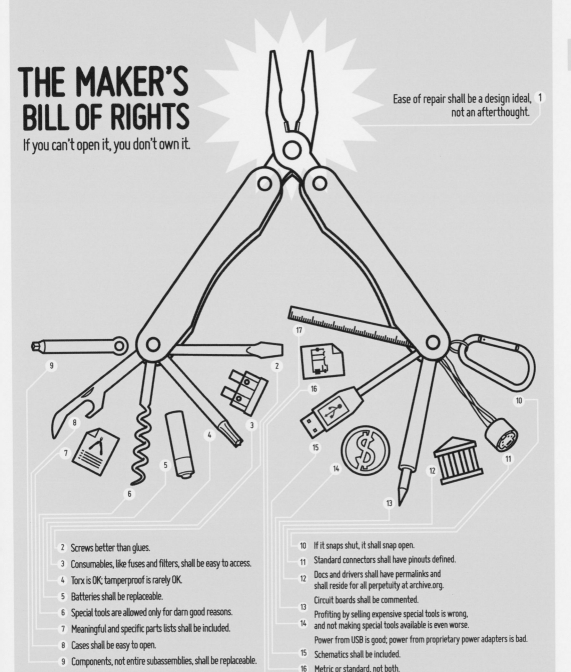

2 Screws better than glues.

3 Consumables, like fuses and filters, shall be easy to access.

4 Torx is OK; tamperproof is rarely OK.

5 Batteries shall be replaceable.

6 Special tools are allowed only for darn good reasons.

7 Meaningful and specific parts lists shall be included.

8 Cases shall be easy to open.

9 Components, not entire subassemblies, shall be replaceable.

10 If it snaps shut, it shall snap open.

11 Standard connectors shall have pinouts defined.

12 Docs and drivers shall have permalinks and
shall reside for all perpetuity at archive.org.

Circuit boards shall be commented.

13 Profiting by selling expensive special tools is wrong,

14 and not making special tools available is even worse.

Power from USB is good; power from proprietary power adapters is bad.

15 Schematics shall be included.

16 Metric or standard, not both.

17

Illustrated by James Provost. The Maker's Bill of Rights by Mister Jalopy.

D

103 SHAWL LASERCUT PATTERNS

104 LASERCUT SUNGLASSES MADE WITH MAGIC BOX, STUDIO LUDENS → P.237

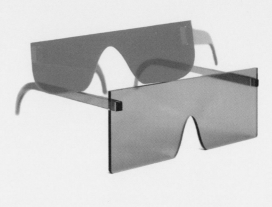

105 *FRUIT BOWL 128* BY SILVIE VAN DE LOO → P.236

106 128 LASERCUT PIECES MAKE A FRUIT BOWL

DOWNLOADABLE DESIGN

Back in the day, The Pirate Bay was an infamous P2P file-sharing service, used to exchange illegal CAD files for products of global brands like Mercedes, Apple and Gucci, which were fed into every household's 3D microwave to replace the household's car parts, PCs or clothing. It became legal again when the world government placed a very high sales tax on the liquid copy medium for those 3D prints. If this is to become our future, if digital files will be so easy to distribute and turn into physical products, what will become of our post-industrial age?

107 WOODEN BOX MADE WITH MAGIC BOX

E

108 CONGRESS OF THE BIGGEST EUROPEAN HACKER ASSOCIATION

109 NOTORIOUS FESTIVAL OPEN TO INNOVATION IN CULTURE → P.36

110 HAR '09: LAUNCH OF (UN)LIMITED DESIGN CONTEST → P.110

111 GUZMAN, LOGO OF ROBÖXOTICA, EVENT FOR COCKTAIL ROBOTS → P.17

112 THE ANNUAL GATHERING OF THE FAB LAB COMMUNITY → P.94

113 (UN)LIMITED DUTCH DESIGN AT DMY MAKERLAB, BERLIN → P.320

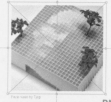

114 GENERATIVE POSTER DESIGN FOR MAKE ART, FRANCE

115 EVERYWHERE AND ALL THE TIME: MAKER FAIRES

E

EVENTS

The more time we spend online, the more time we want to share face to face. Communication intensifies because of technology and we intensify communication because we are intensified. Modes of presentation change, since a growing amount of culture is hands-on and process-oriented. We therefore need more festivities and festivals to celebrate collaborative and open design. We used to go to exhibitions and concerts, but since we are the exhibition ourselves, as we are the performers, different get-togethers pop up faster, in ever-changing format and line-up.

116 OPEN DESIGN CITY MARKET: CREATIVITY AND INVENTIVENESS RUN WILD

117 EXPLORING OPEN DESIGN FOR A BELGIAN EXPOSITION → P.129

118 EXHIBITING DESIGN IN A POST-INDUSTRIAL ERA → P.28

119 BAMBOO BIKE BY BAMBOOSERO

120 HANDMADE BATTERY LIGHTING → P.192

G

121 WATER BOILER MADE FROM SCRAP

122 AUTOMATIC HAMSTER SPINNER

123 THE BEST IDEA OF THE NETHERLANDS (TELEVISION SHOW, SBS6)

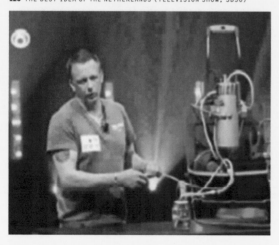

GRASSROOTS INVENTION

Innovation is everywhere, spreading thanks to the power of the Information Age, not only distributing information around the globe and across cultural boundaries, but also revitalizing notions of informal knowledge and sharing. Accompanying a growing awareness of resource depletion and the need to find renewable energy sources, grassroots invention will be taken more seriously by science and commerce. Another name for grassroots invention could simply be affordable innovation (for necessity and play).

124 CONVERTIBLE ROOF FOR HOT ROD WHEELCHAIR BY DARK RUBY MOON

125 CUSTOM ASSISTIVE SPOON BY FRENZY

G

126 FAB LABS WORLDWIDE → P.44

127 TESTING THE FAB FI WIRELESS NETWORK IN AFGHANISTAN

128 FAB LAB BOSTON → P.154

129 MOBILE FAB LAB

130 PREHISTORIC TOOLS FROM HACKED STONES → P.173

131 BIOTECHNOLOGY: HACKED VEGETABLES

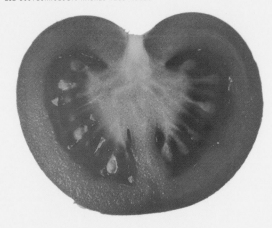

H

132 I HACKED YAHOO AND ALL I GOT WAS THIS LOUSY T-SHIRT

133 HACKED ROADSIGN

134 HALLOWEEN AT THE MASSACHUSETTS INSTITUTE OF TECHNOLOGY

135 THE HACKER LOGO, BASED ON THE GAME OF LIFE → P.90

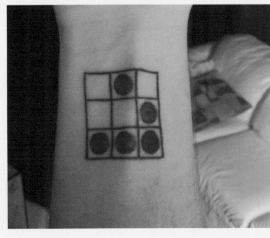

136 SWAPPING ELECTRONIC G.I. JOE AND BARBIE, THE YES MEN

HACKING

Hacking is well-known, dating back to the early days computing. Hacking is about exploring and understanding systems and products, and modifying and personalizing them. As a strategy, hacking is a world-wide phenomenon. Many things can be hacked, from politics (TheYesMen.org) to the newest Nintendo GameBoy; a stand-up comedian might 'hack' jokes by other comedians. You could even say that hacking is as old as human history. But then again: this theory is ready to be hacked!

H

137 A NEW GAMEBOY INSIDE AN OLD GAMEBOY

138 A CLASSIC MAC RUNNING ON OSX

139 HACKING FOR DUMMIES

140 ANONYMOUS

141 SIMULACRA – HACK BY BAS VAN BEEK

142 PLATONIC SUNS – HACK BY DANIEL SAAKES → P.233

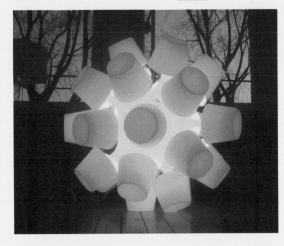

143 ÖLKE BÖLKE – HACK BY REMY&VEENHUIZEN

144 LAMPANBETWEENTWOBLANDAS – HACK BY STUDIO PLUS

145 ASTRID - HACKED BY LISETTE HAASNOOT

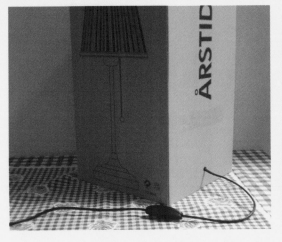

146 ASTRID HACKED BY LISETTE HAASNOOT

147 FLATPACK RE-ARRANGED – HACK BY KIEREN JONES

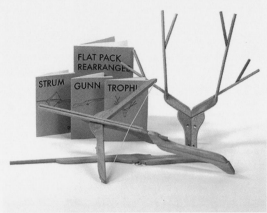

148 FLATPACK RE-ARRANGED – HACK BY KIEREN JONES

149 IKEA COFFIN – HACK BY JOE SCANLAN

150 HEX (IKEA HEX KEY NECKLACE) – HACK BY CYNTHIA HATHAWAY

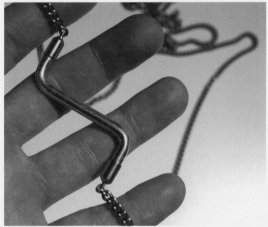

HACKING DESIGN

Echoing Joseph Beuys, IKEA once campaigned that 'everybody is a designer', celebrating their consumers armoured with an Allen key. Today, besides software, people hack politics, the military, cuisine, DNA, Barbie™ and also design. Hacking design not only results in many new products that are copied instantly, but is also an interesting driver for innovation, as is clear from the hacks that were shown at the exhibition *Platform21 = Hacking IKEA*, but also reminiscent of the 'phone phreaking' streak that inspired Steve Wozniac and Steve Jobs to start Apple.

151 BEACH BAG – HACK BY SARAH KUENG AND LOVIS KAPUTO → P.17

HELLO WORLD

The Hello World programme has traditionally been used to test new computer languages, starting with C. The whistles shown here are the Hello World of DIY 3D printing, first designed by Eberhard Rensch. The whistles have taken over Hello World. They are a fine representation of communication expressed as an object. If hello and whistle symbolize communication, what symbol will be produced by the genesis of the DIY bio-printer? Vocal cord tissue?

H

152 3D DRAWING OF A WHISTLE BY EBERHARD RENSCH FROM GERMANY → P.235

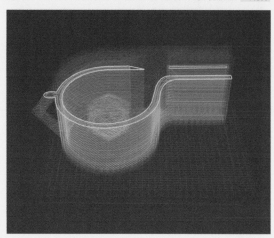

153 3D-PRINTED WHISTLES BY ANU FROM THE NETHERLANDS

154 3D-PRINTED WHISTLE BY SEBASTIAN FROM GERMANY

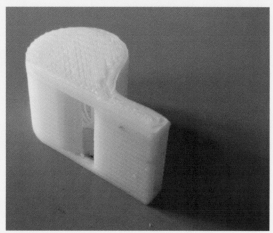

155 3D-PRINTED WHISTLES BY DAVE MENNINGER FROM THE USA

156 3D-PRINTED WHISTLE BY CHRIS PALMER FROM THE UK

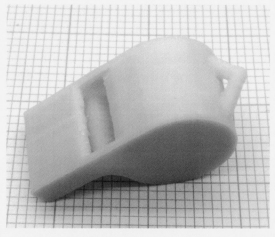

157 3D-RINTED WHISTLE BY ERIK DE BRUIJN FROM THE NETHERLANDS

158 3D-PRINTED WHISTLE BY BRADLEY RIGDON FROM THE USA

H

159 3D-PRINTED WHISTLE BY BEAK90 FROM THE USA

160 3D-PRINTED WHISTLE BY SIERT WIJNIA FROM THE NETHERLANDS

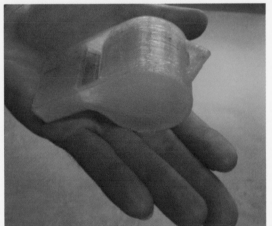

161 3D-PRINTED WHISTLE BY JUAN GONZALEZ FROM SPAIN

162 GERMAN HACKER'S 3D PRINTS OF DUTCH POLICE HANDCUFF KEY → P.78

163 2001, A SPACE ODYSSEY: PASSING KNOWLEDGE ON

164 SHARING KNOWLEDGE: LASCAUX CAVE PAINTINGS

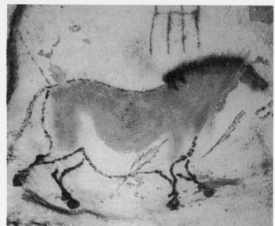

165 PASSING KNOWLEDGE FROM GENERATION TO GENERATION → P.164

166 BOOK OF KNOWLEDGE

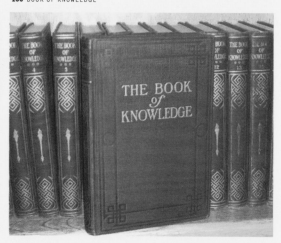

167 THE PIONEER PLAQUE: PASSING KNOWLEDGE TO ALIEN LIFE FORMS → P.51

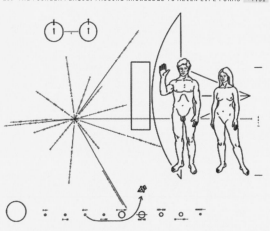

168 THE TREE OF KNOWLEDGE

169 GOOGLE POWER

KNOWLEDGE

Knowledge production is no longer the exclusive domain of science. Moving large chunks of information around at the push of a button has become democratized, at least in the strongly networked part of the globe. The information we access feels increasingly Wikipedized and Googlized and more and more 'informal' knowledge is produced and shared. Many initiatives are born around notions of peer and alternative knowledge production, fueLled by network communities, sharing both knowledge and actual practice.

170 FLÅMMA: A BASIC NEED → P.44

171 OLD KNOWLEDGE IN CONTEMPORARY TIMES

K

172 MAKING FIRE WITH IKEA PRODUCTS

173 IKEA HACK BY HELMUT SMITS

174 1963: MAKE THE RIGHT CHOICES AS A DESIGNER!

MANIFESTOS

Openness is still very much a choice, not a default. If it were a default, there would be no need for directions, ideological or not. Ideological efforts need rules, codes of conduct, manuals, bills, declarations, manifestos, often very precise and helpful, sometimes too dogmatic ('wannabe blueprints'), sometimes agnostic, on occasion hilarious. Like the revolution of digitally sharing designs that can be executed all over the world just by pushing a button, wouldn't it be super if a revolution manifesto took effect by default?

175 1986: CONSCIENTIOUS HACKING → P.93

176 1998: BE IMPERFECT!

177 2005: MAKE THINGS! → P.88

178 2006: GIVE AWAY TYPEFACES!

M

179 2009: RIP YOUR OWN CULTURE!

180 RIP!: THE PAST ALWAYS TRIES TO CONTROL THE FUTURE

181 2010: DO IT NOW!

Yes. Now.

I am an artist. • I take initiative • I do the work, not the job. • Without critics, there is no art. • I am a Linchpin. I am not easily replaced. • If it's never been done before, even better. • The work is personal, too important to phone in. • The lizard brain is powerless in the face of art. • I make it happen. Every day. • Every interaction is an opportunity to make a connection. • The past is gone. It has no power. The future depends on choices I make now. • I own the means of production—the system isn't as important as my contribution to it. • I see the essential truth unclouded by worldview, and that truth drives my decisions. • I lean into the work, not away from it. Trivial work doesn't require leaning. • Busywork is too easy. Rule-breaking works better and is worth the effort. • Energy is contagious. The more I put in, the more the world gives back. • It doesn't matter if I'm always right. It matters that I'm always moving. • I raise the bar. I know yesterday's innovation is today's standard. • I will not be brainwashed into believing in the status quo. • Artists don't care about credit. We care about change. • There is no resistance if I don't allow it to defeat me. • I embrace a lack of structure to find a new path. • I am surprising. (And often surprised). • I donate energy and risk to the cause. • I turn charisma into leadership. • The work matters. • Go. Make something happen.

Find out more

Feel to share. Make your own. Print it.

182 2009: STOP RECYCLING, START REPAIRING! → P.214

Platform21's

Repair Manifesto

1. Make your products live longer!
Repairing means taking the opportunity to give your product a second life. Don't ditch it, stitch it!
Don't end it, mend it! Repairing is not anti-consumption. It is anti- needlessly throwing things away.

2. Things should be designed so that they can be repaired.
Product designers: Make your products repairable. Share clear, understandable information about DIY repairs.
Consumers: Buy things you know can be repaired, or else find out why they don't exist. Be critical and inquisitive.

3. Repair is not replacement.
Replacement is throwing away the broken bit. This is NOT the kind of repair that we're talking about.

4. What doesn't kill it makes it stronger.
Every time we repair something, we add to its potential, its history, its soul and its inherent beauty.

5. Repairing is a creative challenge.
Making repairs is good for the imagination. Using new techniques, tools and materials ushers in possibility rather than dead ends.

183 GUERRILLA GARDENING, A MANUALFESTO

184 2010: REPAIR YOURSELF!

MASS CUSTOMIZATION

Open design, hacking, sharing, co-creation
is becoming truly fashionable and therefore
valuable to corporations and advertising
agencies. A characteristic example is
the mass customization of sportswear.
Frontrunner NIKE launched its NIKEiD
service campaign back in 1999. It was a
blank canvas for almost anyone to fill,
and simultaneously a crowdsourced market
study for the ad agencies working for
the sportswear manufacturer. What does
the average 17-year-old Asian sweatshop
employee think about this book?

185 NIKEiD logo

186 SELECT YOUR MODEL ...

187 CHOOSE FROM A WIDE RANGE OF COLOURS ...

188 ADD THE JUICY DETAILS ...

189 AND ORDER! → P.114

M

190 NIHILIZT → P.36

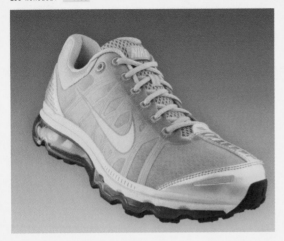

191 PINK CLOUD

192 GLOBAL SALVATION

193 UNITE

M

194 NEXT NATURE

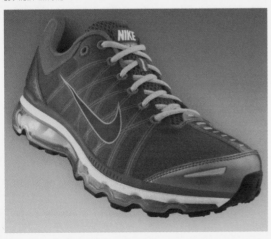

195 SAMOTHRACE

OPEN EVERYTHING

Open source describes practices that promote access to the end product's source materials. Some consider open source a philosophy; others consider it a pragmatic methodology. Fact is, open is spreading. Open source originated from software coding, but many other realms are seen as potentially open. Some claim they can solve urgent social, economic and ethical issues; others are for play and provocation. With so many creative terrains that can and should be open, defining what shouldn't be open might be more efficient.

196 THE OPEN SOURCE INITIATIVE LOGO, BUILT FROM GENERIC SHAPES

197 OPEN HARDWARE: ARDUINO UNO MICROCONTROLLER BOARD → P.206

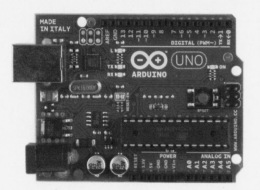

198 A FRITZING SKETCH SHOULD BE FAIRLY SELF-EXPLANATORY → P.221

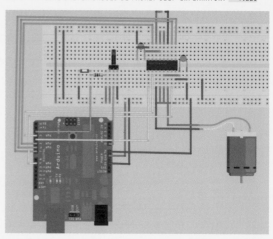

199 OPEN PCR: MOLECULAR BIOLOGY FOR THE HOBBYISTS AND CURIOUS

200 OPEN SOURCE INSTRUMENTS: DJ MIXER

0

201 THE CHOICE OF AN OPEN GENERATION: OPEN COLA

202 I'M FEELING OPEN → P.240

203 OPEN SOURCE ANIMATION SOFTWARE: BLENDER

204 OPEN SOURCE GAMING: LIN CITY, THE OPEN SOURCE NEPHEW OF SIM CITY

205 OPEN SOURCE SCIENCE: OPEN WET WARE

206 OPEN BEVERAGES: VORES ØL OPEN SOURCE BEER

207 EARLY, GUTENBERG-STYLE PRINTING PRESS → P.64

208 COMMODORE MPS801 MATRIX PRINTER

209 POLAROID: INSTANT IMAGES FROM THE PALM OF YOUR HAND

P

PRINTING

Printing represents a revolutionary way of reproducing symbols, but it takes on added impact when it comes to reproducing objects. 2D and 3D printing are no longer unusual; even scents and microscopic organic tissue can be printed now. The required hardware is entering the consumer market, and it is also being made in open backyard industries. These DIY initiatives can expect to run up against copyright and patent agents: a challenge and an opportunity for an open, sustainist prosumption society.

210 BIOPRINTING: PRINTING ORGANIC TISSUE AND BONE STRUCTURES

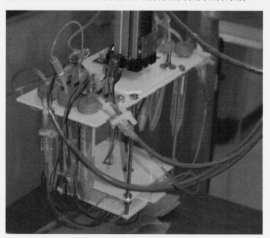

211 RAPID PROTOTYPING: PRINTING OBJECTS FROM YOUR DESKTOP → P.130

212 SPRAY-ON-CLOTHING BY FABRICAN: PRINTING CLOTHES

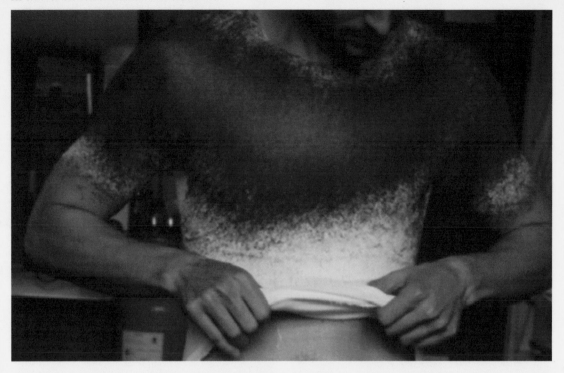

213 FOOD PRINTER PROTOTYPE BY PHILIPS DESIGN: DOWNLOAD RECIPE, ADD NUTRITION VALUE AND PRINT YOUR DAILY BREAD

P

214 GUIYU IS ONE OF THE BIGGEST E-WASTE CENTRES OF THE WORLD → P.192

215 A LOT OF INTERNATIONAL BRANDED GADGETS END UP ILLEGALLY IN GUIYU

216 E-WASTE

217 THIS MAN ASSEMBLES PLASTIC WASTE TO TRY TO RESELL IT

R

RECYCLING

Waste is one of the first modern products. Did it exist a few millennia ago? Raw materials do not get depleted; they just change their composition. One has to mine them elsewhere, often in a more accessible site, such as a local dump, or 'catch' them just before the dump. The challenge is to create the aura of the new while working with used materials, thus meeting the demand for alternative production. Sooner than you think, every day of the week will be a Freitag.

218 GEEK RECYCLING: LASER-ETCHED CIRCUIT BOARD CLOCK, BY JOE

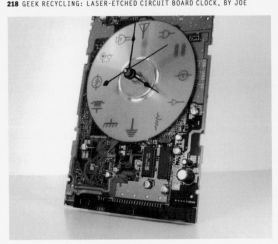

219 EXPORTING BEER MINUS WASTE: HEINEKEN WOBO BOTTLE, 1963

220 WHY WASN'T WOBO SUCCESSFUL?

221 MIELE SPACE STATION, 2012 ARCHITECTEN

222 MIELE SPACE STATION (DETAIL) → P.193

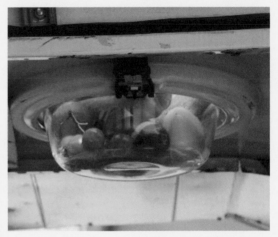

223 FREITAG BAG FROM RECYCLED TRUCK TARPAULIN → P.216

224 MAARTEN BAAS: A CRUEL WAY TO RECYCLE A RIETVELD ZIG ZAG CHAIR

R

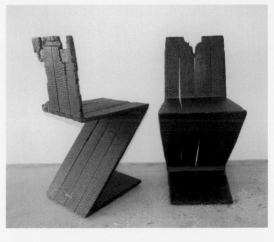

REMIX

Remixing is something that comes from deep within us. A child learns by remixing his or her parents' behavior. Nothing novel is so new it does not relate to anything remotely similar. Originality can be regarded a strange obstacle to innovation, comparing the Western world to China. The remixing mindset is an enormous source of creativity – the Chinese refer to it as *Shanzhai*. Would open design be possible without it? Would culture be possible without it? What is the difference between jazz and casemodding?

225 FORM FOLLOWS FUN: SHANZHAI TERRACOTTA ARMY PHONE

226 FORM FOLLOWS FUN: SHANZHAI POOH-PHONE

227 FORM FOLLOWS FUN: SHANZHAI CIGARETTE BOX PHONE

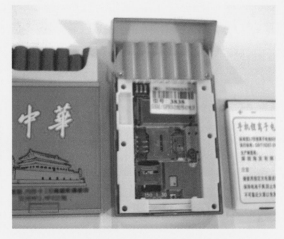

228 CHANEL-STYLE PILLBOX PHONE

229 CHANEL-STYLE PILLBOX PHONE

R

230 SUPERSIZE ME: SHANZHAI PHONE WITH A TELELENS

231 IPOD STYLE SHANZHAI PHONE

232 EXTRA FEATURES: SHANZHAI PHONE THAT RUNS ON WINDOWS 98

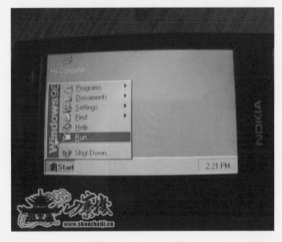

233 EXTRA FEATURES: WATCHING CCTV ON YOUR SHANZHAI PHONE → P.237

234 COUNTERFEIT BECOMES COUNTER CULTURE

235 WYSIWYG: THE OFFICE OF CHINESE LIQUOR BRAND WU LIANG YE

R

236 REPAIRING = CARING → P.207

237 EVERYTHING IS WORTH REPAIRING

238 PLATFORM 21 = REPAIRING IN NEW YORK

239 PLATFORM 21 = REPAIRING IN NEW YORK

R

240 PLATFORM 21 = REPAIRING

241 PLATFORM 21 = REPAIRING

242 YOUR GRANDPARENTS REPAIRED ON A DAILY BASIS → P.214

243 MOBILE REPAIR SERVICES IN INDIA → P.142

244 ANTIQUES ROADSHOW: TRASH OR TREASURE?

245 WHEN WILL WE BRING OUR ELECTRONIC DEVICES TO A CRAFTSMAN?

REPAIRING

The global repair network is still changing. It used to be very local: you used to bring your broken radio around the block. Now you just throw it away; at best, it is disassembled and reassembled into something else in Asia or Africa. You used to bring your car to the mechanic; now it is put on a bulk carrier shipped to Lagos. But repairing isn't only fun, it also changes your perspective on materiality. Soon askthemechanic.com will be bought by instructables.com.

246 THERE, I FIXED IT - REDNECK REPAIRS™

R

REPRODUCTION

Reproduction means accessibility for the
many; reproduction of production even more so.
In contrast to the increasingly specialized
machinery of industrial production at
large, nowadays peer and open workshops
equip themselves with 'self-replicating'
3D printers like RepRap and MakerBot. Do
these machines have the potential to pose
a challenge to industrial production? Will
the peers pair that challenge and change the
global production landscape as Gutenberg and
the steam engine once did? Can digitization
really affect the physical?

247 REPRAP PARTS, PRINTED OUT BY... A REPRAP 3D PRINTER

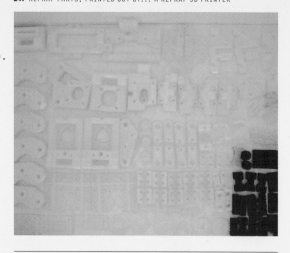

248 THE REPRAP

249 THE REPRAP

R

250 L'ARTISAN ELECTRONIQUE: DIGITAL CERAMIC PRINTING BY UNFOLD

251 ENDLESS CHAIR, DIRK VAN DER KOOIJ, 2010

252 A BABY REPRAP'S PARENT → P.232

253 THE CHILD MADE ITS FIRST GRANDCHILD PART IMMEDIATELY...!

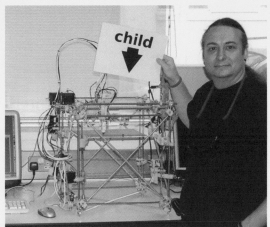

254 THE MAKERBOT, AN AFFORDABLE, OPEN SOURCE 3D PRINTER → P.78

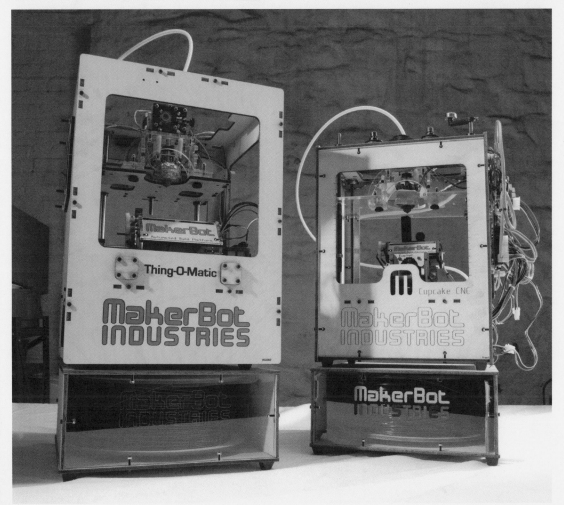

R

255 10,000 BC, AGRICULTURAL REVOLUTION

256 1815-1914, INDUSTRIAL REVOLUTION → P.27

R

257 1980, SERVICE REVOLUTION

258 1990, DIGITAL REVOLUTION → P.234

R

259 *SHARE THIS* ICON (DESIGNED AND COPYRIGHTED BY ALEX KING)

SHARING

What would the share-by-default option mean for a global society where Wikileaks is able to stir things up for weeks? What if everyone could follow every move you and I make? Big Brother would become blind instantly, and a lot of intellectual property would get lost. Would innovation still happen? Will you and I be able to find each other and get lost in a co-creative Babel? We don't know, but it is time we find out, if we are taking the worldwide open experiment seriously. Share this!

260 CONNECTING THE DOTS: BONJOUR NETWORKING, APPLE

261 CONNECTING THE DOTS: SHARE ICON, USED BY FRAMESBYMAIL

262 FIRST AID FOR SHARING: SHAREABLE EMBLEM → P.234

263 SHARE ICON ZIDDU

S

264 FACEBOOK SHARE BUTTON

265 FLICKR SHARE BUTTON → P.154

266 *SHARE.EPFS* LOGO, STUDENT PORTAL BY GOOGLE

267 FAB LAB LOGO → P.38

268 AMAZON SHARE ICON

269 SHARE ICON *CLICKOVA* FOR MOBILE PHONES

S

270 OPEN SOURCE HOUSING PROJECT, EMERGING GHANA, BY BLAANC AND JOÃO CAEIRO → P.180

271 FAIRPHONE: CELL PHONE DESIGN WITHOUT ANY CONFLICT MINERALS, A FAIRER PHONE FOR THE THIRD WORLD → P.217

S

272 THE $50 LEG: A CHEAP PROSTHESIS FOR DEVELOPING COUNTRIES → P.218

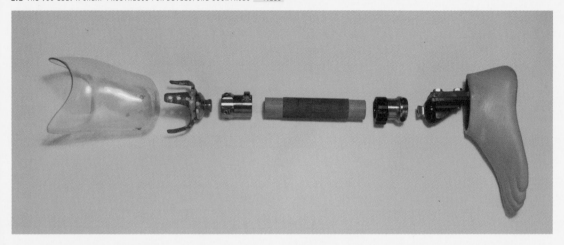

273 BAMBOO INSTEAD OF ALUMINIUM

274 TRYING DIFFERENT MATERIALS

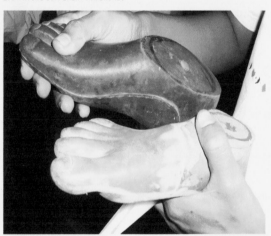

275 THE $50LEG: A COLLABORATIVE EFFORT

SOCIAL DESIGN

S

Social design covers a range between products and services, creating to change society and build a better world. SocialDesignSite.com bears the slogan 'We cannot *not* change the world'. Doesn't that say enough? Design is a collective and collaborative responsibility, which has a solution-seeking aesthetic that goes beyond beauty. If it regards every situation to be possibly designed, openness is an evolutionary asset of its mission and copying an obligation of all its participants. It's a different proposition than the average CSR.

STANDARDS

Standards enable translingual communication. They enable Lego to be a profitable enterprise. They have been nice for kids, but also for designers and hackers. Standardization wars consume a lot of energy for the sake of open market competition, leaving consumers with a new harvest of hardware plugs every season. What is a good balance between minimal standardization and maximum bandwidth for diversity and creativity? What comprises the architecture of digital co-creation, and distributed open fabrication, to share and sustain open design?

276 NAPOLEON TEMPORARILY SUSPENDED THE 1795 METRIC SYSTEM

277 PAPER SIZE STANDARDS

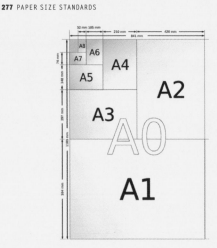

278 EUROPEAN PARLIAMENT ELECTION CAMPAIGN

279 STANDARDIZING INTERACTION: A GESTURE LIBRARY FOR TOUCH SCREENS

one-finger double tap

280 QWERTY: AN OLD STANDARD THAT SURVIVED NEW MEDIA

S

281 LEGO SINCE 1949 → P.88

282 ESPERANTO, AN EASY-TO-LEARN AND POLITICALLY NEUTRAL LANGUAGE

283 DETAIL FROM OPEN DESIGN MANUAL BY INTRASTRUCTURES

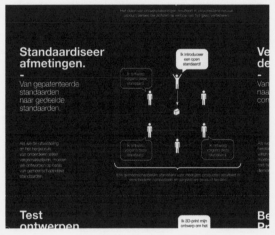

284 *OPEN STRUCTURES GRID* BY THOMAS LOMMÉE → P.229

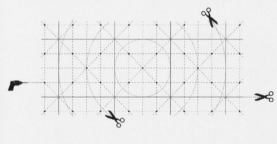

285 A 20 TO 5 MM PLUG BEING ADDED TO *OPEN STRUCTURES* → P.229

286 *OPEN STRUCTURES* KITCHEN → P.229

S

287 SOCIAL MESSAGING PLATFORM TEMPLATE

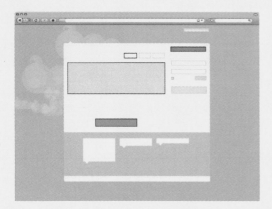

288 ENTERTAINMENT PLATFORM WEBSITE TEMPLATE

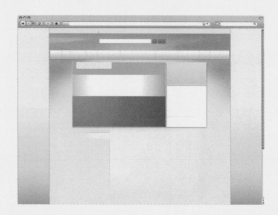

289 COLLABORATIVE ONLINE ENCYCLOPEDIA TEMPLATE

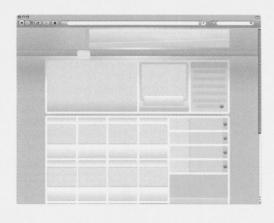

290 SOCIAL NETWORK WEBSITE TEMPLATE

291 COLLABORATIVE ONLINE ENCYCLOPEDIA TEMPLATE

292 SEARCH ENGINE TEMPLATE

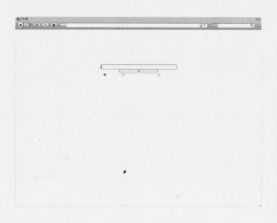

T

293 SWEDISH FURNITURE STORE WEBSITE TEMPLATE

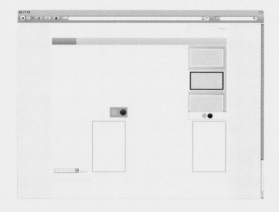

294 ONLINE BOOKSTORE TEMPLATE

295 AUCTION WEBSITE TEMPLATE

296 SECURITY SERVICE WEBSITE TEMPLATE

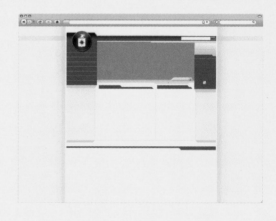

297 SECURITY SERVICE WEBSITE TEMPLATE

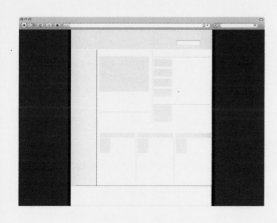

298 SOCIAL BOOKMARKING WEBSITE TEMPLATE

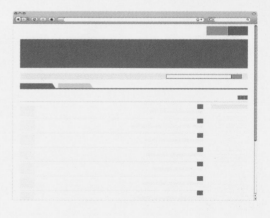

T

299 GLOBAL BRANDING: MORE PEOPLE CAN DRINK COKE THAN BOTTLED WATER

300 IMMIGRATION: NOT ALL CITIZENS ARE TREATED EQUALLY IN THE GLOBAL VILLAGE → P.180

T

301 CHEAP CLOTHES OFTEN MEAN: CHEAP LABOUR

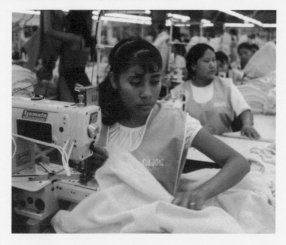

302 GLOCALIZATION: GLOBAL BRANDS, LOCAL CUSTOMS → P.135

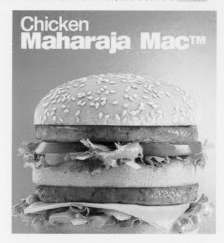

303 AFGHAN RUG: OLD TRADITIONS, CONTEMPORARY INFLUENCES

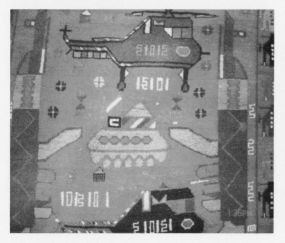

304 THE 1ST PHOTOGRAPH OF OUR PLANET: THE *BLUE MARBLE* PICTURE, 1972

GLOBALIZATION

Most of the world's consumer goods are made in China. Most of our debts are produced in the US. Most of our meat and soy comes from Latin America. Can neoliberal capitalism ultimately sustain a truly globalized world with one integrated economy? How free is a free market economy when there is only one market left? Is it possible that the entire planet will, from that moment, suddenly adopt collaborative, open design and innovation?

305 NEW MARKETS ARE EMERGING: WHERE DO YOU GO SHOPPING?

T

306 THE ULTIMATE DECENTRALIZATION MACHINE: THE INTERNET, AS IT WAS MAPPED ON 3 AUGUST 2009

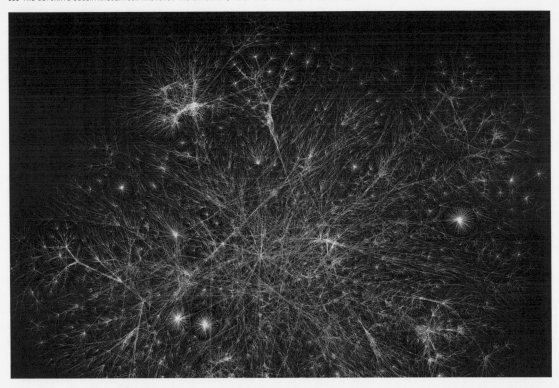

307 ONLINE EVERYWHERE YOU GO, 24 HOURS A DAY → P.64

T

308 UP FRONT, PERSONABLE AND FACE-TO-FACE → P.182

309 HOME IS WHERE I PLUG IN MY LAPTOP

310 DECENTRALIZATION = RETRIBALIZATION (BURNING MAN FESTIVAL, USA)

311 MOBILE PEER-TO-WORLD REPORTING

NETWORK SOCIETY

In the network society, information will travel at light speed. In the network society, no one will be offline anymore. In the network society, the boundaries between public and private will blur so much that it will become unclear whether innovation comes from the industry or from households. The spectrum between one-to-one and many-to-many will fully be utilized by both humans and machines, messages will still be broadcast, but objects will too.

312 TWITTER VISUALIZED BY FLOWING DATA → P.154

T

313 MASS-DEFORESTATION IN THE AMAZON → P.45

314 OLD STYLE STRIP MINING

T

315 CONFLICT MINERALS → P.217

316 COLTAN, CONFLICT MINERAL IN EVERY CELL PHONE

317 OIL SLICK AFTER DISASTER IN THE GULF OF MEXICO, MAY 24 2010

318 BURNING OIL WELLS, KUWAIT 1992 → P.227

SCARCITY OF RESOURCES

Fear of resource depletion is or will become the driving force behind a repair economy — to the extent that it does not already exist in most people's lives. The use of raw materials just reshuffles them around the globe. In a few centuries, coltan mining will mean digging for ancient mobile phones in the rubble of former cities. Every openness emerges from physicality, and an average Google server plant consumes as much electricity as a city of 500,000. Who knows about 'open mining'?

319 COVER OF NATIONAL GEOGRAPHIC MAGAZINE, JUNE 2004 → P.234

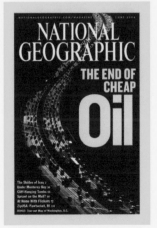

T

320 CITROËN MEHARI CAR ENGINE: WYS = WYG → P.226

321 HASSELBLAD CAMERA: WYS = WYG

322 OLD TELEPHONE: WYS = WYG → P.204

323 CELLULOID: WYS = WYG

324 WATCH: WYS = WYG

W

WYS ≠ WYG

Automated production processes have become so refined that it has become virtually impossible for enthusiasts to re-engineer microscopic parts of machines. That sets limits on to how open an open design can be, for instance if it comes to open hardware projects: what parts does one still buy because they are too tiny to produce and which ones can you truly produce openly? Will new fabbing machinery win the industrial race? What about growing hardware when biotechnology and electronics merge and become the premium hardware supplier?

325 AUDI R5 ENGINE: WYS ≠ WYG → P.93

326 DIGITAL CAMERA: WYS ≠ WYG

327 IPHONE: WYS ≠ WYG

328 DVD: WYS ≠ WYG

329 IF YOU CAN'T OPEN IT, YOU DON'T OWN IT

330 NOT EVERYONE IS AN ENGINEER

W

DO IT YOURSELF

96 COURTESY OF BLACK & DECKER
97 PHOTO: MIKE NEILSON
98 COURTESY OF THE DAILY BUNGALOW @ FLICKR
99 AUTHOR UNKNOWN
100 PHOTO: THOMAS VAN DE WEERT
101 ILLUSTRATION: JAMES PROVOST
    → WWW.JAMESPROVOST.COM

DOWNLOADABLE DESIGN

102 PHOTO: MAARTEN VAN DER MEER
    → WWW.MAARTENVANDERMEER.NL
103 PHOTO: MAARTEN VAN DER MEER
    → WWW.TOETERS.NET
104 PHOTO: WOUTER WALMINK & STUDIO:LUDENS
    → WWW.STUDIOLUDENS.COM
105 PHOTO: NORBERT WAALBOER
    → WWW.DEBESTEFOTOGRAAF.NL
106 PHOTO: NORBERT WAALBOER
    → WWW.SEMDESIGN.NL
107 PHOTO: WOUTER WALMINK & STUDIO:LUDENS
    → WWW.WALMINK.COM

EVENTS

108 CHAOS COMPUTER CLUB → HTTP://CCC.DE
109 ARTWORK FOR PICNIC '10 → DESIGN BY
    MARTINE EYZENGA, MARCEL KAMPMAN,
    WWW.KAMPMAN.NL, PICNICNETWORKS.ORG
110 LOGO HACKIN AT RANDOM → DESIGN BY
    HELEEN KLOPPER→ HTTP://HAR2009.ORG
111 ORIGINAL DRAWING LOGO BY RICHARD
    WIENTZEK → WWW.ROBOEXOTICA.ORG
112 PHOTO AND DESIGN: FIONA VAN DER GEIJN,
    'FAB 6 BAG' → HTTP://FAB6.NL
113 ARTWORK (UN)LIMITED DUTCH DESIGN BY
    ERIK NAP
114 MAKE ART → HTTP://MAKEART.GOTO10.
    ORG/2010/?PAGE=POSTERS
115 MAKE → WWW.MAKERFAIRE.COM
116 PHOTO: CHRISTOPHER DOERING, JAY
    COUSINS, AND DANIELA MARZAVAN, OF OPEN
    DESIGN CITY, BERLIN
117 ARTWORK: INTRASTRUCTURES.NET
118 EXHIBITION CURATED BY PAUL ATKINSON,
    FOR HUB: NATIONAL CENTRE FOR CRAFT &
    DESIGN

GRASSROOTS INVENTION

119 ERIK (HASH) HERSMAN → WWW.FLICKR.COM/
121 PEOPLE/WHITEAFRICAN
122 COURTESY OF HERALD POST
123 HET BESTE IDEE VAN NEDERLAND,
    SBS6 / SBS BROADCASTING
124 ERIC OVELGONE (DARKRUBYMOON),

    → WWW.CAFEPRESS.COM/DARKRUBYMOON
125 GREGG HORTON → WWW.INSTRUCTABLES.COM/
    ID/CUSTOM-ASSISTIVE-SPOON
126 SOURCE: WWW.FABACADEMY.ORG
127 PHOTO: KEITH BERKOBEN
128 PHOTO: FAB LAB BOSTON
129 SOURCE: HTTP://WEB.MIT.EDU/SPOTLIGHT/
    MOBILE-FABLAB

HACKING

130 PHOTO: EL ÁGORA
    → HTTP://COMMONS.WIKIMEDIA.ORG
131 PHOTO: FOENYX
    → HTTP://COMMONS.WIKIMEDIA.ORG
132 PHOTO: PREMSHREE PILLAI
    → WWW.FLICKR.COM/PHOTOS/PREMSHREE
133 BRUCE DOWNS
134 PAUL → SOURCE: WWW.MITADMISSIONS.
    ORG/TOPICS/LIFE/HACKS_TRADITIONS/
    HACK_OR_TREAT.SHTML
135 AUTHOR/OWNER UNKNOWN
    SOURCE: HTTP://CATB.ORG
136 THE YES MEN → HTTP://THEYESMEN.ORG
137 PHOTO: CRTDRONE → WWW.FLICKR.COM/
    PHOTOS/56035206@N00/SETS/72157624009
    019424/
138 PHOTO: WILLIE LÓPEZ → WWW.FLICKR.COM/
    PHOTOS/PIXELMANIATIK/2133750549/
139 WWW.ETHICALHACKERGUIDE.COM
140 PHOTO: VINCENT DIAMANTE
    → HTTP://EN.WIKIPEDIA.ORG/WIKI/
    ANONYMOUS_(GROUP)

HACKING DESIGN

141 PHOTO: PLATFORM 21 / PREMSELA
    → WWW.BASVANBEEK.COM
142 PHOTO: PLATFORM 21 / PREMSELA
    → HTTP://LOG.SAAKES.NET
143 PHOTO: PLATFORM 21 / PREMSELA
    → WWW.REMYVEENHUIZEN.NL
144 PHOTO: PLATFORM 21 / PREMSELA
    → WWW.WOUTERVANNIEUWENDIJK.NL
145 PHOTO: LISETTE HAASNOOT
146 WWW.LISETTEHAASNOOT.NL
147 PHOTO: KIEREN JONES
148 WWW.KIERENJONES.COM
149 PHOTO: PLATFORM 21 / PREMSELA → WWW.
    THINGSTHATFALL.COM/JOESCANLAN.PHP
150 PHOTO: PLATFORM 21 / PREMSELA →
    WWW.HATHAWAYDESIGNS.ORG
151 PHOTO: SARAH KUENG & LOVIS CAPUTO
    → WWW.KUENG-CAPUTO.CH

HELLO WORLD

152 EBERHARD RENSCH
    → WWW.THINGIVERSE.COM/IMAGE:5199
153 WHISTLE ANU
    → WWW.THINGIVERSE.COM/DERIVATIVE:2655
154 SEBASTIAN
    → WWW.THINGIVERSE.COM/DERIVATIVE:3243
155 DAVE MENNINGER
    → WWW.THINGIVERSE.COM/DERIVATIVE:1779
156 CHRIS PALMER
    → WWW.THINGIVERSE.COM/DERIVATIVE:1302
157 ERIK DE BRUIJN
    → WWW.THINGIVERSE.COM/DERIVATIVE:700
158 BRADLEY RIGDON
    → WWW.THINGIVERSE.COM/DERIVATIVE:701
159 BEAK90
    → WWW.THINGIVERSE.COM/DERIVATIVE:2959
160 SIERT WIJNIA
    → WWW.THINGIVERSE.COM/IMAGE:15962
161 JUAN GONZALEZ
    → WWW.THINGIVERSE.COM/DERIVATIVE:4600
162 DESIGN BY RAY AKA MR. HANDCUFF,
    SOURCE: TWEAKERS.NET

KNOWLEDGE

163 CLASSIC INTRODUCTION SCENE FROM
    STANLEY KUBRICK'S 2001: A SPACE ODYSSEY
164 SOURCE: HTTP://COMMONS.WIKIMEDIA.ORG
165 PHOTO BY JULIAN COCHRANE, 1904;
    COURTESY OF ROB OECHSLE COLLECTION
166 SOURCE: HTTP://COMMONS.WIKIMEDIA.ORG
167 DESIGN: NASA → HTTP://EN.WIKIPEDIA.
    ORG/WIKI/PIONEER_PLAQUE
168 THE FALL OF MAN, JACOB JORDAENS →
    SOURCE: HTTP://COMMONS.WIKIMEDIA.ORG
169 ACES4HIRE
170 DESIGN AND IMAGES: HELMUT SMITS -
173 HTTP://HELMUTSMITS.NL/DESIGN

MANIFESTOS

174 FIRST THINGS FIRST, MANIFESTO BY
    DESIGNER KEN GARLAND
175 AUTHOR UNKNOWN, MORE AT:
    WWW.PHRACK.ORG/ISSUES.HTML?
    ISSUE=7&ID=3&MODE=TXT
176 BRUCE MAU → WW.BRUCEMAUDESIGN.COM
177 MAKEZINE → HTTP://CDN.MAKEZINE.COM/
    MAKE/MAKERS_RIGHTS.PDF
178 SCREENSHOT: WWW.DESIGNWRITING
    RESEARCH.ORG/FREE_FONTS.HTML
179 DVD RIP! A REMIX MANIFESTO
    → HTTP://RIPREMIX.COM/
180 STILL FROM RIP! A REMIX MANIFESTO
    → HTTP://RIPREMIX.COM/
181 SOURCE: HTTP://SETHGODIN.TYPEPAD.COM/
    FILES/THELINCHPINMANIFESTO.PDF
183 PLATFORM 21 — WWW.PLATFORM21.NL/

317

DOWNLOAD/4375
183 DAVID TRACEY, WWW.DAVIDTRACEY.CA
184 SOURCE: WWW.IFIXIT.COM/MANIFESTO

MASS CUSTOMIZATION

185 JUST DO IT: WWW.NIKEID.COM OR WATCH IT
195 AT WWW.FLICKR.COM/GROUPS/NIKE-ID

OPEN EVERYTHING

196 'THIS IMAGE OF SIMPLE GEOMETRY IS
INELIGIBLE FOR COPYRIGHT AND THEREFORE
IN THE PUBLIC DOMAIN'
197 PHOTO: THE ARDUINO TEAM, SOURCE:
HTTP://ARDUINO.CC/EN/MAIN/HARDWARE
198 SKETCH: FRITZING TEAM,
SOURCE: WWW.FRITZING.ORG
199 PHOTO: ROBERT GOODIER, SOURCE:
WWW.FLICKR.COM/PHOTOS/44221799@N08/
200 AURORA → WWW.AURORAMIXER.COM
201 PHOTO: UNUKORNO,
SOURCE: HTTP://EN.WIKIPEDIA.ORG/WIKI/
OPENCOLA_(DRINK)
202 AUTHOR UNKNOWN, SOURCE: HTTP://
TINKERLONDON.COM/NOW/WP-CONTENT/
UPLOADS/2010/09/OPEN-BAG.JPG
203 PHOTO: RPGSIMMASTER,
SOURCE: HTTPS://SECURE.WIKIMEDIA.ORG/
WIKIPEDIA/EN/WIKI/USER:RPGSIMMASTER
204 SOURCE: HTTP://COMMONS.WIKIMEDIA.ORG
205 DESIGN: JENNIFER COOK-CHRYSOS,
INFO: HTTP://OPENWETWARE.ORG
206 VORES ØL → SOURCE:HTTP://EN.WIKIPEDIA.
ORG/WIKI/FREE_BEER

PRINTING

207 GUTENBERG PRESS (15TH CENTURY) –
HTTP://COMMONS.WIKIMEDIA.ORG
208 COMMODORE MATRIX PRINTER (1984) –
HTTP://COMMONS.WIKIMEDIA.ORG
209 MIKE AKA SQUEAKY MARMOT
→ WWW.FLICKR.COM/PHOTOS/SQUEAKYMARMOT/
210 MARIA KONOVALENKO, PICTURE TAKEN AT
WAKE FOREST INSTITUTE FOR REGENERATIVE
MEDICINE
211 DIMENSION UPRINT BY STRATASYS
212 PHOTO: CAROLINE PREW/IMPERIAL COLLEGE
LONDON – TECHNOLOGY: FABRICAN,
WWW.FABRICANLTD.COM
213 FOOD PRINTER CONCEPT FROM THE PHILIPS
DESIGN *FOOD PROBE*, COURTESY OF PHILIPS

RECYCLING

214 PHOTO: BERT VAN DIJK. MORE IMAGES
217 OF GUIYU → WWW.FLICKR.COM/PHOTOS/
ZILPHO/2994217039/
218 COURTESY OF WWW.GEEKGEARSTORE.COM
219 COURTESY OF HEINEKEN INTERNATIONAL
220 COURTESY OF HEINEKEN INTERNATIONAL
221 2012ARCHITECTEN, ROTTERDAM
222 →WWW.2012ARCHITECTEN.NL
223 PHOTO: ROBAN KRAMER →
WWW.FLICKR.COM/PHOTOS/ROBANHK
224 WHERE THERE'S SMOKE...ZIG ZAG CHAIR
(RIETVELD) WWW.MAARTENBAAS.COM,
PHOTOGRAPHY: DANE JENSEN

REMIX

225 ALL THESE IMAGES ARE READILY AVAILABLE
235 IN VARIOUS PLACES ON THE INTERNET AND
BELIEVED TO BE IN PUBLIC DOMAIN. MANY
THANKS TO FOLLOWING BLOGS:
WWW.SHANZHAIJI.CN, WWW.M8COOL.COM

REPAIRING

236 CLAIRE & TIM, WINCHESTER
→WWW.LEARNINGTOLOVEYOUMORE.COM
/REPORTS/67/CLAIRE_TIM.PHP
237 KIRSTEN GOEMAERE, GENT
→WWW.LEARNING TOLOVEYOUMORE.COM/
REPORTS/67/GOEMAERE_KIRSTEN.PHP
238 PHOTO: LINDSAY BLATT -
239 WWW.LINDSAYBLATT.COM
240 *DISPATCHWORK AMSTERDAM*, JAN VORMANN
AND PLATFORM21. PHOTOGRAPHY JOHANNES
ABELING
241 PLATFORM 21 – WWW.PLATFORM21.NL
242 DEUTSCHE FOTOTHEK
243 PHOTO: JAN CHIPCHASE
→ HTTP://JANCHIPCHASE.COM
244 *TUSSEN KUNST & KITSCH* – AVRO
245 *REPAIR & SHINE*, NY SHOE REPAIRMEN BY
LINDSAY BLATT →WWW.LINDSAYBLATT.COM
246 AUTHOR UNKNOWN, SOURCE:
WWW.THEREIFIXEDIT.COM

REPRODUCTION

247 PHOTO: TONY BUSER
→ WWW.FLICKR.COM/PHOTOS/TBUSER
248 PHOTO: ZACH HOEKEN
→ WWW.FLICKR.COM/PHOTOS/HOEKEN
249 PHOTO: CHRIS HELENIUS
→ WWW.FLICKR.COM/PEOPLE/ORANSE-/
250 DESIGN: UNFOLD →WWW.UNFOLD.BE,
PHOTO: KRISTOF VRANCKEN FOR Z33
→WWW.FLICKR.COM/PHOTOS/Z33BE

251 PHOTO: DIRK VANDER KOOIJ
→ HTTP://DIRKVANDERKOOIJ.NL
252 HTTP://REPRAP.ORG
253 HTTP://REPRAP.ORG
254 MAKERBOT →WWW.MAKERBOT.COM

REVOLUTION

255 PHOTO: JEFF CAYLOR
→ WWW.FLICKR.COM/PHOTOS/JEFFCAYLOR
256 *COTTONPOLIS*, ENGRAVING BY EDWARD
GOODALL (1795-1870)
257 PHOTO: ANGELA ANDERSON-COBB
→ WWW.FLICKR.COM/PHOTOS/ANGELARIEL65
258 PHOTO: HUGO VAN MEIJEREN

SHARING

259 = SHARED...
269

SOCIAL DESIGN

270 PHOTO: BLAANC AND JOÃO CAEIRO
271 IDEA: WORKING-5-TO-9, IMAGE: CHRIS
KARTHAUS AND FLORIS WIEGERINCK
272 PHOTO: ALEX SCHAUB,
275 FAB LAB AMSTERDAM
→ HTTP://FABLAB.WAAG.ORG

STANDARDS

276 JACQUES-LOUIS DAVID 'NAPOLEON CROSSES
THE ST. BERNARD'
277 –
278 CAMPAIGN FOR EUROPEAN PARLIAMENT
279 SOURCE: OPEN SOURCE GESTURE LIBRARY,
CHAD PERSON
280 SOURCE: HTTP://COMMONS.WIKIMEDIA.ORG
281 ALAN CHIA → WWW.FLICKR.COM/PHOTOS/
SEVEN13AVENUE
282 L.L. ZAMENHOF →HTTP://EN.WIKIPEDIA.
ORG/WIKI/ESPERANTO
283 MANUAL FOR PARTICIPATING IN THE OPEN
DESIGN PROCESS BY INTRASTRUCTURES
284 DESIGN AND PHOTO: PHILIP LUSCHEN
285 DESIGN: INTRASTRUCTURES
286 DESIGN: CHRISTIANE HOEGNER, LUCAS
MAASSEN, THOMAS LOMMÉE, JO VAN
BOSTRAETEN, BIOGAS-E VZW & MICHOU
NANON DEBRUIJN. PHOTO: KRISTOF
VRANCKEN FOR Z33.

TEMPLATE CULTURE

287 *TEMPLATE CULTURE: FORM FOLLOWS FORMAT.*
298 MANIPULATED WEBSITE SCREENSHOTS BY
HENDRIKJAN GRIEVINK

TREND: GLOBALIZATION

299 PHOTO: RICHARD ALLAWAY
300 PHOTO: PHILIPPE LEROYER
→ WWW.FLICKR.COM/PHOTOS/
PHILIPPELEROYER
301 PHOTO: MARISSA ORTON
302 MC DONALD'S INDIA
303 PHOTO: GREG SCRATCHLEY → WWW.FLICKR.
COM/PHOTOS/SCRATCH/119524328
304 ASTRONAUT PHOTOGRAPH AS17-148-22727,
A.K.A. THE *BLUE MARBLE* PICTURE, TAKEN
ON DECEMBER 7, 1972. COURTESY OF NASA
JOHNSON SPACE CENTER
305 BUSINESSWEEK COVER DECEMBER 2004 —
BLOOMBERG

TREND: NETWORK SOCIETY

306 PHOTO: MATT BRITT
→ HTTP://COMMONS.WIKIMEDIA.ORG
307 PHOTO: BEATE PALAND → WWW.FLICKR.COM/
PHOTOS/ALICE_C/4554189742
308 SCREENSHOT
309 PHOTO: KEVIN MCSHANE → WWW.FLICKR.
COM/PHOTOS/LOBRAUMEISTER/4126174862
310 PHOTO: CHRISTOPHER MICHEL →
WWW.FLICKR.COM/PHOTOS/CMICHEL67
/4966958892
311 STILL FROM AMATEUR VIDEO
→ GOOGLE SEARCH ENTRY= 'NEDA + IRAN'
312 PHOTO: YOAN BLANC → WWW.FLICKR.COM/
PHOTOS/GREUT/502095764

TREND: SCARCITY OF RESOURCES

313 PHOTO: LEONARDO F FREITAS
→ WWW.FLICKR.COM/PHOTOS/LEOFFREITAS/
1469376131
314 PHOTO: STEPHEN COLDRINGTON
→ HTTP://COMMONS.WIKIMEDIA.ORG
315 PHOTO: ROB LAVINSKY → IROCKS.COM
316 PHOTO: KAREN HAYES → PACT, INC
317 PHOTO: NASA GODDARD SPACE FLIGHT
CENTER WWW.FLICKR.COM/PHOTOS/GSFC
318 PHOTO: US MILITARY
→ WWW.DEFENSEIMAGERY.MIL
319 COVER PHOTO: SARAH LEEN →
NATIONAL GEOGRAPHIC, HTTP://NGM.
NATIONALGEOGRAPHIC.COM

WYS≠WYG

320 PHOTO: YOSHIN YAMADA → WWW.FLICKR.
COM/PHOTOS/OCEANYAMAHA/185130670/
321 PHOTO: JOE HARPER → WWW.FLICKR.COM/
PHOTOS/JOEHARPER/3872936498/
322 PHOTO: MATTI MATTILA → WWW.FLICKR.
COM/PHOTOS/MATTIMATTILA/4863056891/
323 PHOTO: EDITOR B → HTTP://B.ROX.COM/
324 PHOTO: AUSTIN CONNELL → WWW.FLICKR.
COM/PHOTOS/AUSTINCONNELL/
325 PHOTO: AARON PATTERSON → WWW.FLICKR.
COM/PHOTOS/AARONINDENVER/2562904844/
326 PHOTO: FABIAN SCHLENZ → WWW.FLICKR.
COM/PHOTOS/FABIANONLINE
327 PHOTO: MARK HOEKSTRA → WWW.FLICKR.
COM/PHOTOS/GEEKTECHNIQUE/1676622189/
328 –
329 AUTHOR UNKNOWN, PART OF THE
MAKER'S BILL OF RIGHTS CAMPAIGN
BY MAKE → WWW.MAKEZINE.COM
330 SOURCE: THE BLOGOSPHERE, SAID TO BE
APRIL'S FOOL DAY CAMPAIGN FOR IKEA

319

COLOPHON

EDITORS
Bas van Abel
Lucas Evers
Roel Klaassen
Peter Troxler

PROJECT MANAGEMENT
Aart Helder

VISUAL CONCEPT AND DESIGN
Hendrik-Jan Grievink

IMAGE EDITING
Bas van Abel
Lucas Evers
Hendrik-Jan Grievink
Aart Helder

PROOFREADING
Joy Maul-Phillips

ACKNOWLEDGEMENTS
Special thanks to Michel Avital, Gianfranco
Chicco, Matt Cottam, Ronen Kadushin,
Tommi Laitio and Michelle Thorne, who
collaborated with the project team to
form the Tempelhof Group and helped to lay
the foundations for this book at the DMY
International Design Festival 2010 in Berlin
Tempelhof, Germany.

This publication is made possible with the
kind support of the Dutch Design Fashion
Architecture programme. DutchDFA aims to
strengthen the international position of
the most prominent sectors of the Dutch
creative industries — design, fashion and
architecture — by facilitating a collective
and inclusive approach.

320

ADDRESSES

PUBLISHER
BIS Publishers
Building Het Sieraad
Postjesweg 1
1057DT Amsterdam
The Netherlands
T +31 (0)20 515 02 30
F +31 (0)20 515 02 39

bis@bispublishers.nl
www.bispublishers.nl

INITIATORS
Creative Commons Netherlands
PO Box 2960
1000CZ Amsterdam
The Netherlands
T +31 (0)20 575 67 20
F +31 (0)20 575 67 21
info@creativecommons.nl
www.creativecommons.nl

*Premsela, the Netherlands
Institute for Design and Fashion*
PO Box 75905
1070AX Amsterdam
The Netherlands
T +31 (0)20 344 94 49
F +31 (0) 20 344 94 43
secretariaat@premsela.org
www.premsela.org

Waag Society
Nieuwmarkt 4
1012CR Amsterdam
The Netherlands
T +31 (0)20 557 98 98
F +31 (0)20 557 98 80
society@waag.org
www.waag.org

PROPERTY OF
SENECA COLLEGE
LIBRARIES
@ YORK CAMPUS